LANGUAGE & READING

LANGUAGE & READING

AN INTERDISCIPLINARY APPROACH

COMPILED BY DORIS V. GUNDERSON

CENTER FOR APPLIED LINGUISTICS : 1970

The publication of this work has been made possible by a grant from the Ford Foundation to the Center for Applied Linguistics in support of the Interdisciplinary Committee on Reading Problems.

Library of Congress Catalog Card Number: 79-120747
International Standard Book Number: 87281-002-X

Printed in the United States of America

Cover design: Frank A. Rice

PREFACE

The interdisciplinary process often results in a realization of the interrelationship among disciplines which share in an attach upon a common problem. The Interdisciplinary Committee on Reading Problems was organized to focus attention upon reading problems by individuals representing the fields of linguistics, anthropology, education, sociology, psychology, economics, and the specialized fields of medicine such as pediatrics, ophthalmology, neurology, and psychiatry. In order to make writings of various disciplines concerning reading problems accessible to the committee members, articles from professional journals were circulated in a monthly newsletter. The articles were drawn from such a wide variety of discipline-centered publications as to be far beyond the normal reading diet of most individuals. Because of the enthusiastic interest of committee members in these papers, it was decided to publish a representative selection.

The first section includes papers concerned with language, theories of reading, and some discussion of beginning reading. Papers in section two deal with research: the direction in which reading research should go, a conceptual analysis of reading, and a research study on perceptual training. The third section includes several articles which discuss factors contributing to reading disability, a discussion of the confusing use of the term dyslexia, and a paper on reading disability in Japan. The final paper is a current look at reading instruction.

Reading is a process of recognizing that printed words represent spoken words and is a part of the total language spectrum. Reading cannot be considered independently of language. Language can be studied from several points of view, e.g. cultural, social, etc., and an investigator's particular inclinations are revealed in his explanations of language. Lenneberg, who is interested in man as a biological species, cites six characteristics of language which relate language to developmental biology and discusses those aspects of language to which biological concepts are most appropriately applied

Although the learning process has received considerable emphasis recently, reading as a process has received little attention. Carroll discusses the complex nature of the reading process and notes that mature reading ability is acquired over a period of time. He specifies eight components of reading skill which must be learned and practiced before the beginning reader acquires the competencies which characterize the mature reader.

Venezky et al. say that reading success is usually attributed to teacher, home, or reading program variables, while reading failure is attributed to such sources as brain damage, emotional distress, motivational deficit, or inappropriateness of the content of primary reading texts for the child's social or cultural background. The skills possessed by good readers but not present in the poorer readers are rarely analyzed. Venezky focuses on reading as a skill behavior with emphasis on the decoding process, presents theoretical models for the process, and examines the skills required by each model.

Jenkinson states that after 75 years of research in reading, a coherent construct for examining reading has not yet evolved and cites some reasons for the failure to produce theories. She notes the current interest in model making in education and stresses the need for more sophisticated models in reading. The contributions that the fields of philosophy, psychology, and linguistics have to make to a theory of reading emphasize the need for an interdisciplinary approach.

Shuy discusses two areas in which linguistic research can be related to children with reading disabilities: one, which is concerned with the child's cultural environment, is termed positional, and the other, concerned with the learning of language symbolization, is called processive. He calls attention to the lack of consistency in syllabication in the teaching of reading and lists five rules which "constitute a beginning toward a linguistic theory of syllabication which can apply to the syllables of both oral and written language." The positional dimension is further developed in a second paper concerned with factors to be considered in developing beginning reading materials for ghetto children. Shuy suggests that materials which avoid linguistic mismatch of the ghetto child's oral language and the written text may draw on three levels of data: lexical, phonological, and grammatical, but recommends that the focus be placed on the avoidance of grammatical mismatch rather than the other two.

Reed analyzes the textbooks used in four approaches to teaching beginning reading: the basal series, the language-experience series,

the phonic readers, and the linguistic readers. He cites strengths
and weaknesses in each of the approaches, emphasizing the failure
of some to distinguish between the process and the use of reading.

Goodman disagrees with the commonly held notion that reading
consists of precise, sequential identification. Rather, he considers
it a psycholinguistic guessing game which involves an interaction
between thought and language. He presents a model which uses
long and short term memory in which the sequence of steps as well
as the time devoted to each step may vary with the individual.

Two of the papers in the second section discuss research in reading, and the third is a report of a research project. Similar to
Reed's distinction of reading as a two-stage process is Levin's
breakdown of reading into two broad categories with the first the
skill of decoding the writing system into its associated language,
and the second the uses of reading. Levin points out that research
in reading has not concentrated on these areas but rather on meth-
odology. Researchers should first look at the fundamental question:
"What is reading?"; then other areas of reading research such as
the sequencing of sub-skills can receive attention.

After analyzing many definitions of reading, Wiener and Cromer
found that certain issues emerged from their examination related
to different usages of the term "reading", but an examination of
the term "reading difficulty" reveals other issues. The authors
"explain" reading problems and present six models, using Handlon's
model as a starting point, relating the variables associated with
reading (antecedents) to the variables associated with reading difficulties (consequents). Confusion arises because some investigators consider reading as identification while others treat it as comprehension; Wiener and Cromer integrate the two approaches by
conceptualizing reading as a two-step process involving identification first and then comprehension.

Basing their research on a theoretical rather than a pragmatic
orientation, the perceptual development theory propounded by
Piaget, Elkind and Deblinger conducted a study concerned with
reading achievement in disadvantaged children. They found that
training children in processes which they considered basic to
particular aspects of reading achievement resulted in improved
performance on those aspects.

That many children experience problems in learning to read has
been discussed widely; blame has been attributed to the materials
used in teaching beginning reading, the teachers, the school structure, the language of the school as opposed to the language of the
community, and the framework of society itself. No single cause
can be established; rather, because individual children learn in different ways and respond to various stimuli, there are many factors

responsible for the large number of cases of reading retardation. Reed and Sawyer discuss linguistic considerations in reading disability, proceeding from the point of view that language is "an intellectual component of the disabilities suffered by some persons in learning to read."

Eisenberg views reading retardation from a psychiatric and sociological point of view and stresses several factors which underlie reading disability. He outlines a pediatric action program and also focuses on the importance of the school's identifying the child who is not beginning to read by the second semester of first grade and providing appropriate instruction for him rather than waiting until he is in second or third grade and experiencing difficulty.

The relationship of reading failure to peer-group status in the urban ghetto has been investigated by Labov and Robins. Although lip service is given to the school's acceptance of the culture of the ghetto, their research indicates that the schools are not fully aware of the culture. They suggest some unique practices for the schools such as granting special licenses to young men to serve an intermediary function between the school and the social structure of the ghetto.

Use of the term dyslexia probably compounds more confusion in reading than any other single term. To some it is synonymous with reading difficulty; to others the term suggests the presence of "soft neurological signs". Reid discusses the term and its connotations, not from the point of view of a single discipline but from the point of view of professions as diverse as education and medicine, and notes the confusion that results from the use of the term, considering it a communication problem.

Many articles attest to the prevalence of reading disability in the United States but seldom, if ever, are transcultural comparisons made. The incidence in Japan is some ten times lower than in Western countries, according to Makita. He considers the specificity of the language used as the major factor in the formation of reading disability, so that it is primarily a philological rather than a neuropsychiatric problem.

Sheldon provides an overview of the state of the art of reading instruction in the United States today. He discusses the teaching of reading to preschool, kindergarten, and elementary school children, and also surveys the teaching of reading in the secondary school and to illiterate adolescents and adults.

Doris V. Gunderson, Executive Director
Interdisciplinary Committee on Reading Problems
Center for Applied Linguistics, Washington, D. C.

December 1969

CONTENTS

II. READING RESEARCH

III. READING PROBLEMS

IV. THE TEACHING OF READING: THE STATE OF THE ART

I. READING AND LANGUAGE

ON EXPLAINING LANGUAGE

by Eric H. Lenneberg

Many explanations have been offered for many aspects of language; there is little agreement, however, on how to explain various problems or even on what there is to be explained. Of course, explanations differ with the personal inclinations and interests of the investigator. My interests are in man as a biological species, and I believe that the study of language is relevant to these interests because language has the following six characteristics. (i) It is a form of behavior present in all cultures of the world. (ii) In all cultures its onset is age correlated. (iii) There is only one acquisition strategy--it is the same for all babies everywhere in the world. (iv) It is based intrinsically upon the same formal operating characteristics whatever its outward form (1). (v) Throughout man's recorded history these operating characteristics have been constant. (vi) It is a form of behavior that may be impaired specifically by circumscribed brain lesions which may leave other mental and motor skills relatively unaffected.

Any form of human behavior that has all of these six characteristics may likewise be assumed to have a rather specific biological foundation. This, of course, does not mean that language cannot be studied from different points of view; it can, for example, be investigated for its cultural or social variations, its capacity to reflect individual differences, or its applications. The purpose of this article, however, is to discuss the aspects of language to which biological concepts are applied most appropriately (2). Further, my concern is with the development of language in children--not with its origin in the species.

Predictability of Language Development

A little boy starts washing his hands before dinner no sonner than when his parents decide that training in cleanliness should

---

Reprinted by permission from Science 164:3880. 635-643 (May 9 1969). Copyright 1969 by the American Association for the Advancement of Science.

Table 1. Correlation of motor and language development

Age (years)	Motor milestones	Language milestones
0.5	Sits using hands for support; unilateral reaching	Cooing sounds change to babbling by introduction of consonantal sounds
1	Stands; walks when held by one hand	Syllabic reduplication; signs of understanding some words; applies some sounds regularly to signify persons or objects, that is, the first words
1.5	Prehension and release fully developed; gait propulsive; creeps downstairs backward	Repertoire of 3 to 50 words not joined in phrases; trains of sounds and intonation patterns resembling discourse; good progress in understanding
2	Runs (with falls); walks stairs with one foot forward only	More than 50 words; two-word phrases most common; more interest in verbal communication; no more babbling
2.5	Jumps with both feet; stands on one foot for 1 second; builds tower of six cubes	Every day new words; utterances of three and more words; seems to understand almost everything said to him; still many grammatical deviations
3	Tiptoes 3 yards (2.7 meters); walks stairs with alternating feet; jumps 0.9 meter	Vocabulary of some 1000 words; about 80 percent intelligibility; grammar of utterances close approximation to colloquial adult; syntactic mistakes fewer in variety, systematic, predictable
4.5	Jumps over rope; hops on one foot; walks on line	Language well established; grammatical anomalies restricted either to unusual constructions or to the more literate aspects of discourse

Source: 3, pp. 128-130.

begin. However, children begin to speak no sooner and no later than when they reach a given stage of physical maturation (Table 1). There are individual variations in development, particularly with respect to age correlation. It is interesting that language development correlates better with motor development than it does with chronological age. If we take these two variables (motor and language development) and make ordinal scales out of the stages shown in Table 1 and then use them for a correlation matrix, the result is a remarkably small degree of scatter. Since motor development is one of the most important indices of maturation, it is not unreasonable to propose that language development, too, is related to physical growth and development. This impression is further corroborated by examination of retarded children. Here the age correlation is very poor, whereas the correlation between motor and language development continues to be high (3). Nevertheless, there is evidence that the statistical relation between motor and language development is not due to any immediate, causal relation; peripheral motor disabilities can occur that do not delay language acquisition.

Just as it is possible to correlate the variable language development with the variables chronological age or motor development, it is possible to relate it to the physical indications of brain maturation, such as the gross weight of the brain, neurodensity in the cerebral cortex, of the changing weight proportions of given substances in either gray or white matter. On almost all counts, language begins when such maturational indices have attained at least 65 percent of their mature values. (Inversely, language acquisition becomes more difficult when the physical maturation of the brain is complete.) These correlations do not prove causal connections, although they suggest some interesting questions for further research.

Effect of Certain Variations in Social Environment

In most of the studies on this topic the language development of children in orphanages or socially deprived households has been compared with that of children in so-called normal, middle-class environments. Statistically significant differences are usually reported, which is sometimes taken as a demonstration that language development is contingent on specific language training. That certain aspects of the environment are absolutely essential for language development is undeniable, but it is important to distinguish between what the children actually do, and what they can do.

There is nothing particularly surprising or revealing in the demonstration that language deficits occur in children who hear no language, or only the discourse of uneducated persons. But what interests us is the underlying capacity for language. This is not a spurious question; for instance, some children have the capacity for language but do not use it, either because of peripheral handicaps such as congenital deafness or because of psychiatric disturbances such as childhood schizophrenia; other children may not speak because they do not have a sufficient capacity for language, on account of certain severely retarding diseases.

There is a simple technique for ascertaining the degree of development of the capacity for speech and language. Instead of assessing it by means of an inventory of the vocabulary, the grammatical complexity of the utterances, the clarity of pronunciation, and the like, and computing a score derived from several subtests of this kind, it is preferable to describe the children's ability in terms of a few broad and general developmental stages, such as those shown in Table 1. Tests which are essentially inventories of vocabulary and syntactic constructions are likely to reflect simply the deficiencies of the environment; they obscure the child's potentialities and capabilities.

I have used the schema described to compare the speech development of children in many different societies, some of them much more primitive than our own. In none of these studies could I find evidence of variation in developmental rate, despite the enormous differences in social enviornment.

I have also had an opportunity to study the effect of a dramatically different speech environment upon the development of vocalizations during the first 3 months of life (4). It is very common in our culture for congenitally deaf individuals to marry one another, creating households in which all vocal sounds are decidedly different from those normally heard and in which the sounds of babies cannot be attended to directly. Six deaf mothers and ten hearing mothers were asked, during their last month of pregnancy, to participate in our study. The babies were visited at home when they were no more than 10 days old and were seen biweekly thereafter for at least 3 months. Each visit consisted of 3 hours of observation and 24 hours of mechanical recording of all sounds made and heard by the baby. Data were analyzed quantitatively and qualitatively. Figure 1 shows that although the environment was quantitatively quite different in the experimental and the control groups, the frequency distributions of various baby noises did not differ significantly; as seen in Figure 2, the developmental histories of cooing noises are also remarkably alike in the two groups. Figure 3 demonstrates that the babies of deaf parents tend to fuss

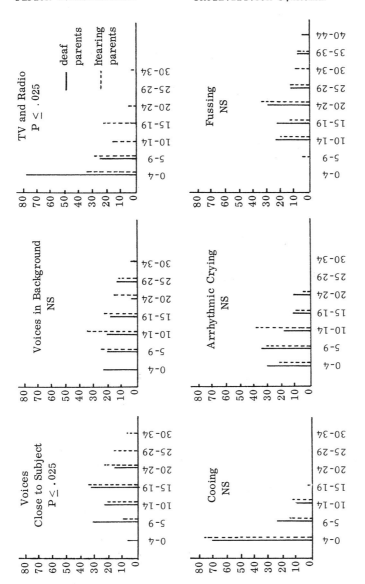

Fig. 1. Frequency distributions of various noises. The basic counting unit is individual recording days.

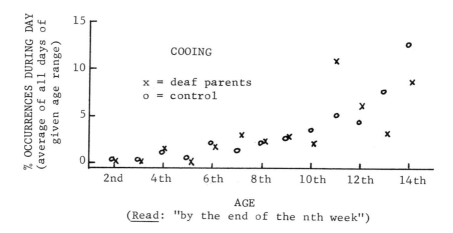

(Read: "by the end of the nth week")

Fig. 2. Each baby's day was divided into 6-minute
periods; the presence or absence of cooing was noted
for each period; this yielded a percentage for each
baby's day; days of all babies were ordered by their
ages, and the average was taken for all days of identical age. Nonaveraged data were published in (4).

an equal amount, even though the hearing parents are much more
likely to come to the child when it fusses. Thus the earliest development of human sounds appears to be relatively independent of
the amount, nature, or timing of the sounds made by parents.

I have observed this type of child-rearing through later stages,
as well. The hearing children of deaf parents eventually learn two
languages and sound systems: those of their deaf parents and those
of the rest of the community. In some instances, communication
between children and parents is predominantly by gestures. In no
case have I found any adverse effects upon the language development of standard English in these children. Although the mothers
made sounds different from the children's, and although the children's vocalizations had no significant effect upon attaining what
they wanted during early infancy, language in these children in-
variably began at the usual time and went through the same stages
as is normally encountered.

Also of interest may be the following observations on fairly retarded children growing up in state institutions that are badly under-
staffed. During the day the children play in large, bare rooms,
attended by only one person, often an older retardate who herself
lacks a perfect command of language. The children's only entertainment is provided by a large television set, playing all day at

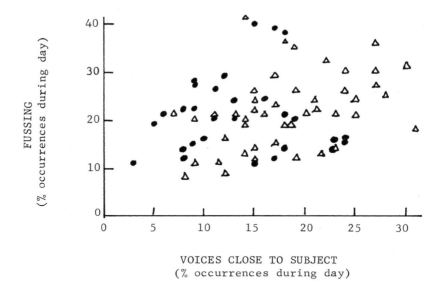

Fig. 3. Relation between the amount of parents'
noises heard by the baby and the amount of fussing
noises made by the baby. Each symbol is one baby's
day; (solid circles) deaf parents; (triangles) hearing
parents.

full strength. Although most of these retarded children have only
primitive beginnings of language, there are always some among
them who manage, even under these extremely deprived circumstances, to pick up an amazing degree of language skill. Apparently they learn language partly though the television programs,
whose level is often quite adequate for them!

From these instances we see that language capacity follows its
own natural history. The child can avail himself of this capacity
if the environment provides a minimum of stimulation and opportunity. His engagement in language activity can be limited by his
environmental circumstances, but the underlying capacity is not
easily arrested. Impoverished environments are not conducive
to good language development, but good language development is
not contingent on specific training measures (5); a wide variety of
rather haphazard factors seems to be sufficient.

Effect of Variations in Genetic Background

Man is an unsatisfactory subject for the study of genetic influences; we cannot do breeding experiments on him and can use only statistical controls. Practically any evidence adduced is susceptible to a variety of interpretations. Nevertheless, there are indications that inheritance is at least partially responsible for deviations in verbal skills, as in the familial occurence of a deficit termed congenital language disability (2, chapter 6). Studies, with complete pedigrees, have been published on the occurrence and distribution of stuttering, of hyperfluencies, of voice qualities, and of many other traits, which constitute supporting though not conclusive evidence that inheritance plays a role in language acquisition. In addition to such family studies, much research has been carried out on twins. Particularly notable are the studies of Luchsinger, who reported on the concordance of developmental histories and of many aspects of speech and language. Zygosity was established in these cases by serology (Figure 4). Developmental data of this kind are, in my opinion, of greater relevance to our speculations on genetic background than are pedigrees.

The nonbiologist frequently and mistakenly thinks of genes as being directly responsible for one property or another; this leads him to the fallacy, especially when behavior is concerned, of dichotomizing everything as being dependent on either genes or environment. Genes act merely on intracellular biochemical processes, although these processes have indirect effects on events in the individual's developmental history. Many alterations in structure and function indirectly attributable to genes are more immediately the consequence of alterations in the schedule of developmental events. Therefore, the studies on twins are important in that they show that homozygotes reach milestones in language development at the same age, in contrast to heterozygotes, in whom divergences are relatively common. It is also interesting that the nature of the deviations--the symptoms, if you wish--are, in the vast majority, identical in homozygotes but not in heterozygotes.

Such evidence indicates that man's biological heritage endows him with sensitivities and propensities that lead to language development in children, who are spoken to (in contrast to chimpanzee infants, who do not automatically develop language--either receptive or productive--under identical treatment). The endowment has a genetic foundation, but this is not to say that there are "genes for language," or that the environment is of no importance.

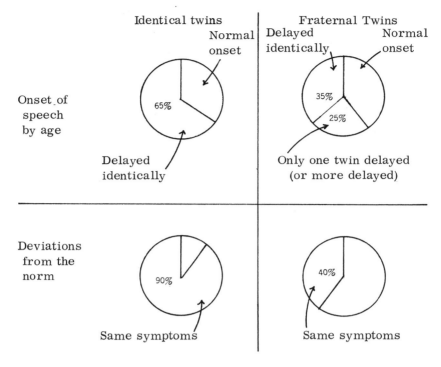

Fig. 4. The onset of speech and its subsequent development tend to be more uniform among identical twins than fraternal twins.

Attempts to Modify Language Development

Let us now consider children who have the capacity for language acquisition but fail to develop it for lack of exposure. This is the case with the congenitally deaf, who are allowed to grow up without either language or speech until school age, when suddenly language is brought to them in very unnatural ways. Before this time they may have half a dozen words they can utter, read, write, or finger-spell, but I have known of no profoundly deaf child (in New England, where my investigations were conducted) with whom one could communicate by use of the English language before school age.

When deaf children enter an oralist school, lipreading and speech become the major preoccupation of training. However, in most children these activities remain poor for many more years, and in some, throughout life. Their knowledge of language comes through learning to read and write. However, teachers in the oral tradition

restrict expression in the graphic medium on the hypothesis that it
interferes with lipreading and speech skills. Thus, exposure to
language (i) comes much later in these children's lives than is
normal, (ii) is dramatically reduced in quantity, (iii) is presented
through a different medium and sensory modality, and (iv) is
taught to the children rather as a second language is taught, instead
of through the simple immersion into a sea of language that most
children experience. The deaf children are immediately required
to use grammatically correct sentences, and every mistake is
discussed and explained to them.

The results of this procedure are interesting but not very en-
couraging from the educational point of view. During the early
years of schooling, the children's spontaneous writings have a very
unusual pattern; there is little evidence that the teachers' instruction in "how to compose correct sentences" is of any avail. Yet,
careful analysis of their compositions shows that some subtleties
of English syntax that are usually not part of the grammar taught
in the school do make their appearance, sometimes quite early.
There can be no question that the children do not simply imitate
what they see; some of the teachings fall by the wayside, whereas
a number of aspects of language are automatically absorbed from
the written material given to the children.

There are other instances in which efforts are made to change a
child's language skills by special training, as in the mildly retarded, for example. Many parents believe that their retarded
child would function quite normally if somebody could just teach
him to speak. At Children's Hospital in Boston I undertook a pilot
study in which a speech therapist saw a small number of children
with Downe's syndrome (mongolism) for several hours each week,
in as effort to speed up language development. Later, two graduate
students in linguistics investigated the children's phonetic skills
and tried to assess the capacities of each child for clearer enuncia-
tion. Throughout these attempts, it was found that if a child had a
small repertoire of single words, it was always possible to teach
him yet another word, but if he was not joining these words spontaneously into phrases, there was nothing that could be done to induce him to do so. The articulatory skills were somewhat different. It was often possible to make a child who had always had
slurred speech say a specific word more clearly. However, the
moment the child returned to spontaneous utterances, he would fall
back to the style that was usual for him. The most interesting results were obtained when the retarded children were required
simply to repeat well-formed sentences. A child who had not developed to a stage in which he used certain grammatical rules
spontaneously, who was still missing the syntactic foundations and

prerequisites, could not be taught to repeat a sentence that was formed by such higher rules. This was true even in sentences of very few words. Similar observations have since been made on normal children (6), with uniformly similar results; normal children, too, can repeat correctly only that which is formed by rules they have already mastered. This is the best indication that language does not come about by simple imitation, but that the child abstracts regularities or relations from the language he hears, which he then applies to building up language for himself as an apparatus of principles.

What Sets the Pace of Language Development?

There is a widespread belief that the development of language is dependent on the motor skills of the articulating organs. Some psychologists believe that species other than man fail to develop language only because of anatomical differences in their structures. However, we have evidence that this is not so.

It is important that we are clear about the essential nature of language. Since my interests are in language capacities, I am concerned with the development of the child's knowledge of how language works. This is not the same as the acquisition of "the first word." The best test for the presence and development of this knowledge is the manner in which discourse is understood. In most instances, it is true that there is a relation between speech and understanding, but this relation is not a necessary one (7).

By understanding, I mean something quite specific. In the realm of phonology, understanding involves a process that roughly corresponds to the linguists' phonematization (in contrast, for example, to a "pictographic" understanding: phonematization results in seeing similarities between speech sounds, whereas pictographic understanding would treat a word as an indivisible sound pattern). In the realm of semantics, understanding involves seeing the basis on which objects are categorized, thus enabling a child to name an object correctly that he has never seen before. (The child does not start out with a hypothesis that "table" is the proper name of a unique object or that it refers to all things that have four appendages.) In the realm of grammar, understanding involves the extraction of relations between word classes; an example is the understanding of prediction. By application of these tests, it can be shown empirically that Aunt Pauline's favorite lap dog does not have a little language knowledge, but, in fact, fails the test of understanding on all counts.

A survey of children with a variety of handicaps shows that their grasp of how language works is intimately related to their general cognitive growth, which, in turn, is partly dependent on physical maturation and partly on opportunities to interact with a stimulus-rich environment. In many retarding diseases, for example, language development is predicted best by the rate of advancement in mental age (using tests of nonverbal intelligence). In an investigation of congenitally blind children (8), we are again finding that major milestones for language development are highly correlated with physical development. A naive conception of language development as an accumulation of associations between visual and auditory patterns would be hard put to explain this.

Brain Correlates

In adults, language functions take place predominantly in the left hemisphere. A number of cortical fields have been related to specific aspects of language. The details are still somewhat controversial and need not concern us here. It is certain, however, that precentral areas of the frontal lobe are principally involved in the production of language, whereas the postcentral parietal and superior temporal fields are involved in sensory functions. These cortical specializations are not present at birth, but become only gradually established during childhood, in a process very similar to that of embryological history; there is evidence of differentiation and regulation of function. In the adult, traumata causing large left-sided central cortical lesions carry a highly predictable prognosis; in 70 percent of all cases, aphasia occurs, and in about half of these, the condition is irreversible (I am basing these figures on our experience with penetrating head injuries incurred in war).

Comparable traumatic lesions in childhood have quite different consequences, the prognosis being directly related to the age at which the insult is incurred. Lesions of the left hemisphere in children under age 2 are no more injurious to future language development than are lesions of the right hemisphere. Children whose brain is traumatized after the onset of language but before the age of 4 usually have transient aphasias; language is quickly reestablished, however, if the right hemisphere remains intact. Often these children regain language by going through stages of language development similar to those of the 2-year-old, but they traverse each stage at greater speed. Lesions incurred before the very early teens also carry an excellent prognosis, permanent residues of symptoms being extremely rare.

The prognosis becomes rapidly worse for lesions that occur after this period; the young men who become casualties of war have symptoms virtually identical with those of stroke patients of advanced age. Experience with the surgical removal of an entire cerebral hemisphere closely parallels this picture. The basis for prognosticating operative success is, again, the age at which the disease has been contracted for which the operation is performed.

If a disturbance in the left hemisphere occurs early enough in life, the right hemisphere remains competent for language throughout life. Apparently this process is comparable to regulation, as we know it from morphogenesis. If the disease occurs after a certain critical period of life, namely, the early teens, this regulative capacity is lost and language is interfered with permanently. Thus the time at which the hemispherectomy is performed is less important than the time of the lesion.

Critical Age for Language Acquisition

The most reasonable interpretation of this picture of recovery from aphasia in childhood is not that there is vicarious functioning, or taking over, by the right hemisphere because of need, but rather that language functions are not yet confined to the left hemisphere during early life. Apparently both hemispheres are involved at the beginning, and a specialization takes place later (which is the characteristic of differentiation), resulting in a kind of left-right polarization of functions. Therefore, the recovery from aphasia during preteen years may partly be regarded as a reinstatement of activities that had never been lost. There is evidence that children at this age are capable of developing language in the same natural way as do very young children. Not only do symptoms subside, but active language development continues to occur. Similarly, we see that healthy children have a quite different propensity for acquiring foreign languages before the early teens than after the late teens, the period in between being transitional. For the young adult, second-language learning is an academic exercise, and there is a vast variety in degree of proficiency. It rapidly becomes more and more difficult to overcome the accent and interfering influences of the mother tongue.

Neurological material strongly suggests that something happens in the brain during the early teens that changes the propensity for language acquisition. We do not know the factors involved, but it is interesting that the critical period coincides with the time at which the human brain attains its final state of maturity in terms

of structure, function, and biochemistry (electroencephalographic
patterns slightly lag behind but become stabilized by about 16
years). Apparently the maturation of the brain marks the end of
regulation and locks certain functions into place.

There is further evidence that corroborates the notion of a critical period for primary language acquisition, most importantly,
the developmental histories of retarded children. It is dangerous
to make sweeping generalizations about all retarded children, because so much depends on the specific disease that causes the
retardation. But if we concentrate on diseases in which the patho-
logical condition is essentially stationary, such as microcephaly
vera or mongolism, it is possible to make fairly general predic-
tions about language development. If the child's mental developmental age is 2 when he is 4 years old (that is, his IQ is 50), one
may safely predict that some small progress will be made in language development. He will slowly move through the usual stages
of infant language, although the rate of development will gradually
slow down. In virtually all of these cases, language development
comes to a complete standstill in the early teens, so that these
individuals are arrested in primitive stages of language development that are perpetuated for the rest of their lives. Training and
motivation are of little help.

Development in the congenitally deaf is also revealing. When they
first enter school, their language acquisition is usually quite spec-
tacular, considering the enormous odds against them. However,
children who by their early teens have still not mastered all of the
principles that underlie the production of sentences appear to encounter almost unsurmountable difficulties in perfecting verbal
skills.

There is also evidence of the converse. Children who suddenly
lose their hearing (usually a consequence of meningitis) show very
different degrees of language skill, depending on whether the
disease strikes before the onset of language or after. If it occurs
before they are 18 months old, such children encounter difficulties
with language development that are very much the same as those
encountered by the congenitally deaf. Children who lose their
hearing after they have acquired language, however, at age 3 to 4,
have a different prospect. Their speech deteriorates rapidly;
usually within weeks they stop using language and so far it has
proved impossible to maintain the skill by educational procedures
(although new techniques developed in England and described by
Fry (9) give promise of great improvement). Many such children
then live without language for a relatively long time, often 2 to 3
years, and when they enter the schools for the deaf, must be
trained in the same way that other deaf children are trained. How-

ever, training is much more successful, and their language habits
stand out dramatically against those of their less fortunate colleagues. There appears to be a direct relation between the length
of time during which a child has been exposed to language and the
proficiency seen at the time of retraining.

Biological Approach: Defining Language Further

Some investigators propose that language is an artifact--a tool
that man has shaped for himself to serve a purpose. This assumption induces the view that language consists of many individual
traits, each independent of the other. However, the panorama of
observations presented above suggests a biological predisposition
for the development of language that is anchored in the operating
characteristics of the human brain (10). Man's cognitive apparatus
apparently becomes a language receiver and transmitter, provided
the growing organism is exposed to minimum and haphazard environmental events.

However, this assumption leads to a view different from that
suggested by the artifact assumption. Instead of thinking of language as a collection of separate and mutually independent traits,
one comes to see it as a profoundly integrated activity. Language
is to be understood as an operation rather than a static product of
the mind. Its modus operandi reflects that of human cognition,
because language is an intimate part of cognition. Thus the biological view denies that language is the cause of cognition, or even
its effect, since language is not an object (like a tool) that exists
apart from a living human brain.

As biologists, we are interested in the operating principles of
language because we hope that this will give us some clues about
the operating principles of the human brain. We know there is
just one species Homo sapiens, and it is therefore reasonable to
assume that individuals who speak Turkish, English, or Basque
(or who spoke Sanskrit some millennia ago) all have (or had) the
same kind of brain, that is, a computer with the same operating
principles and the same sensorium. Therefore, in a biological
investigation one must try to disregard the differences between the
languages of the world and to discover the general principles of
operation that are common to all of them. This is not an easy
matter; in fact, there are social scientists who doubt the existence
of language universals. As students of language we cannot fail to
be impressed with the enormous differences among languages. Yet
every normal child learns the language to which he is exposed.

Perhaps we are simply claiming that common denominators must exist; can we prove their existence? If we discovered a totally isolated tribe with a language unknown to any outsider, how could we find out whether this language is generated by a computer that has the same biological characteristics as do our brains, and how could we prove that it shares the universal features of all languages?

As a start, we could exchange children between our two cultures to discover whether the same language developmental history would occur in those exchanged. Our data would be gross developmental stages, correlated with the emergence of motor milestones. A bioassay of this kind (already performed many times, always with positive results) gives only part of the answer.

In theory, one may also adduce more rigorous proof of similarity among languages. The conception of language universals is difficult to grasp intuitively, because we find it so hard to translate from one language to another and because the grammars appear, on the surface, to be so different. But it is entirely possible that underneath the structural difference that makes it so difficult for the adult speaker to learn a second language (particularly one that is not a cognate of his own) there are significant formal identities.

Virtually every aspect of language is the expression of relations. This is true of phonology (as stressed by Roman Jakobson and his school), semantics, and syntax. For instance, in all languages of the world words label a set of relational principles instead of being labels of specific objects. Knowing a word is never a simple association between an object and an acoustic pattern, but the successful operation of those principles, or application of those rules, that lead to using the word "table" or "house" for objects never before encountered. The language universal in this instance is not the type of object that comes to have a word, nor the particular relations involved; the universal is the generality that words stand for relations instead of being unique names for one object.

Further, no language has ever been described that does not have a second order of relational principles, namely, principles in which relations are being related, that is, syntax in which relations between words are being specified. Once again, the universal is not a particular relation that occurs in all languages (though there are several such relations) but that all languages have relations of relations.

Mathematics may be used as a highly abstract form of description, not of scattered facts but of the dynamic interrelations--the operating principles--found in nature. Chomsky and his students have done this. Their aim has been to develop algorithms for specific languages, primarily English, that make explicit the series of computations that may account for the structure of sentences. The

fact that these attempts have only been partially successful is irrelevant to the argument here. (Since every native speaker of
English can tell a well-formed sentence from an ill-formed one,
it it evident that some principles must exist; the question is merely
whether the Chomskyites have discovered the correct ones). The
development of algorithms is only one province of mathematics,
and in the eyes of many mathematicians a relatively limited one.
There is a more exciting prospect; once we know something about
the basic relational operating principles underlying a few languages,
it should be possible to characterize formally the abstract system
language as a whole (11). If our assumption of the existence of
basic, structural language universals is correct, one ought to be
able to adduce rigorous proof for the existence of homeomorphisms
between any natural languages, that is, any of the systems characterized formally. If a category calculus were developed for this
sort of thing, there would be one level of generality on which a
common denominator could be found; this may be done trivially
(for instance by using the product of all systems). However, our
present knowledge of the relations, and the relations of relations,
found in the languages so far investigated in depth encourages us to
expect a significant solution.

Environment and Maturation

   Everything in life, including behavior and language, is interaction of the individual with its milieu. But the milieu is not constant. The organism itself helps to shape it (this is true of cells
and organs as much as of animals and man). Thus, the organism
and its environment is a dynamic system and, phylogenetically, developed as such.
   The development of language in the child may be elucidated by
applying to it the conceptual framework of developmental biology.
Maturation may be characterized as a sequence of states. At each
state, the growing organism is capable of accepting some specific
input; this it breaks down and resynthesizes in such a way that it
makes itself develop into a new state. This new state makes the
organism sensitive to new and different types of input, whose acceptance transforms it to yet a further state, which opens the way
to still different input, and so on. This is called epigenesis. It
is the story of embryological development observable in the formation of the body, as well as in certain aspects of behavior.
   At various epigenetic states, the organism may be susceptible
to more than one sort of input--it may be susceptible to two or

more distinct kinds or even to an infinite variety of inputs, as
long as they are within determined limits--and the developmental
history varies with the nature of the input accepted. In other words,
the organism, during development, comes to crossroads; if condition A is present, it goes one way; if condition B is present, it
goes another. We speak of states here, but this is, of course, an
abstraction. Every stage of maturation is unstable. It is prone
to change into specific directions, but requires a trigger from the
environment.

When language acquisition in the child is studied from the point
of view of developmental biology, one makes an effort to describe
developmental stages together with their tendencies for change and
the conditions that bring about that change. I believe that the
schema of physical maturation is applicable to the study of language development because children appear to be sensitive to successively different aspects of the language environment. The
child first reacts only to intonation patterns. With continued exposure to these patterns as they occur in a given language, mechanisms develop that allow him to process the patterns, and in most
instances to reproduce them (although the latter is not a necessary
condition for further development). This changes him so that he
reaches a new state, a new potential for language development.
Now he becomes aware of certain articulatory aspects, can process them and possibly also reproduce them, and so on. A similar sequence of acceptance can be demonstrated on the level of
semantics and syntax.

That the embryological concepts of differentiation, as well as
of determination and regulation, are applicable to the brain processes associated with language development is best illustrated
by the material discussed above under the headings "brain correlates" and "critical age for language acquisition." Furthermore, the correlation between language development and other
maturational indices suggests that there are anatomical and
physiological processes whose maturation sets the pace for both
cognitive and language development; it is to these maturational
processes that the concept differentiation refers. We often transfer the meaning of the word to the verbal behavior itself, which is
not unreasonable, although, strictly speaking, it is the physical
correlates only that differentiate.

Pseudo-Homologies and Naive "Evolutionizing"

The relation between species is established on the basis of
structural, physiological, biochemical, and often behavioral

correspondences, called homologies. The identification of homologies frequently poses heuristic problems. Common sense may
be very misleading in this matter. Unless there is cogent evidence
that the correspondences noted are due to a common phylogenetic
origin, one must entertain the possibility that resemblances are
spurious (though perhaps due to convergence). In other words,
not all criteria are equally reliable for the discovery of true homologies. The criteria must pass the following two tests if they are
to reveal common biological origins. (i) They must be applicable
to traits that have a demonstrable (or at least conceivable) genetic
basis; and (ii) the traits to which they apply must not have a spo-
radic and seemingly random distribution over the taxa of the entire
animal kingdom. Homologies cannot be established by relying on
similarity that rests on superficial inspection (a whale is not a
fish); on logical rather than biological aspects (animals that move
at 14 miles per hour are not necessarily related to one another);
and on anthropocentric imputation of motives (a squirrel's hoarding
of nuts may have nothing in common with man's provisions for his
future).

Comparisons of language with animal communication that pur-
port to throw light on the problem of its phylogenetic origins in-
fringe on every one of these guidelines. Attempts to write generative grammars for the language of the bees in order to discover
in what respect that language is similar to and different from
man's language fail to pass test (i). Syntax does not have a genetic basis any more than do arithmetic or algebra; these are
calculi used to describe relations. It may be that the activities or
circumstances to which the calculi are applied are in some way
related to genetically determined capacities. However, merely the
fact that the calculus may or may not be applied obviously does not
settle that issue.

The common practice of searching the entire animal kingdom for
communication behavior that resembles man's in one aspect or
another fails test (ii). The fact that some bird species and perhaps two or three cetaceans can make noises that sound like words,
that some insects use discrete signals when they communicate, or
that recombination of signals has been observed to occur in communication systems of a dozen totally unrelated species are not
signs of a common phylogeny or genetically based relationship to
language. Furthermore, the similarities noted between human language and animal communication all rest on superficial intuition.
The resemblances that exist between human language and the language of the bees and the birds are spurious. The comparative
criteria are usually logical (12) instead of biological; and the very

idea that there must be a common denominator underlying all
communication systems of animals and man is based on an anthropocentric imputation.

Everything in biology has a history, and so every communication
system is the result of evolution. But traits or skills do not have
an evolutionary history of their own, that is, a history that is independent of the history of the species. Contemporary species are
discontinuous groups (except for those in the process of branching)
with discontinuous communication behavior. Therefore, historical
continuity need not lead to continuity between contemporary communication systems, many of which (including man's) constitute
unique developments.

Another recent practice is to give speculative accounts of just
how, why, and when human language developed. This is a somewhat futile undertaking. The knowledge that we have gained about
the mechanisms of evolution does not enable us to give specific
accounts of every event of the past. Paleontological evidence
points to the nature of its fauna, flora, and climate. The precursors of modern man have left for us their bones, teeth, and
primitive tools. None of these bears any necessary or assured
relation to any type of communication system. Most speculations
on the nature of the most primitive sounds, on the first discovery
of their usefulness, on the reasons for the hypertrophy of the
brain, or the consequences of a narrow pelvis are in vain. We can
no longer reconstruct what the selection pressures were or in
what order they came, because we know too little that is securely
established by hard evidence about the ecological and social conditions of fossil man. Moreover, we do not even know what the
targets of actual selection were. This is particularly troublesome
because every genetic alteration brings about several changes at
once, some of which must be quite incidental to the selective
process.

Species Specificities and Cognitive Specialization

In the 19th century it was demonstrated that man is not in a
category apart from that of animals. Today it seems to be necessary to defend the view (before many psychologists) that man is
not identical with all other animals--in fact, that every animal
species is unique, and that most of the commonalities that exist
are, at best, homologies. It is frequently claimed that the principles of behavioral function are identical--in all vertebrates, for
example--and that the differences between species are differences

of magnitude, rather than quality. At other times, it is assumed that cognitive functions are alike in two species except that one of the two may have additionally acquired a capacity for a specific activity. I find fault with both views.

Since behavioral capacities (I prefer the term cognition) are the product of brain function, my point can well be illustrated by considering some aspects of brain evolution. Every mammalian species has an anatomically distinct brain. Homologies are common, but innovations can also be demonstrated. When man's brain is compared with the brain of other primates, extensive correspondences can be found, but there are major problems when it comes to the identification of homologies. Dramatic differences exist not only in size but also in details of the developmental histories; together with differences in cerebrocortical histology, topography, and extent, there are differences in subcortical fiber-connections, as pointed out by Geschwind (13) most recently and by others before him. The problem is, what do we make of the innovations? Is it possible that each innovation (usually an innovation is not a clear-cut anatomical entity) is like an independent component that is simply added to the components common to all the more old-fashioned brains? And if so, is it likely that the new component is simply adding a routine to the computational facilities already available? Both presumptions are naive. A brain is an integrated organ, and cognition results from the integrated operation of all its tissues and suborgans. Man's brain is not a chimpanzee's brain plus added "association facilities." Its functions have undergone reintegration at the same pace as its evolutionary developments.

The identical argument applies to cognitive functions. Cognition is not made up of isolated processes such as perception, storing, and retrieval. Animals do not all have an identical memory mechanism except that some have a larger storage capacity. As the structure of most proteins, the morphology of most cells, and the gross anatomy of most animals show certain species specificities (as do details of behavioral repertoires), so we may expect that cognition, too, in all of its aspects, has its species specificities. My assumption, therefore, is that man's cognition is not essentially that of every other primate with merely the addition of the capacity for language; instead, I propose that his entire cognitive function, of which his capacity for language is an integral part, is species-specific. I repeat once more that I make this assumption not because I think man is in a category all his own, but because every animal species must be assumed to have cognitive specificities.

Conclusion

The human brain is a biochemical machine; it computes the relations expressed in sentences and their components. It has a print-out consisting of acoustic patterns that are capable of similar relational computation by machines of the same constitution using the same program. Linguists, biologists, and psychologists have all discussed certain aspects of the machine.

Linguists, particularly those developing generative grammar, aim at a formal description of the machine's behavior; they search mathematics for a calculus to describe it adequately. Different calculations are matched against the behavior to test their descriptive adequacy. This is an empirical procedure. The raw data are the way a speaker of a language understands collections of words or the relationships he sees. A totally adequate calculus has not yet been discovered. Once available, it will merely describe, in formal terms, the process of relational interpretation in the realm of verbal behavior. It will describe a set of operations; however, it will not make any claims of isomorphism between the formal operations and the biological operations they describe.

Biologists try to understand the nature, growth, and function of the machine (the human brain) itself. They make little inroads here and there and generally play catch-as-catch-can; everything about the machine interests them (including the descriptions furnished by linguists).

Traditionally, learning theory has been involved neither in a specific description of this particular machine's behavior nor in its physical constitution. Its concern has been with the use of the machine: What makes it go? Can one make it operate more or less often? What purposes does it serve?

Answers provided by each of these inquiries into language are not intrinsically anatagonistic, as has often been claimed. It is only certain overgeneralizations that come into conflict. This is especially so when claims are made that any one of these approaches provides answers to all the questions that matter.

REFERENCES AND NOTES

1.   E. H. Lenneberg, in The Structure of Language; Readings in the Philosophy of Language, J. A. Fodor and J. J. Katz, eds. (Prentice-Hall, Englewood Cliffs, N. J., 1964).

2.   For complete treatment, see E. H. Lenneberg, Biological
     Foundations of Language (Wiley, New York, 1967).

3.   E. H. Lenneberg, I. A. Nichols, E. F. Rosenberger, in Dis-
     orders of Communication, D. Rioch, ed. (Research Publica-
     tions of Association for Research in Nervous and Mental Dis-
     orders, New York, 1964), vol. 42.

4.   E. H. Lenneberg, F. G. Rebelsky, I. A. Nichols, Hum.
     Develop. 8, 23 (1965).

5.   R. Brown, C. Cazden, U. Bellugi, in The 1967 Minnesota Sym-
     posium on Child Psychology, J. P. Hill, ed. (Univ. of Minne-
     sota Press, Minneapolis, in press).

6.   D. Slobin, personal communication.

7.   E. H. Lenneberg, J. Abnorm. Soc. Psychol. 65, 419 (1962).

8.   -----, S. Fraiberg, N. Stein, research in progress.

9.   D. B. Fry, in The Genesis of Language: A Psycholinguistic
     Approach, F. Smith and G. A. Miller, eds. (M. I. T. Press,
     Cambridge, 1966).

10. For details, see E. H. Lenneberg, Perception and Language,
     in preparation.

11. N. Chomsky, "The formal nature of language" (in 2, Appendix
     A).

12. See, for instance, C. F. Hockett, in Animal Communication,
     W. E. Lanyon and W. N. Tavelga, eds. (American Institute of
     Biological Sciences, Washington, D. C. , 1960); and in Sci.
     Amer. 203, 89 (1960).

13. N. Geschwind, Brain 88, 237, 585 (1965).

14. I thank H. Levin and M. Seligman for comments and criticisms.

THE NATURE OF THE READING PROCESS

by John B. Carroll

As you silently read this very paragraph, what are you doing?
If you are a skilled reader and are attending carefully to what this
paragraph is trying to say, you will notice the following. First,
what are your eyes doing? Moving together in a swift and well-
coordinated way, your eyes are making a series of fixations,
jumping from place to place on the page of print. The jumps are
exceedingly rapid; you see little while your eyes are jumping.
What is important are the fixations, when your eyes come to rest.
Most of these fixations are actually on or close to the line of print,
but unless you are reading quite slowly you cannot easily predict
or control where your eyes will fixate. The fixations are usually
quite short in duration; each one will last about one-quarter of a
second on the average.
Usually the fixations progress from left to right along the first
line of print, then back to the beginning of the next line and again
from left to right across the line, and so on. For the average
adult reader there will be about two fixations per inch of ordinary
type like this. Some of these fixations may be very brief, amount-
ing to minor adjustments in order to bring the print better into
view. During most of the fixations, you receive an impression of
a certain amount of printed material; that is, you instantaneously
perceive and recognize one or more words, perhaps up to four or
five in some cases. You are more likely to recognize the words
that are in the immediate area of fixation; words outside this immediate area may be less well recognized, but some of them have
been recognized in a previous fixation, and others may be more
clearly recognized in a future fixation. Some of the words may
never be clearly recognized, but you apprehend enough of the
stimulus to fill them in from the general drift of what you are
reading.

Prepared for the HEW Secretary's Advisory Committee on Dyslexia
and Related Reading Disorders.

Let us just think about this process of instantaneous word recognition. Most of the words you see are words you have seen many times before; even though in actuality they may be relatively rare, they are familiar enough to you to permit "instantaneous" recognition. Of course recognition is not really instantaneous; it takes a certain amount of time. Experiments in which words are exposed very briefly show that common words can be recognized quite accurately in less than 1/10 of a second; even words that are quite rare can be recognized with at least 50 percent accuracy in exposures of about 1/5 of a second. During the average fixation lasting 1/4 of a second it is often possible to take in several words. The point is that most words are recognized extremely rapidly. If you are a skilled reader you do not have to stop to figure out the pronunciation of a familiar word from its spelling; you are hardly conscious of the spelling at all. Still less do you attend to the particular phonetic values of the letters; in reading the word <u>women</u> it would scarcely occur to you to note that the "o" in the first syllable stands for a sound that rhymes with /i/ in <u>whim</u>. The printed word <u>women</u> is a Gestalt-like total stimulus that immediately calls to mind the spoken word that corresponds to it, or if not the spoken word itself, some underlying response which is also made when the word is spoken. As a skilled reader, you can consider yourself lucky to have a large "sight" vocabulary.

The actual process by which we recognize words is not well understood, simply because the whole process of "pattern perception", as it is called, is one of the most mysterious problems in psychology. How, for example, do we recognize a table, a goblet, or a flagpole for what it is, regardless of the angle of regard? Nevertheless, it is a simple fact that we <u>can</u> learn to recognize words even though the words may be printed in different typefaces or written in different cursive styles, and in different sizes. Now even though word recognition is rapid, it obviously depends to a large extent on cues from the letters composing the word. There is little confusion among such highly similar items as <u>cob</u>, <u>rob</u>, <u>mob</u>, and <u>nob</u> even in fast single exposures. We do know that in recognizing longer words, the letters standing at the beginning and end are more critical than letters in the middle, for in fast exposures these middle letters can sometimes be altered or replaced without this being noticed by the reader. In ordinary reading we frequently fail to notice words that contain printer's errors. But there is little evidence to support the idea that a mature reader recognizes words merely by their outlines or general shape. It is unlikely that if you see the shape ⬤⬤⬤ you will recognize the word <u>dog</u>; you might just as well think it to be <u>day</u> or <u>dug</u>. Beginning readers sometimes use more shape cues in trying to recognize words, but they will be overwhelmed with confusion if they depend solely on such cues apart from the recognition of the letters themselves. In the mature reader the process of rapid word recognition seems to depend upon his ability to integrate the information provided by the separate letters composing the word, some letters being more critical as cues than others. Because the recognizability of a word is apparently correlated rather highly with its frequency of use, word perception seems to be a skill that depends upon large amounts of practice and exposure.

Suppose, however, that the skilled reader comes to a word that he has never seen before, like dossal, cunctation, or latescent, or an unfamiliar proper name like Vukmanovich or Sharra. Though the skilled reader can hardly be said to "recognize" a word he has never seen before, he nevertheless recognizes elements of it-- letters and patterns of letters that give him reasonably good cues as to how the word should be pronounced. Dossal may be recognized as similar to fossil and pronounced to rhyme with it, the first letter cuing the /f/ sound. Cunctation may give a little more difficulty but be recognized as somewhat similar to punctuation and at the same time to mutation; by following the total pattern of cues the reader may be able to infer the correct pronunciation. Latescent will probably be recognized not as a compound of late and scent, but as a member of a family of words like quiescent, fluorescent, etc. Somewhat the same principles apply to the reading of foreign proper names; even if he is not familiar with the foreign language involved, the skilled reader will be sensitive to the possible values of the letters and letter-combinations in the name, and come up with a reasonable pronunciation.

It should be noted that thus far we have been speaking of the recognition of words as particular combinations of letters. Actually, in English there are numerous instances of homographs-- words that are pronounced in different ways depending on their use. The word READ is an interesting example: in the context to read it rhymes with bead, but in the context to have read, it rhymes with bed. The skilled reader instantaneously interprets the word in its proper "reading" or pronunciation depending upon the context, i.e. the surrounding words and their meanings.

This takes us, in fact, to the next stage of our analysis of the reading process. As you take in material recognized in the succession of rapid fixations that is characteristic of skilled reading, it somehow merges together in such a way as to build up in your mind an impression of a meaningful message, --a message that is in many ways analogous to the message you would apprehend if someone read the paragraph aloud to you, all its proper inflections and accents.

Some people report that as they read they can "hear" (in the form of internal auditory images) the message as it might be spoken; at least they report that they "hear" snatches of such a message. Other readers feel that they apprehend a meaning from the printed message directly, --that is, without the intervention of any auditory images. In slow readers, or even in skilled readers reading very difficult material, one may notice slight articulatory movements that suggest that the reader is trying to pronounce the words subvocally.

The process of scanning a paragraph for a meaningful message does not, of course, always run smoothly. As one reads, there may be momentary lapses of attention (which can be due to lack of interest, distractions, or even stimulation from the content itself), or of comprehension (which can be due to the difficulty of the material, poor writing, or other conditions). The process of comprehension seems to have some influence on the movements of the eyes: when the reader fails to attend or comprehend, his eyes may "regress", moving back to fixate on a portion of the material already scanned. Difficulties in recognizing particular words may cause the eyes to dwell on or around a particular point in the text longer than the usual amount of time. There are large differences among individuals in all the reading processes we have mentioned. Some readers can read with markedly fewer fixations per line; some read with an abnormally high number of fixations per line and exhibit many more regressions than normal. Few individuals have the same pattern of eye movements, even when they read at approximately the same speed. Obviously, there are wide individual differences in rate and accuracy of comprehension.

The essential skill in reading is getting meaning from a printed or written message. In many ways this is similar to getting meaning from a spoken message, but there are differences, because the cues are different. Spoken messages contain cues that are not evident in printed messages, and conversely. In either case, understanding language is itself a tremendous feat, when one thinks about it. When you get the meaning of a verbal message, you have not only recognized the words themselves; you have interpreted the words in their particular grammatical functions and you have somehow apprehended the general grammatical patterning of each sentence. You have unconsciously recognized what words or phrases constitute the subjects and predicates of the sentence, what words or phrases modify those subjects or predicates, and so on. In addition, you have given a "semantic" interpretation of the sentence, assigning meanings to the key words in the sentence. For example, in reading the sentence "He understood that he was coming tonight" you would know who each "he" refers to, and you

would interpret the word <u>understood</u> as meaning "had been caused
to believe" rather than "comprehended". Somehow you put all
these things together in order to understand the "plain sense" of
what the message says.

Even beyond getting the simple meaning of the material you are
reading, you are probably reacting to it in numerous ways. You
may be trying to evaluate it for its truth, validity, significance, or
importance. You may be checking it against your own experience
or knowledge. You may find that it is reminding you of previous
thoughts or experiences, or you may be starting to think about its
implications for your future actions. You may be making inferences
or drawing conclusions from what you read that go far beyond what
is explicitly stated in the text. In doing any or all of these things,
you are "reasoning" or "thinking". Nobody can tell you exactly
what to think; much of your thinking will be dependent upon your
particular background and experience. At the same time, some
thinking is logical and justified by the facts and ideas one reads,
while other kinds of thinking are illogical and not adequately justified by the facts and ideas one reads. One aspect of a mature
reader's skill consists in his being able to think about what he reads
in a logical and well-informed way. This aspect of reading skill
sometimes takes years to attain.

We have described the process of reading in the skilled reader,
--a process that is obviously very complex. How is this process
learned or attained?

As in the case of any skill, reading skill is not learned all at
once. It takes a considerable amount of time. Furthermore, the
process of learning to read is not simply a "slow-motion" imitation
of the mature reading process. It has numerous components, and
each component has to be learned and practiced.

There are probably a great many ways to attain reading skill,
depending upon the order in which the various components are
learned and mastered. It may be the case that some ways are always better than others. On the other hand, children differ in their
aptitudes, talents, and inclinations so much that it may also be the
case that a particular way of learning is better for one child while
another way is better for another child. It all depends upon which
components of reading skill a given child finds easier to learn at a
given stage of his development. In referring to different orders in
which component skills would be learned, we do not mean to imply
a lock-step procedure in which the child first learns and masters
one skill, than goes on to learn and master another skill, and so on.
Actually, a child can be learning a number of skills simultaneously,
but will reach mastery of them at different periods in his development. From the standpoint of the teacher, this means that different

skills may need to be emphasized at different periods, depending
upon the characteristics of the individual child. This is particularly true in the case of the child who is having difficulty in learning to read.

Let us try to specify the components of reading skill. Some of
these components come out of our analysis of the mature reading
process; others out of a further analysis of those components.

1. The child must know the language that he is going to learn to
read. Normally, this means that the child can speak and understand the language at least to a certain level of skill before he
starts to learn to read, because the purpose of reading is to help
him get messages from print that are similar to the messages he
can already understand if they are spoken. But language learning
is a lifelong process, and normally there are many aspects of language that the individual learns solely or mainly through reading.
And speaking and understanding the language is not an absolute
prerequisite for beginning to learn to read; there are cases on
record of children who learn to read before they can speak, and of
course many deaf children learn the language only through learning
to read. Foreign-born children sometimes learn English mainly
through reading. Children who, before they begin to read, do not
know the language, or who only understand but do not speak, will
very likely require a mode of instruction specially adapted to them.

2. The child must learn to dissect spoken words into component
sounds. In order to be able to use the alphabetic principle by which
English words are spelled, the child must be able to recognize the
separate sounds composing a word and the temporal order in which
they are spoken, --the consonants and vowels that compose spoken
words. This does not mean that he must acquire a precise knowledge of phonetics, but it does mean that he must recognize those
aspects of speech sound that are likely to be represented in spelling.
For example, in hearing the word straight, the child must be able
to decompose the sounds into the sequence /s, t, r, ey, t/.

3. The child must learn to recognize and discriminate the letters
of the alphabet in their various forms (capitals, lower-case letters,
printed, and cursive). (He should also know the names and alphabetic ordering of the letters.) This skill is required if the child
is to make progress in finding correspondences between letters and
sounds.

4. The child must learn the left-to-right principle by which words
are spelled and put in order in continuous text. This is, as we
have noted, a very general principle, although there are certain
aspects of letter-sound correspondences that violate the principle,
--e.g. the reverse order of wh in representing the sound cluster
/hw/.

5. The child must learn that there are patterns of highly probable correspondence between letters and sounds, and he must learn those patterns of correspondence that will help him recognize words that he already knows in his spoken language or that will help him determine the pronunciation of unfamiliar words. There are few if any letters in English orthography that always have the same sound values; nevertheless, spellings tend to give good clues to the pronunciation of words. Often a letter will have highly predictable sound values if it is considered in conjunction with surrounding letters. Partly through direct instruction and partly through a little-understood process of inference, the normal child can fairly readily acquire the ability to respond to these complex patterns of letter-sound correspondences.

6. The child must learn to recognize printed words from whatever cues he can use, --their total configuration, the letters composing them, the sounds represented by those letters, and/or the meanings suggested by the context. By "recognition" we mean not only becoming aware that he has seen the word before, but also knowing the pronunciation of the word. This skill is one of the most essential in the reading process, because it yields for the reader the equivalent of a speech signal.

7. The child must learn that printed words are signals for spoken words and that they have meanings analogous to those of spoken words. While "decoding" a printed message into its spoken equivalent, the child must be able to apprehend the meaning of the total message in the same way that he would apprehend the meaning of the corresponding spoken message. As in the case of adult reading, the "spoken equivalent" may be apprehended solely internally, although it is usual, in early reading efforts, to expect the child to be able to read aloud, at first with much hesitation, but later with fluency and expression.

8. The child must learn to reason and think about what he reads, within the limits of his talent and experience.

It will be noticed that each of these eight components of learning to read is somehow involved in the adult reading process, -- knowing the language, dissecting spoken words into component sounds, and so forth. Adult reading is skilled only because all the eight components are so highly practiced that they merge together, as it were, into one unified performance. The well-coordinated, swift eye movements of the adult reader are a result, not a cause, of good reading; the child does not have to be taught eye movements and therefore we have not listed eye-coordination as a component skill. Rather, skilled eye movements represent the highest form of the skill we have listed as (4), --the learning of the left-to-right principle. The instantaneous word recognition ability of the

mature reader is the highest form of the skill we have listed as
(6), --recognition of printed words from whatever cues are available; and usually that skill in turn depends upon the mastery of
some of the other skills, in particular (5), --learning patterns of
correspondence between letters and sounds. The ability of the
adult reader to apprehend meaning quickly is an advanced form of
skill (7), and his ability to think about what he reads is an advanced form of skill (8).

The great "debate" about how reading should be taught is really
a debate about the order in which the child should be started on the
road toward learning each of the skills. Few will question that
mature reading involves all eight skills; the only question is which
skills should be introduced and mastered first. Many points of
view are possible. On the one hand there are those who believe
that the skills should be introduced in approximately the order in
which they have been listed; this is the view of those who believe
that there should be an early emphasis on the "decoding" of print
into sound via letter-sound relations. On the other hand, there are
those who believe that the skills should be introduced approximately
in the following order:

(1)   The child should learn the language he is going to read.
(6)   The child should learn to recognize printed words from
      whatever cues he can use initially, but only from total con-
      figurations.
(7)   The child should learn that printed words are signals for
      spoken words, and that meanings can be apprehended from
      these printed words.
(8)   The child must learn to reason and think about what he
      reads.
(4)   The child should learn the left-to-right principle, but ini-
      tially only as it applies to complete words in continuous
      text.
(3)   The child should learn to recognize and discriminate the
      letters of the alphabet.
(2)   The child should learn to dissect spoken words into compo-
      nent sounds.
(5)   The child should learn patterns of correspondence between
      letters and sounds, to help him in the advanced phases of
      skill (6).

This latter view is held by those who argue that there should be
an early emphasis on getting the meaning from print, and that the
child should advance as quickly as possible toward the word-
recognition and meaning-apprehension capacities of the mature
reader. Skills (2), (3), and (5) are introduced only after the child
has achieved considerable progress towards mastery of skills (4),
(6), (7), and (8).

These are the two main views about the process of teaching
reading. If each one is taken quite strictly and seriously, there
can be very clear differences in the kinds of instructional materials
and procedures that are used. It is beyond our scope to discuss
whether the two methods differ in effectiveness. We would emphasize, rather, that methods may differ in effectiveness from child
to child. Furthermore, it is possible to construct other reasonable
orders in which the various components of reading skill can be introduced to the child. There is currently a tendency to interlace
the approaches distinguished above in such a way that the child can
attain rapid sight recognition of words at the same time that he is
learning letter-sound correspondences that will help him "attack"
words that he does not already know.

For the child who is having difficulty in learning to read, it may
be necessary to determine exactly which skills are causing most
difficulty. The "dyslexic" child may be "hung up" on the acquisition
of just one or two skills. For example, he may be having particular trouble with skill (3), --the recognition and discrimination of
the letters of the alphabet; or with skill (2), --the dissection of
spoken words into component sounds. On determining what skills
pose obstacles for a particular child, it is usually necessary to
give special attention to those skills while capitalizing on those
skills which are easier for the child to master.

Uncertainties and Research Problems

The above description of the nature of the reading process is
based on the findings of nearly three-quarters of a century of research. A good deal is known about reading behavior, yet there
are many questions that have not been answered with precision and
certainty. We shall list the most important of these.

Questions about the mature reading process:

1. How does the individual's ability to recognize words "instan-
    taneously" develop? What clues for word recognition are most
    important? How and when does awareness of spelling clues
    and "inner speech" representation recede, if at all? What is
    the "sight vocabulary" of the mature reader? (It should be
    noted that most studies of word recognition processes have
    been conducted with adults; there is need for developmental
    studies in which word recognition processes would be investi-
    gated over different chronological age levels.)

2. How do skilled readers process unfamiliar words? To what
    extent, and how, do they use patterns of letter-sound corre-
    spondences?
3. How do skilled readers find the proper "readings" of homo-
    graphs and other types of ambiguous words?
4. What are the detailed psychological processes by which skilled
    readers comprehend the simple meaning of what they read?
    In what way do lexico-semantic, syntactical and typographical
    factors interact to yield this comprehension?
5. How are eye movements controlled by comprehension proces-
    ses, and how does the individual develop skill in scanning
    print?
6. How does the mature reader acquire skill in reading and infer-
    ential processes?
7. What are the major sources of individual differences in rate
    and accuracy of comprehension in mature readers?

Questions about certain components of reading skill as they affect
   learning:

1. In what way does knowledge of the spoken language interact
    with learning to read? What kinds and amounts of competence
    are desirable before the child undertakes any given task in
    learning to read?
2. What is the nature of the ability to discriminate sounds in the
    spoken language and to "dissect" words in terms of these
    sounds? How does it develop, and what role does it play in the
    beginning reader's learning of letter-sound correspondences?
    How can this ability be taught?
3. How do children learn to recognize and discriminate alphabetic
    letters in their various forms? When children have difficulty
    with letter recognition, how can these difficulties be overcome?
4. How do children learn the left-to-right principle in orthography
    (both as applied to individual words, and to the order of words
    in continuous text)? Are there children with special difficul-
    ties in learning this component of reading skill?
5. Exactly what are the most useful and functional patterns of
    letter-sound correspondence in English orthography, and in
    what order should they be learned? How, indeed, are they
    learned? Is it better to give direct instruction in them, or is
    it better to rely upon the child's capacity to infer these pat-
    terns from the experience he acquires as he learns to read?
    Should the characteristics of particular children be taken
    into account in deciding this?

6.   When a child has acquired the ability to recognize words and
     read them in order, yet does not appear to comprehend the
     message as he would if it were spoken to him, what is the
     nature of the difficulty?

Questions about the ordering of the components of reading skill in
   the teaching process:

1.   In what way are the various skills prerequisite for each other?
     What aspects of each skill are necessary to facilitate progress
     in another skill?
2.   Is there one best order in which to introduce the components of
     reading skill in the learning process, or are there different
     orders depending upon characteristics of individual children
     or groups of children? If so, how can these individual or
     group characteristics be determined?
3.   On the assumption that there is an optimal ordering of skills
     for any given child, how much mastery of a given skill is
     desirable before another skill is introduced?

SKILLS REQUIRED FOR LEARNING TO READ

by Richard L. Venezky, Robert C. Calfee, and Robin S. Chapman

INTRODUCTION

After decades of debate and expenditures of millions of research dollars, the teaching of reading remains on questionable psychological and linguistic grounds. The history and current practices of reading instruction, as summarized in Matthew (1966) and Chall (1967), show an overwhelming concern by educators, psychologists, linguists, and publishers with the content of reading texts and the methods of reading instruction, but little interest in the skills employed by the beginning reader. As the competing nostrums for literacy pains have come and gone, assumptions about the reading process have changed also--with little relevant research to justify the transitions (Fries 1962).

Characteristic of these changes has been a continual desire for the "right way", a desire that has led to rather strange behavior by otherwise sober and intelligent men. Thorndike, a psychologist, became the authoritative source of linguistic knowledge for reading, and Bloomfield, a linguist, became the primary reference for the psychology of reading. Flesch, neither a linguist nor a psychologist, has been taken by some as an authority on both. Thorndike's influence on the linguistic basis of reading has been underestimated. Besides the constrictive influence of the Thorndike and Lorge (1944) word counts on the selection of reading vocabulary.

The research reported herein was performed pursuant to a contract with the United States Office of Education Department of Health, Education, and Welfare, under the provisions of the Cooperative Research Program. This article first appeared as Working Paper No. 10, Wisconsin Research and Development Center for Cognitive Learning, University of Wisconsin, Madison, Wisconsin, September 1968.

lary, there are also a number of other influential language analyses prepared by Thorndike. Chief among these is The Teaching of English Suffixes (1932). Bloomfield, one of America's greatest linguists, was narrow-minded in psychological matters, having been converted to behaviorism by his colleague at Ohio State University, A. P. Weiss. While there was room for dissent in the linguistic domain, the stimulus-response approach to learning was not questioned (c.f. Bloomfield 1942).

In the teaching of reading, as in most topics which relate to education, research and development have been forced to yield stage-center to politics, economics, and frequently uninformed sentiment. The concern of publishers to be solvent, of politicians to capitalize on parental concern, and of assorted entrepreneurs to impose their executive experiences on school systems have left little room for linguists, psychologists, and educators to apply their seldom startling discoveries to the teaching of reading. But even if these extraneous influences on the educational system were reduced, immediate improvements of reading instruction would probably not be forthcoming, since basic information about the skills the child uses in the reading process is not available.

Reading success is generally attributed to teacher, home, or reading program variables, while reading failure is attributed to such sources as brain damage, emotional distress, motivational deficit, or inappropriateness of the content of primary reading texts for the child's social or cultural background. Analyses of the skills present in the good readers and lacking in the poorer ones are rarely made.

In this paper we attempt to focus on the conception of reading as a skill behavior. For the present, we are interested primarily in the decoding operation, the process used in translating from meaningless alphabetical symbols to that form of language from which the native speaker already derives meaning. (Learning to read ideographic signs is quite different.) We consider briefly several models for the decoding process and examine the skills required by each for efficient decoding. The problem of increasing instructional efficiency will not be considered further in this paper.

THE READING PROCESS

What is Reading?

For the purposes of this discussion, which focuses on the teaching of reading in the early grades, reading has been interpreted as the process of translating from alphabetical symbols to that form of language from which the native speaker can already derive meaning.

The narrowness of this definition is intended to avert confusions about the teaching of reading. To teach reading is not to teach language. By the time the normal child comes to the reading task, he already speaks a language--he has mastered a system of signals for communicating in a meaningful fashion with other people. The child can make himself understood and can understand others. While there are some features of this system which he has not yet mastered by the age of five or six, he can still communicate effectively with both his peers and adults (Lenneberg 1967). Once a child learns to read, he can employ this new skill to enlarge his vocabulary or to increase his usage of certain syntactic forms. However, the use of reading to improve competence in language should not be confused with learning to read.

Any complete description of the reading process must include the transition from written symbols to meaning. However, it may be that the only part of this process which is different from listening to speech is the initial translation from written symbols to some representation of language to which the reader can assign meaning, a representation that may be common to listening and reading. It seems unlikely that in learning to read, a child acquires meanings, new syntax or a new morphology. Rather, the problem can be viewed as the learning of an alternate representational scheme for an existing system.

In rapid, silent reading by a competent reader, translation may at times proceed from graphical patterns directly (in some sense) to meaning, especially when nonlinguistic cues are utilized: paragraph indentations, position of headings, quotations, etc. But to become a skilled speed reader, it appears that one must first pass through various stages of reading--including those that require translation from graphical forms to spoken language.

Cognitive Skills and Reading

A few years ago, Harry Levin, coordinator of Project Literacy research, wrote: "Reading is a skill rather than a body of curricular content.... To think of reading as a complex skill is to borrow an analogy from the research on other skill-learnings in which the total process is analyzed into component parts" (Levin 1966). Levin suggested that the traditional approach to reading research, involving comparisons of different methods of presenting material

or different materials, could be profitably superseded by investigation of the specific cognitive skills necessary for the development of reading proficiency.

In view of the vagueness of the term cognitive skill, it is not
suprising that there is no useful taxonomy of such behaviors. We
shall not try to construct a taxonomy here, but rather shall consider a preliminary analysis of selected skills which most investigators would agree are related to reading and are cognitive in
nature, i.e. are associated in one way or another to language,
thinking, or information processing. In following our narrow
definition of the initial reading task, we will be deliberately ignoring many skills which are employed in reading, e.g. the use of
context and pictorial clues in comprehension or the development of
search strategies in speed reading.

Models of the Reading Process

Statements about the component skills necessary to read imply
that certain assumptions have been made about the reading process, i.e. that one has assumed a particular model of reading.
By a reading model is meant a psychological description of the
processes used in reading. Different models have been proposed,
and readers probably do operate in different ways from time to
time. In fact, one might hope that by the end of the first grade
the better readers have learned to apply different reading strategies
to different types of material. No one reading model will be general enough to account for all reading behavior, whatever the background of instruction and experience, material, and purpose for
reading. However, it is useful to examine the implications of
certain general assumptions. (This discussion will be limited to
oral reading in first graders, primarily reading of single words,
but with extensions to the reading of sentences and other connected
material.)

In one model that might be proposed, the child is assumed to
store by rote association an exact visual replica of each word he
learns. In reading, the visual form is matched against replicas
until a match is made, thus making available the associated pronunciation pattern. In an alternative model, the visual information is analyzed sequentially (letter by letter), the appropriate
sounds or sound patterns identified, and then integrated for pronunciation.

It is interesting to ask what skills are required by each of these
models for oral reading, disregarding comprehension. First, the

student must be able to identify and differentiate visual patterns.
Second, organized access to and utilization of memory is necessary.
In the first model, the necessary memory capacity rapidly becomes
large, unless one begins to expand the notion of similarity. That
is, one might assume that a written word is segmented, using
vowels as breakpoints, and matched against partial replicas until
a similar spelling pattern is found for each segment. The word
splint might be broken into spl- and -int, pronunciations for each
segment recovered from more familiar words (e.g. from splash
and hint) and integrated. In the second model, demands on as-
sociative memory are smaller, but the amount of processing and
the level of cognitive ability required are greater.

Finally, there is a cluster of skills related to articulation of the
word. If a child is asked to pronounce spray, and he says /θpre/,
the mispronunciation may reflect the fact that the child tries but
cannot articulate the correct phoneme pattern, is missing his
front teeth, cannot discriminate between /s/ and /θ/ and hence
has no basis for different pronunciation, has made mistakes in
visual processing of the letter patterns, or has failed to come up
with the correct correspondence between the visual pattern and pronunciation. Typically, reading (as decoding) has concerned itself
only with his last possibility, but each of the other problems is
quite plausible.

To account for comprehension, another dimension must be added
to the models. For example, in the first model above, comprehension might be most simply handled by assuming that the meaning is
stored together with the replica and pronunciation. The reader
would have simultaneous access to articulation and comprehension
for any word he has learned to read. An alternative assumption
might be that the student links each visual pattern to a meaning and
that articulation depends upon this identification. That is, the
written word is used to retrieve some meaningful concept which then
determines pronunciation.

In the letter-by-letter model, one can also imagine at least two
ways in which comprehension could be handled. On the one hand,
the visual pattern may be associated directly with its semantic
referent so that, during decoding, comprehension takes place
simultaneously with pronunciation. Comprehension and articulation would be more or less independent. The reader might make
a decoding mistake and pronounce the word incorrectly, although
understanding quite well what it meant. On the other hand, he
might wait until the decoding process was complete and use the
spoken representation of the word (or some equivalent thereof) for
comprehension. The word would be comprehended only after it was
pronounced.

If context is available, as when a word is part of a sentence or there are pictures or other cues to identification, comprehension may be achieved in other ways. For one thing, the reader may simply guess. It is common practice for the teacher to present to the children a list of "new words" just prior to the oral reading exercises. The set of reasonable guesses may be thereby sufficiently limited so that guessing as a reasonable strategy. Goodman (1968) has suggested that reading models include explicit references to such strategies. He points out the potential significance of visual cues that permit readers to focus on selected words in connected material by matching the available information against expectations. Little is known about those cognitive skills necessary to acquire "psycholinguistic guessing" strategies in reading.

The models considered above point to several component skills that are possibly related to beginning reading ability. Some are basically perceptual-motor skills--visual, auditory, and articulatory. A child must be able to discriminate auditory and visual patterns that differ on certain critical (but not easily discriminable) dimensions, and at the same time perceive identities or similarities among patterns that are in most respects quite different. For example, a right-left transformation is an essential clue for contrasting letter pairs such as b-d and p-q. On the other hand, a child must learn to ignore the differences between the various type forms of a lower-case letter, as in primary type, cursive script, and the particular style used by his first-grade teacher.

Reading also involves memory. The student is called upon for information that will not be explicitly taught in the classroom; he must also be able to acquire new information and to store it in a retrievable fashion. In this connection, it appears that a well developed vocabulary and familiarity with the language help the beginning reader for a variety of reasons, some of which (e.g. ability to follow instructions) are not directly related to reading as decoding or comprehension. There is undoubtedly an implicit premium on problem solving or thinking capabilities. As one example, it has been suggested (Chall 1967) that children taught by non-phonic reading programs develop adequate word attack skills to the extent they can induce letter—sound regularities.

SKILLS REQUIRED FOR LEARNING TO READ

General Categories of Skills

In kindergarten and first grade, learning to read involves both training and testing. Typically, a reading readiness test is administered towards the end of kindergarten, and from the results of this test and the teacher's evaluation, each child is assigned to a first-grade reading track (high, medium, or low). The child is likely to remain at this level thereafter. One may conclude that the preliminary tests are superb predictors of subsequent performance, or that assignment constitutes a self-fulfilling prophecy.

As a start at skill analysis, first-grade reading instruction includes (a) presentation of information of simple (rote, serial memorization of the alphabet) and complex (learning to use context cues) sorts; (b) informal testing by interrogation or workbooks; and (c) a formal achievement test near the end of the school year. The question to be asked is, what task skills are required for a child to perform adequately on the tests and for the instruction to be effective? It is standard practice to check a child's eyesight and hearing, since if either of these are faulty, the testing and training procedures are obviously invalid. It is less obvious that there should be equal concern with basic cognitive skills such as ability to follow instructions, and that for a child without these skills, the teaching and testing procedures are as inappropriate as if the child were deaf and blind.

In the discussion which follows, attention will be directed first to task skills, the ability to follow directions and carry out various tasks; then to oral language skills; and finally to skills directly related to acquisition of letter-sound relationship. The intention here is not to attempt a comprehensive listing of skills--appropriate research is much too scarce--but to raise questions and thereby illustrate what research is needed.[1]

Task Skills

Any assessment of skills related to reading necessarily takes place in the context of a specific task. The test-taking situation is demanding at best, especially for group tests. Directions must be remembered; responses must be quick and recall efficient; set to perform in a particular fashion must often change considerably from one subtest to another (e.g. emphasis shifts from speed to accuracy); attention must be maintained and anxiety suppressed. Poor performance may be the result of excessive task requirements and have little to do with the ability presumed to be under investigation. For example, in one procedure found in several readiness tests, the child is presented with one or more exemplars beginning with the same consonant phoneme (e.g. sand, sun, soap) and asked to select from a test list those items "beginning with the same sound". It is assumed that the child is able to:

(a) distinguish the initial position in a word from middle or last;
(b) isolate individual sounds;
(c) use the concept of "same" as intended by the adult tester;
(d) retain the sound (or exemplar) in memory; and,
(e) compare speech sounds.

None of these skills has been adequately examined, but there is some evidence that normal middle-class five-year-olds have difficulty with all of them.

In our experience, same-different responses are difficult for many kindergarteners. The child's overall language development may be important in this regard. There is no reason to believe that a child has the same concept of identity as adults, or uses the same labels, that adults do (e.g. "alike" vs. "not alike" may work where "same-different" has failed). It may not be clear to the child which features of a pair of items are relevant, particularly with such abstract concepts as "sound the same". A child may hear a difference between /græs/ and /gwæs/, yet say they sound alike because the two pronunciations are semantically equivalent for him. For these reasons, tests such as the Wepman Auditory Discrimination Test which require same-different responses may be poor diagnostics for speech discrimination.

Oral Language Skills

By kindergarten, most children are reasonably competent speakers and listeners. A sizable experimental literature exists on the development of language abilities in children (McCarthy 1954; Templin 1957; Strickland 1962). However, articulation and phonemic discrimination--skills of potential importance for reading--have not been adequately examined.

Many reports on articulation exhibit technical deficiencies, e.g. investigators have neglected to separate idiolect and dialect forms from articulation errors. Articulation problems may reflect perceptual confusions (a failure to hear the differences between similar sound patterns and consequent inability to produce a difference) or a lack of motor coordination. (Organic disorders, as in aphasia, may also result in articulation problems.) Most techniques for speech correction appear to be based on the assumption that perceptual difficulties underlie articulation errors. Children with severe functional defects in articulation do tend to score lower on speech sound discrimination tests than children with normal articulation. This correlation does not show, however, that articulation errors in specific phoneme groups are matched by discrimination errors involving the same phonemes, or that there is a cause-and-effect relationship between discrimination and articulation inabilities, as is sometimes assumed. For example, Cohen and Diehl (1963) found that children with severe articulation defects scored significantly lower on the Templin Speech Sound Discrimination Test than children with normal speech. From this data the authors concluded that "major emphasis should be placed on improving sound discrimination ability in children with articulation problems who demonstrate poor auditory discrimination" (p. 190). Such a conclusion might be better viewed as a hypothesis to be tested experimentally.

More exact knowledge about the relation between articulation and discrimination is of potential importance in reading instruction as well as treatment of speech defects. If a child is to respond appropriately to both skin and kin, for example, he must be able to articulate the sounds in these words. If he cannot produce /sk/, but gives /k/ instead, there might be some reason to question whether he is ready to read. Even if it is found that a child with speech problems is ready for reading (i. e. gives evidence of distinguishing between skin and kin in other ways than oral reading), it is important to know what the underlying difficulties are so that the proper remedy can be chosen.

The nature of confusion errors among simple consonant contrasts has been investigated in adults (Miller & Nicely 1955) and shown to relate to articulatory patterns (Liberman et al. 1963). Development of the ability to discriminate these elementary patterns remains to be explored. For example, there is no information about the role played by frequency of occurrence of contrasting patterns in the child's environment.

If a child is to determine whether or not a new (written) word is in his speaking vocabulary, he must be able to compare phonological patterns (or some representation thereof) and decide whether they are the same. The assumption being made is that the child pronounces the new word, either aloud or subvocally, and decides whether the word is familiar.

Knowledge of the process by which speech patterns are segmented should be important for the development of a reading program. Segmentation may be considered at various levels. For example, one may ask about the basic units or "words" in a child's lexicon at different developmental stages. It seems likely that the first units comprehended are the names of familiar objects and people in the child's environment. Later, sentence-like sequences are probably handled as integrated units, e.g. /hwə čədum?/. Only after the child has achieved considerable speaking competence are sequences comprehended or produced as strings of units. Even in adult speech, it seems probable that certain "pat" phrases or clichés function as units.

Segmentation of speech sounds within a word or syllable would appear to be essential in the early stages of reading, because English orthography is alphabetic. We have in mind those skills used to recognize or produce rhymes or Pig Latin. We suspect that many children have not developed these skills by kindergarten, although we have not yet developed adequate tests for proving or disproving this. Are consonant clusters perceived as single units or combinations of units? Is the /r/-colored vowel in bird perceived as a unit, or as vowel plus /r/ as in for?

It may be important to have the ability to vary the sound (or sounds) in a word in order to search for a familiar sounding word. For example, a child may have the word /waild/ in his speaking vocabulary, yet not recognize immediately how to pronounce wild. If he says /wild/ and then recognizes that this is similar to /waild/, he may try the latter pronunciation.

Decoding Skills

Perhaps the most interesting question about skills essential for the transition from the spoken to the written form of the language concerns acquisition of the letter—sound code. There appear to be severe limits on the number of written word patterns that may be held in memory as "rote" associations. When a child has cracked the code, so to speak, it appears that he has a general strategy for handling new words in reading. If each letter has a single sound and if stress were marked, the task of learning to read might require few skills other than learning the pairings between letters and sounds.[2] English orthography is not, however, a simple letter—sound system. Instead, it is a more complex system in which many letters have alternate pronunciations, depending frequently upon their graphemic, morphemic, or phonemic environment (Venezky 1967). Accordingly, in order to make use of letter—sound correspondences, the reader must learn efficient strategies for scanning words. Studies of word attack strategies suggest that most readers observe the beginning of a word first, then the end, and finally the middle (Camp & Harcum 1964). Details about how the visual cues are processed and used to generate a word are still scarce.[3]

It is generally impossible to read aloud by scanning left to right in a single pass, pronouncing in sequence. The pronunciation of initial k, for example, cannot be predicted until the next letter is

determined. If it is n̲, the k̲ is silent; otherwise, it is pronounced
/k/. Given ho̲-, there is no way to predict the pronunciation of
either the h̲ or the o̲ until more letters are seen. Compare, for h̲
pronunciation, hour̲ and ho̲t; for o̲ pronunciations, home̲, ho̲t, ho̲o̲t,
house̲, ho̲g (Upper Midwestern /ɔ/), ho̲ok, hone̲y, and ho̲ist.

For a child to pronounce correctly pairs such as ha̲t : ha̲te,
cu̲t : cu̲te, and si̲t : si̲te, he not only must have alternate pronunciations for the vowel letters, but also must recognize the graphemic
environments which mark these pronunciations. Such patterns are
composed of vowel and consonant letters--classes which the child
must differentiate. For the long pronunciation of the vowel, the
pattern is $V_s + C_s + e̲$, where V_s is a simple vowel (a̲, e̲, i̲, y̲, o̲,
or u̲) and C_s is a simple consonant unit. (A simple consonant is
any single consonant, except x̲ or digraphs such as ch̲, th̲, sh̲, and
wh̲, but not dg̲, ck̲, and tch̲; dg̲, ck̲, and tch̲ function as compound
consonant units in English orthography. Simple vowels have short
pronunciations before compound consonants.) If a person learns
the rule as vowel + consonant + e̲, he will make the wrong response
for words like a̲xe, ba̲the, clo̲the, and a̲che. Many people may
learn the rule in this latter form and treat a̲xe, ba̲the, etc., as
exceptions.

Pronunciation Strategies

In one of our studies (Calfee et al. 1968), student subjects were
asked to pronounce synthetic words such as ci̲pe, under instructions
to treat each word as an English word. The better students, rated
by IQ, reading achievement, or college grade point average, generally pronounced this word /saip/. What produced this uniformity
of behavior, assuming the ci̲pe was unfamiliar?

One technique apparently not often employed was conscious application of letter-sound rules. Few people can verbalize these
rules, and even if they could the recorded reaction times seem
quite short for such rules to be consulted.

A second possible technique is rapid search through memory for
similar spelling patterns. To pronounce ci̲pe, the subject would
recall and pronounce to himself whose words beginning with ci̲-,
and then repeat this process on the -i̲pe entries. If the pattern to
be processed had only one pronunciation, as in the case of initial
c̲ before i̲, then the subject's task would be fairly simple. If,
however, there were no single, predictable pronunciations, then
the subject would not only have to search for the various possible
pronunciations of that pattern, but also decide which one to produce.

While relatively little is known about storage and retrieval of language data, we can speculate that the decision-making procedure depends on those processes. In pronouncing yook, for example, a subject may not look for all oo words, but instead only those with -ook, like look, book, and crook, thus responding /ʊ/ for oo. The most frequent pronunciation for oo is /u/, yet oo before k is almost always /ʊ/.

A third pronunciation strategy would be for the subject to search for one or two words with spellings similar to the new word, pronounce the test item silently by analogy with these retrieved items, and then compare the resulting pronunciation with stored pronunciations to ensure that it is both possible and probable. If the trial response did not pass this test, then it would be modified on the basis of these last comparisons and retested. The process may be nearly identical to the preceding one for single syllable words. With more complex words, however, the two techniques differ in that the latter assumes considerably more trial and error. From an introspective standpoint, trial-and-error efforts are important for the pronunciation of words of more than one syllable where the complexities of stress patterns, vowel reductions, and syllable divisions arise. There is some chance that through studies of letter—sound habits with subjects who subvocalize, it can be determined whether or not such silent testing occurs (Hardyck & Petrinovich 1967).

If the second technique outlined above is employed, word memory should be directly accessible by spelling patterns. If the third technique is used, however, then memory should be organized by both spelling and sound. (There is evidence that words which sound alike are confused in memory [Brown & McNeill 1966].) The relevance of this question to the teaching of reading involves the grouping of words in reading texts. Should words be grouped by spellings--regardless of pronunciations--to facilitate spelling linkages; or should words be grouped by sounds--regardless of spellings; or should they be grouped on the basis of both spelling and sound?

One problem with any theory based on storage of spelling patterns is that it implies that poor spellers are poorer readers than good spellers, assuming that other potentially confounded variables are partialled out. There appears to be no evidence to support this conclusion. In fact, spelling ability seems to vary considerably among good readers. People can pronounce, or at least recognize upon hearing or seeing them, many words which they cannot spell correctly. Thus, it appears that the linkages from spelling to sound are considerably stronger than those from sound to spelling.

Additional evidence of asymmetric linkages can be found by observing spelling behavior. A good speller, when attempting to spell a word he is not sure of, generally writes his best guess, looks at it, and then decides whether it is correct. A good speller, by one definition, is a person who knows whether or not to check spellings in the dictionary. Champion spellers may have highly developed visual imagery that allows them to generate the spelling for a word, observe it internally, and decide whether it is correct.

One storage strategy which might produce asymmetry between spelling—sound and sound—spelling is the following. Suppose letter segments are stored with corresponding phonetic segments. For example, associated with the terminal segment /-il/ might be a variety of spellings--ele, eal, eel. These segmental associations might be used except for common words, where the phonetic and graphemic representation would be available as a well integrated unit. Spelling in this scheme is largely divorced from reading, since linkages between complete (phonetic) word units and their graphemic representation is not assumed except for common words.

Whatever the phonetic and graphemic content of memory--whole words or segments--there is probably a second level of storage containing not isolated, single graphemic units, but patterns or generalizations based upon them. This second level of storage may be realized through the structure or organization of the first level of information, rather than as independent storage of generalizations or concepts. Readers can classify spelling units as vowels or consonants, label the letters, assign common pronunciations to each one, and recognize general patterns like the final e or doubled consonant pattern. It is doubtful that a person, when encountering a new word with a doubled consonant like bb, searches for stored occurrences of bb and checks their pronunciation. More likely, there is a general strategy for pronuncing doubled consonant letters as single consonant phonemes, except across certain morpheme boundaries, as in some pronunciations of finally.

The failure of subjects to verbalize or employ letter—sound rules does not preclude verbalizing these rules in the teaching of reading. Such verbalizations may aid the reader in organizing his spelling and sound memories. If, for example, he knows the general rule for pronouncing c, then he can make arcing, cello, and facade as exceptions for this rule, rather than just treating them as possessing low frequency correspondences.

For ea, on the other hand, if the subject is informed that there is no rule--no sure procedure for predicting the correct pronunciation of ea in any given word--then he can organize the various pronunciations of ea in a different fashion than the various pronunciations of c are organized.

Ontogenetically, an individual acquires a store of spoken words
first. Next, he learns to connect graphemic patterns with spoken
words and, perhaps, to recognize the visual patterns as units.
Later he learns to connect spoken words to their spellings. The
spoken word has linked to it syntactic, morphological, semantic,
and articulatory information. The items processed in memory
are probably not spoken words, but tags to the data for a word. In
repeating a sentence which has just been spoken, it is primarily
these tags together with syntactic information which are retained
in immediate memory. If the phonemic or phonetic representations
were retained, then one would expect long familiar words to'take
more room in immediate memory than short familiar ones, but
this does not appear to be the case. However, there is evidence
that the processing time for unfamiliar words is a function of their
graphemic length (Warm & McCray 1967).

Conclusion

This paper has been necessarily speculative. While a great deal
of prose has been prepared on reading skills, little research has
been generated on the nature of these skills in students of differing
backgrounds and ability levels, and at varying stages of training.
Complex models of the reading process have been suggested by
theorists, and reading programs thereby generated. Little work
has been done to clarify the implications of models with regard to
the cognitive skills required--visual and auditory perception, segmentation, long-term and short-term memory load, inductive and
deductive inference, and information processing. These components
of the thinking process have been treated as simple entities; they
are in fact clusters of related skills.

A case in point is the role of memory in reading. Relatively
little work has been done on the problem of natural language and
memory. A few findings are worth noting. For example, sub—
jects seem to handle single digits and letters about as easily as
they do meaningful, common words. Semantic and syntactic relationships facilitate memory for larger units. Synthetic or nonsense words which preserve frequent spelling patterns in the
English language also seem to be easier to remember over short
periods of time. These tidbits of information are interesting, but
need to be greatly expanded. It has been suggested recently that a
distinction be made between structure and function in memory.
That is, one needs to consider separately those storage and processing operations which are unique to some particular set of conditions, and which have been referred to as short-term memory. By

structure is meant those relatively permanent aspects of memory, entailing the storage of well-learned facts about the real world, which because of their number and relatedness may take time to retrieve, but comprise an enormous amount of information.

Information is needed about these two aspects of human memory, based on subjects representing a wider background of reading competence, and tested in a variety of reading tasks. For instance, it is likely that memory processing is very different depending upon whether the material is familiar or not, whether the subject is reading for complete comprehension or for enjoyment, whether a great deal of information must be skimmed for a few relevant facts or complete detail is essential, whether the subject is reading silently or aloud, whether for technical comprehension or for entertainment. The example of oral reading may be quite interesting in its own right. Here is a case where comprehension may play a minimal role but where requirements for correct intonation and phonetic accuracy are important.

Today one hears of "psycholinguistic" approaches to reading. Enough is known about certain aspects of natural language theory and cognitive psychology so that needed improvements in reading instruction might in fact be realized. However, until the correspondences between these facts and the acquisition of reading ability are established empirically, a "psycholinguistic program of reading instruction" remains a challenge, a bird in the bush, not in the hand.

If substantial improvements are to be made in the teaching of reading, component skills of the sort discussed here must be examined. To continually bring out new textbooks and teaching procedures for the classroom without a basic understanding of the learning process is to present occasional palliatives, but no cures. New reading programs seldom fail on their maiden voyage; it is only with the natural attrition of time that the lack of improvement becomes obvious. Dicta for or against pictures in reading texts, for or against nonsense words, for or against irregularly spelled words in early lessons, are pronounced with confidence; yet they are rarely derived from reliable research. The net result after many decades is a surplus of opinions and a dearth of facts. To overcome this state, reading research must be channeled toward an investigation of the reader and the skills he can muster to acquire literacy.

NOTES

1. In particular, visual perception skills will not be considered.
    for recent thought on this area, cf. Neisser (1967) and Gibson
    (1965). Also, cf. Calfee et al. (1968) for a critique of current
    readiness and achievement tests.

2. Experience with ita suggests otherwise. Segmentation of
    auditory patterns and integration of components into a word
    are ancillary requirements that pose problems. Also note that
    variability in pronunciation arises from many sources.

3. The extensive literature on word recognition is relevant
    though not altogether illuminating at present (Haber 1966), but
    cf. Marchbank and Levin (1965). Also, under some circum-
    stances, such as central fixation and tachistoscopic presenta-
    tion, the letters in the center of a word are more readily per-
    ceived (Crovitz and Schiffman 1965).

REFERENCES

Bloomfield, L. Linguistics and reading. Elementary English Review, 1942, 19, 125-131, 183-186.

Brown, R., & McNeill, D. The "tip of the tongue" phenomenon.
Journal of Verbal Learning and Verbal Behavior, 1966, 5, 325-337.

Calfee, R. C., Venezky, R. L., & Chapman, R. S. Pronunciation
of predictable and unpredictable and unpredictable letter—sound
correspondences. Technical Report, Research & Development
Center for Cognitive Learning, University of Wisconsin, 1968.

Camp, D. S., & Harcum, E. R. Visual pattern perception with
varied fixation locus and responses recording. Perceptual Motor
Skills, 1964, 18, 283-296.

Chall, G. Learning to read: The great debate. New York:
McGraw-Hill, 1967.

Cohen, J. H., & Diehl, C. F. Relation of speech-sound discrimination ability to articulation-type speech defects. Journal of Speech
and Hearing Disorders, 1963, 28, 187-190.

Crovitz, H. F. , & Schiffman, H. R. Visual field and the letter span. Journal of Experimental Psychology, 1965, 70, 218-223.

Fries, C. C. Linguistics and reading. New York: Holt, Rinehart & Winston, 1962.

Gibson, E. J. Learning to read. Science, 1965, 148, 1066-1072.

Goodman, K. S. Reading: A psycholinguistic guessing game. Journal of the Reading Specialist, 1967, 4, 126-135. [Reprinted in the present volume, pages 107-119.]

Haber, R. N. Perceptual processes and general cognitive activity. In J. F. Voss (ed.), Approaches to thought. Pittsburgh: University of Pittsburgh Press, in press.

Hardyck, C. D. , & Petrinovich, L. F. The functions of subvocal speech. Project Literacy Reports, No. 8, Cornell University, 1967, 112-115.

Lenneberg, E. Biological foundations of language. New York: Wiley, 1967.

Levin, H. Reading research: What, why, and for whom? Elementary English, 1966, 43, 138-147. [Reprinted in the present volume, pages 123-135.]

Liberman, A. M. , Cooper, F. S. , Harris, K. S. , & MacNeilage, P. F. A motor theory of speech perception. Proceedings of the Speech Communication Seminar, Stockholm, 1962. Stockholm: Royal Institute of Technology, 1963, D3.

Marchbank, G. , & Levin, H. Cues by which children recognize words. Journal of Experimental Psychology, 1965, 56, 57-61.

Matthew, M. M. Teaching to read: Historically considered. Chicago: University of Chicago Press, 1966.

McCarthy, D. A. Language development in children. In L. Carmichael (ed.), A Manual of Child Psychology. New York: Wiley, 1954.

Miller, G. A. , & Nicely, P. E. An analysis of perceptual confusions among some English consonants. Journal of the Acoustical Society of America, 1955, 27, 338-352.

Neisser, U. Cognitive psychology. New York: Appleton-Century-Crofts, 1967.

Strickland, R.G. The language of elementary school children:
Its relationship to the language of reading textbooks and the quality
of reading of selected children. Bulletin of the School of Education,
Indiana University, 38, 1962.

Templin, M. C. Certain language skills in children. Minneapolis:
University of Minnesota Press, 1957.

Thorndike, E. L. The teaching of English suffixes. New York:
Teachers College Press, 1932.

Thorndike, E. L. , & Lorge, I. The teacher's word book of 30,000
words. New York: Columbia University Press, 1944.

Venezky, R. L. English orthography: Its graphical structure and
its relation to sound. Reading Research Quarterly, 1967, 2, 27-
106.

Warm, J. S. & McCray, R. E. Influence of word frequency and
length on apparent duration of tachistoscopic presentations. Paper
presented at Psychonomic Society, Chicago, October 1967.

SOURCES OF KNOWLEDGE FOR THEORIES OF READING

by Marion D. Jenkinson

I am perhaps being bold, not to say foolish, to undertake to speak to the topic of this paper. My reasons for consenting to do so spring from my own need to explore why, after seventy-five years of research and investigation, there has not emerged a coherent construct within which we can examine reading. Two aphorisms point up my dilemma. "Experience keeps a dear school but fools will learn in no other" (Benjamin Franklin). Yet, on the other hand, as an old Welsh proverb states, "Experience is the fool's best teacher; the wise do not need it".

This paper, then, will attempt first to suggest why this failure has occurred, and then will indicate some points of departure which may be productive for the gradual evolution of theories. More questions will be posed than answers given, but it was Einstein who reminded us that the asking of the right questions may lead to greater knowledge than the discovery of scientific facts. Yet again, I must counteract this with another adage: "The greater fool may ask more than the wisest man can answer".

The following topics will be discussed briefly in the remainder of this paper: The reasons for the failure to evolve theories, model making in reading, some questions concerning the assimilation of meaning, and a triad of sources for a reading model.

Reasons for the Failure to Evolve Theories

The first reason is not peculiar to the reading field, but has great pertinence for it. I have been concerned recently with educational epistemology (Jenkinson, 1967). My own concern has been supported in the United States by Cooper (1967). What are the

Reprinted by permission from the Journal of Reading Behavior
1:1. 11-29 (Winter 1969)

sources of our knowledge in education? It seems to me that the traditional six ways of knowing, identified by philosphers--appeal to authority, intuition, formal logic, empiricism, pragmatism, and scepticism--should all be applied to our endeavours to know more about what is happening in education. Of course, some of these methods are superior to others for certain purposes, and their effectiveness will depend upon the nature of the thing to be known. My quarrel is that because the empirical method has proved so effective in scientific enquiry, we in education have allowed this to influence us too exclusively. Educational evidence which is not labelled "research", or does not present evidence in what is often a pseudo-scientific manner, is usually suspect.

More recently the term "development" or "experiment" has become the magic lamp, by rubbing which we hope to solve our educational problems. On the surface this new dogma appears to espouse pragmatism, the method of evaluating things on the basis of their palpable effects. Yet the variety of conclusions, and the conflicting and partial nature of the evidence from the myriad of reading programs and innovations of the past decade, not only leads to scepticism but also calls for prudence in application of any of the findings. We are still far from codifying the experiential proof of these efforts since we are still at such a primitive stage of collecting significant data. It has been demonstrated frequently that the teacher is the one single important variable contributing to reading success. Yet we are only just beginning to realize that we must examine, in depth, the teacher's behaviour and, particularly language performance, in terms both of linguistic mastery and the ways in which language is used to elicit learning.

Another common error which has crept into our educational thought arises from a mistaken notion even of scientific truth. As Wiseman (1966) has suggested:

Development in the history of science which has lead to a clearer and more widespread realization that the distinguishing marks of a scientific hypothesis, as compared, for example, with an affirmation, or belief, is the fact that it must be intrinsically susceptible to disproof, rather than that it can be proved to be true. The most that can ever be said about the truth of a hypothesis, even in the more highly developed of the physical sciences, is that all the results obtained so far are in line with what we would have predicted from it.

In reading, we frequently fall into the trap of attempting to "prove or produce" evidence that one method or set of materials is superior to another. Sometimes the burden of truth should lie rather with the established mode. The efficacy of innovation might well be subject to disproof rather than proof.

When one examines the epistemology of reading, it appears that superficially we cover the range of sources suggested above. Yet, I would argue that we need to acquire a true appreciation for a balance of all six methods and develop the skills of knowing when to select the most appropriate one or combination of them for the specific reading area we are examining.

This is not just another plea for an eclectic approach to reading. We should rather recognize those specific and peculiar contributions that differing sources of knowledge, as well as different disciplines, can make. Too often the "eclectic approach" has served to camouflage rather than elucidate our concepts.

Model Making in Reading

Model making in many aspects of education, including reading, is playing a new role. Hopefully, this desire to create models will not decline into a mere mystique, but will enable us through their construction to show interrelationships between concepts and to suggest areas of ignorance. The Maccias (1966) have suggested that educational theorizing might profit much through the use of models, though it is acknowledged that model making in education, as in all the social sciences, is of a special kind and perhaps of greater complexity than that encountered in the sciences. However, as Eastwood (1966) suggests, though there are many ways of using the term model, a systematic enquiry model, the end product of which is explanation rather than a solution of various problems, is most appropriate for people in education to consider. Eastwood further suggests that this may be conceived as a system of four dimensions-- the referential, the theoretical, the experimental and the validational. Such systems should provide a.general model which encompasses the framework for the derivation of specific models from which testable hypotheses can be deduced.

One of the most common misunderstandings is that the word model is seen as synonymous for theory. It is not appropriate to discourse at length on the distinctions and variety of definitions of the two words. There is a consensus, however, that the two terms are not identical. George (1966) compares a model to a skeleton, whereas the relevant theory can be compared to the complete organism.

My reference to this current work of enquiry into models and theories is really to suggest that in reading we must become more sophisticated in our model making. Several models have been used in reading. The earliest ones were by Gray (1960) with later

additions by Robinson (1966). Holmes (1965) used factor analysis
to produce his substrata-factor theory of reading, while Smith
(1963) has adapted Guilford's (1959) model of the intellect to the
reading process, and more recently McCullough (1968), Kingston
(1961), and Cleland (1965) have suggested other models.

All these models, it is true, attempt to clarify and explicate the
relationships between one facet of reading and another. Unfortunately, however, until comparatively recently, they have attempted
to cover too many facets in reading. The intellectual, dynamic
activity of the reading process has been confused by linking this
with the techniques and skills which need to be acquired in the
"learning to read" process. In addition, the learning and teaching
activity are rarely examined independently.

As I have suggested elsewhere, it would seem that future models
should not attempt, at least in the beginning, to be all inclusive
(Jenkinson, 1968). We need a series of models of various aspects
of reading which may ultimately be capable of being integrated.
But a model which deals with the reading process as such, which
includes the cognitive interactions, the impact of language and linguistic considerations in the affective as well as in the cognitive
domain, and will then attempt to relate these reading operations to
other aspects of thinking, is perhaps the most urgently needed.
Part of this process may be the differentiation of the reading-
thinking action from every other human activity, including ordinary
thinking. I feel that this may be a productive point of departure.

A quite separate model is needed to show the interrelationship
between the skills, techniques, materials and media involved in the
decoding process. This will then lead to the way in which the child
gradually assimilates the understanding of the word which is decoded. Yet the assimilation of understanding at this period will not
be identical with the very different aptitudes of the mature reader.
It would seem that the acquisition of encoding and decoding in
children as they progress through school is entirely dependent on
their developing perceptual activities and the acquisition of the
appropriate, systematic, cognitive abilities. The extent to which
the developing abilities influence the amount that the child can as-
similate from his reading is still largely a mystery. We do know,
however, that as he matures he can apparently understand increasingly complex material. It would seem to me that we shall
make greater progress if we do not attempt to account, at least in
the same model, for both the developing reader and the mature
reader.

One of the problems that continues to plague us is that we lack
accurate definitions in reading. It has become imperative that we
somehow attempt to agree on some terms within the field. Several

of the contributors to the N.S.S.E. volume <u>Innovation and Change in Reading Instruction</u> (Robinson, 1968) commented on the problems attendant on trying to simplify ideas from research and experimentation because of the lack of agreement on definitions. Spache (1968) also suggested that the confusion has been further confounded because many of the disciplines which have contributed to our knowledge of the field of reading have their own distinctive terminology for the basic components of reading. The varied uses of terms to describe conditions or concepts which are often quite similar not only interfere with our exchange of information but retard our ultimate progress toward greater knowledge.

Many sciences have experienced this problem but the time has come, as it did in the other sciences, when a general acceptance of some definitions is essential. It is true that the way to good definitions is paved with difficulties. As Dewey has reminded us, the twin demons of vagueness and ambiguity frequently impinge upon salient definitions. It is ironical, too, that language itself is a major deterrent in accurate defining. Dewey (1933) wrote with cogency on this point.

A constant source of misunderstanding and mistake is indefiniteness of meaning. Because of vagueness of meaning we misunderstand things ourselves. Because of ambiguity, we distort and pervert. Conscious distortion of meaning may be enjoyed as nonsense; erroneous meanings may be followed up and got rid of. Vague meanings are too indefinite to allow for analysis and too bulky to support other beliefs. Vagueness prevents testing and responsibility and disguises the unconscious mixing together of half understood concepts. It is aboriginal, logical sin, the source from which most bad intellectual consequences flow. To totally eliminate indefiniteness is impossible. To reduce it in extent and force requires sincerity and vigour.

The nature of definitions has plagued us from the time of the Greeks, but recently philosophers such as Robinson (1965) have come to some general conclusions about the attributes of functional definitions, and of these we must become aware. Our definitions at one and the same time must be inclusive but never so restrictive that they cannot function. Definitions in reading as in all other sciences must be relative. They must be capable of changing in both basic concepts and in content, as new ideas appear. Thus, it would seem that the only definitions we can use would be tentative or stipulative definitions, for should rigid definitions be used, these would belie the dynamic character of language and further restrict investigation. Wittgenstein (1958) has aptly stated that definitions should not be permitted to give us mental cramp and rigidly limit exploration. Reading as an act and a process may in the end be the most difficult of all to define. Perhaps reading, like mystery, can only be described and evoked.

Moreover, we are often faced in the field of reading with the sceptics who often exist among the practitioners who deny the use or validity of theories. Perhaps the concept that "it is all right in theory but it won't do in practice" is merely a way of rejecting something which is difficult to understand. Black (1946) has indicated that Schopenhauer (1932) said all that needs to be said about this type of sophistry.

> The assertion is based upon an impossibility: what is right in theory must work in practice. And if it does not there is a mistake in the theory; something has been overlooked and not allowed for and consequently what is wrong in practice is wrong in theory too.

And now having examined several problems which seem to have been major deterrents to the formulation and evolution of useful theories about reading, some questions will be posed concerning the assimilation of meaning, since this is basic to the mature reading process. Then some of the sources of knowledge from which we might seek further enlightenment will be examined briefly.

Some Questions Concerning the Assimilation of Meaning

It is a truism that part of our problem in developing a theory has been the complexity of the process involved. Reading must engage the total organism. The recent distinction made by Wiener and Cromer (1967) between acquisition and assimilation of meaning I think is one we have needed to examine for some time.

(1) Is reading comprehension synonymous with thinking? The converse obviously is not true, but if reading is considered to be a type of thinking which is triggered by the printed rather than by the spoken word, what are the controlling variables of the thinking thus aroused?

(2) How does this thinking differ from all other types of thinking? It obviously must be controlled to an extent by the thought indigenous to the writer, but though the reader's thought is controlled by the content, he frequently has to interpolate and extrapolate in order to get the full impact of the author's meaning.

(3) What are the differences between spoken and written language? This could apply to the ways in which the thoughts are engendered but is also very important in our understanding of the problems that will face the reader but which may or may not be apparent if the ideas are expressed orally.

(4)   What are the respective functions of the lexical and struct-
      ural elements within written material? Again, a beginning
      has been made on this but we need more information.

(5)   What are the variables residing within the reader which en-
      able him to become receptive to the message of the author?
      What is the influence of past experience, of prejudice, of
      bias, of attitudes, of personality variables? What is the
      effect of general and immediate motivation, of interests, of
      attitudes or rigidity, or personality structure, of the cog-
      nitive style of the reader and his ability to initially submerge
      his concepts for those of the author? And these constitute
      but a few of the variables inherent in the reader.

(6)   What problems arise because of the level of abstraction of
      the material that is being presented? This is apposite for
      the mature reader as well as the child learning to read.
      Moreover, undoubtedly the reader will be more or less
      successful according to his familiarity with the content of
      the matter he is reading and the type of "language game"
      which is being undertaken by the author. (Cf. Wittgenstein,
      1958.)

(7)   How do the separate and disparate experiences of individuals
      lead to a common acceptance of general meaning but which
      also permit differences of interpretation? What is going to
      be the future of literacy as compared with "oracy"? (Cf.
      McLuhan, 1964.)

(8)   Perhaps we need to examine the axiology of reading, the
      values gained from reading, particularly in the light of cur-
      rent contentions that "oracy" rather than literacy has be-
      come the pervasive means of the immediate conveying of
      meaning. It appears that written material, however, will
      continue to play an active part in conveying and relating
      meaning from one area to another and from one generation
      to another. Since reading permits more effective thinking,
      the written word will continue to be the most efficacious in-
      fluence in knowledge extension and exchange in every sphere.
      (Cf. McLuhan, 1964, p. 168.)

The answers to these questions will be complex, but by examining
some recent development in "basic" fields we may obtain productive
insights.

A Triad of Sources for a Reading Theory

Although psychology and linguistics were once studied as part of
the philosophy of mind, the three subjects are now pursued separa-

tely. Chomsky (1966) has himself suggested that this resulting
speculation without rational attempts at synthesis has been detrimental to our knowledge of language and its functioning. A very
cursory examination follows of each of these three areas of philosophy, psychology and linguistics as they might contribute to
some of the questions posed above.

(a) <u>Philosophy</u>. Philosphers have been concerned for the past
thirty years with the problems involved in how meaning is obtained
through language. If any current journal of philosphy, either
British or American, is selected it will be noticed that much of
its content is concerned with language and the strategies involved
in language functioning.

Wittgenstein, some thirty years ago, by his insistence that most
philosophical questions turned upon the meaning of the language in
which the questions were posed, inaugurated this movement for
clarity. He emphasized the problems which words impose upon
thought and also the problems which thought imposes upon words
and the ideas these words attempt to convey. He insisted that
meaning was the "meaning of the word in use" and that all communication was dependent upon both parties being aware of the
"language game" in which they were engaged. The language of
science will necessitate an entirely different set of rules and
strategies than the language of poetry. It is a different language
game. (Cf. Wittgenstein, 1958.)

Austin (1962) distinguished between statements and the "performative utterances" and finally replaced this with a more inclusive general theory of "illocutionary" forms which have "perlocutionary" effects. In attempting to analyze the impact of language he termed a "performative" utterance, one in which we
purpose to be doing something in saying something: e.g. "I judge
this to be the best dog in the show", or "I promise ...", or "I
appoint you ...". These sentences are neither true nor false,
but in the event that there is failure to do what is purported, the
utterance becomes null and void. An "illocutionary" utterance is
one which contains some sort of action. It contains the performance of an act in saying something as opposed to the performance
of an act of saying something. Illocutionary acts are those of
informing, ordering, warning, undertaking, etc. "Perlocutionary"
effects are those which are brought about when words such as
"convince", "persuade", "deter", etc., produce the desired results, e.g. "I persuaded him to stop teasing the cat". These
differing yet interlinked utterances producing acts are differing
senses or dimensions of the "use of a sentence", or of "the use of
language". There are, of course, many more differing types of
utterances than the three illustrated. However, discussion of the

purpose of utterance has obvious impact upon assimilation of
meaning.

The noted American philospher Quine (1960) has been exploring
the relationship of the notion of meaning and the linguistic mechanisms of objective references, as expounded in his book Word and
Object. He insists that the meaning of a sentence is not an external entity, but is embodied in the words used. The problems of
translation, explanation, and explication in terms of language are
explored. He examined the anomalies, ambiguities and conflicts
implicit in the referential implications of language. In his most
recent series of lectures--the Dewey Lectures, 1968--Quine (1968)
is exploring "ontological relativity" as it pertains to language.
Quine recognized the complexity of the problems facing us in language learning:

> The semantic part of learning a word is more complex than the
> phonetic part; therefore, even in simple cases, we have to see
> what is stimulating the other speaker. In the case of words not
> directly ascribing observable traits to things, the learning pro-
> cess is increasingly complex and obscure; and obscurity is the
> breeding place of mentalistic semantics. What the naturalist
> insists on is that, even in the complex and obscure parts of lan-
> guage learning, the learner has no data to work with but the
> overt behaviour of other speakers (p. 186).

He includes, however, the problem of extension reference and the
attendant difficulties upon our knowledge of these references.

Langer, on the other hand, found the ordinary language of words
so complex for explaining exact meaning that she continued the
work of Whitehead and emphasized the value of symbolic forms to
convey logical ideas. In her most recent work (Langer, 1967) she
is beginning to throw some light on cognitive functioning and its
relation to language. Her new attack on the problem of mind and
its functioning involves biology, biochemistry and psychology as
well as philosophy. She attempts to contribute to a concept of
mind adequate and acceptable to both the sciences and the humani-
ties.

> The enormous power of language, whereby we are enabled to
> form abstract concepts, concatenate them in propositions, apply
> these to the world of perception and action, making it into a
> world of "facts", and then manipulate its facts by a process of
> reasoning, springs from the simpleness of discursive projection
> (p. 102).

These are but a few of the many philosophers who have turned
their attention to the elucidation and illumination of the way ideas
are conveyed through language and these studies and many others
are of obvious relevance to our study of reading and its comprehension.

Another philosopher (Findley, 1963) has heartened me considerably. He writes:

Modern philosophy is distinguished by the emergence of a new
question: how to give meaning to the expressions used in ordinary
and philosophical discourse. Earlier philosophers simply in-
quired into the truth of this or that assertion, without troubling
to raise the prior question as to what precisely such an assertion
meant, or whether it really meant anything at all. When the
question of sense has been raised, it lead to yet another inquiry:
in what way or ways a sense had been given to some assertion,
or in what way or ways a sense could be given to it. The question led to yet another question ... in what way or ways the sense
of an expression could be taught or imparted, so that many men
could use the expression in an identical way, and give it the same
sense. This obviously is a truly fundamental question. For it is
plain that most expressions acquire sense for use through a process of teaching (p. 72).

At least this indicates that the vital knowledge of language functioning is capable of being learned and, therefore, presumably of
being taught.

(b) Linguistics and Psycho-linguistics. Again, I can only suggest
it is presumptuous of me to attempt in a short period of time to
indicate what further contributions might be obtained from the linguists and particularly now because of their closer relation to
psycho-linguists.

Part of our problem has been in the past that there have been so
many differing schools of thought about language structure and
functions that it has been almost impossible for anyone outside the
field to make any appropriate synthesis of its findings. Perhaps
it was unfortunate, too, that in the fifties the interest of most linguists in reading was concentrated almost exclusively upon the
grapheme-phoneme relationship. It is only more recently that
several of the branches of linguistics and psycho-linguistics have
begun to explore the effect of structure and lexical meaning on the
understanding of language.

Some descriptive linguists, interested primarily in analyzing
non-Western languages in order to provide viable writing systems
for them, produced grammars and alphabets adequate for their
purposes. Applied English linguists relate some of these descriptive methods to the English language and writing system.
Abercrombie (1965) has begun to sharpen our awareness of the
great differences between actual everyday speech, on the one
hand, and the "texts" of spoken English analyzed by linguists and
English deliberately organized for visual presentation (prose), on
the other. And although Abercrombie's book is quite revealing,

it does not indicate the more subtle differences the reader must perceive to obtain a meaning closely approximating what he might obtain from the primary source of speech.

Lefevre (1964) was one of the first to point out the implications for reading of the complex interplay of spoken and written English language patterns--above the level of phonemes and graphemes. He emphasized that in reading instruction we must recognize and teach the essential grammatical and syntactical clues in printed English, particularly those that suggest intonation: stress, tune, and junctures or terminals. Insensitivity to some of these signals, I suspect, may underlie problems of differing interpretations that are accorded to much written material. As Lefevre (1968) said in a recently published paper, intonation and sentence patterns are critically important subsystems of the English structural system and are essential to meaning in both speech and writing; moreover, in addition to their lexical meanings, the syntactical functions of words, signaled by grammatical inflections and derivational affixes, must be perceived as important clues to meaning in reading printed English just as they are in hearing English spoken.

At this point, apparently some linguists are beginning to explore analyses of structures at higher levels than that of the single sentence. This discourse analysis, it seem to me, will have as an important impact on our understanding of meaning as will the tagmemicists' analysis. Both these suggest the possibilities of useful new insights into larger structures of the exposition of all types of prose. The work in this field has primarily been directed towards writing but it seems that it should have pertinence to reading, too.

Undoubtedly the work of Chomsky and the transformational grammarians in revealing that sentences, and thus discourse as a whole, had both a surface and a deep meaning, has had much to offer in expanding our knowledge of how meaning is conveyed. The embeddedness of meaning in deep structures is apparently learned comparatively easily by a child, but although he may use the structures adequately in performance, he may face a very difficult task when he receives these from others. Goodman (1964), in his insistence on the types of miscues which can lead to major errors in understanding, has indicated one of the most productive ways of furthering our understanding, since it is often by examination of errors made rather than by competence revealed, that our knowledge in any field is enhanced. The distinction which linguists have made between linguistic performance and linguistic competence, as Wardhaugh (1968) has suggested, may be a very important one for our assessing the ability of students to obtain meaning from what they need. This competence at the spoken level may vary quite

considerably from the linguistic performance in reading. It may
be that the reader will only catch the superficial interpretation and
will fail to take into account the more deeply embedded structural
elements which occur in the printed word. The printed word tends
to be more complex and thus contains more latent embeddedness.
Incidentally, the discrepancy between linguistic competence and
performance is very evident in children as some recent research
by Lyons and Wales (1966) in Britain has shown.

Again, in a sense, I have only dabbled in this vast field of linguistics. My plea is, however, that we continue to use the emerging findings of the linguists and incorporate these into our theories
and ultimately into our teaching of reading as efficiently and effectively as possible.

(c) Psychology. It is perhaps most difficult to summarize the
contributions of psychology to our knowledge of the reading process
because they are so diverse. A great many of the findings of behavioral analysis, of child development, including child cognition,
of general learning theory, of theories of perception, and of problem solving have been applied to the teaching of reading, but few
have examined these findings in the light of the mature reader obtaining meaning. In addition, there are so few studies which have
focused in depth upon any one area which extend our knowledge of
the reading process per se.

The work on cognition is so far the most fruitful field. Undoubtedly Guilford's (1959) model of the intellect has stimulated
many workers to explain the relationships between the parameters
suggested. When this model, however, was applied to reading
there were obvious gaps, inconsistencies, and invalidities. Ausubel's
(1967) concept of the pervasiveness of receptive learning as opposed
to the less frequent opportunities for discovery learning is also
pertinent. The reading process is obviously one of the main ve-
hicles for such receptive learning. The need to know, the "epistemic
curiosity" described by Berlyne (1965) has also obvious implications, since books are still a prime source of knowledge. Skinner's
concept of verbal behaviour is also pertinent. Perhaps we are in
more need of workers such as Carroll, who synthesized both in
1959 and 1964 the relationships between psychology and language,
than we are of direct researchers.

The concept of the impact of a distinctive cognitive style on all
aspects of personality variables, including those of attitudes, flexibility and ability to tolerate ambivalence, is receiving attention
from a variety of psychologists, but as yet there is little to be applied to reading.

The psychology of motivation, including that of interest, is moving
forward too, but again the results are scattered and still appear to

apply to experimental rather to real life situations. We need to know more than the superficial interest of what and why people read, but also how they read. The attempt by Gray and Rogers (1956) remains the only thorough study which tries to assess the differing levels of adult reading competence linked with their interests.

There have been a few attempts, mostly by people within the field of reading, to analyze the reading process, but again few of these have dealt with mature readers. The majority of these studies have examined errors made in comprehension in an effort to determine what caused differing interpretive responses. Strang (1965) has given an admirable summary of these to 1965.

Thus, from a psychological point of view, the reading process is dependent upon a reader's prerequisites for learning, his language competence (including reading) and his attitudes and goals. Yet, all these may be vitiated by chemical or neurological factors, of which our knowledge is still minimal.

Conclusion

I have merely explored some of the fringes of those areas of knowledge which seem to impinge upon the eternal conundrum of the meaning in reading. To develop an appropriate theory, it is evident that we need to bring together related disciplines in co-ordinated research efforts. The most productive insights frequently emerge from the interplay and friction between the differences of disparate disciplines, from the interfaces where the knowledge of one area borders on another. Regretfully, too, frequently one discipline disparages another, and I can only deplore that too often people in the reading field have reacted negatively to some of the attempts of other disciplines to explain the reading process. But other scholars must also share some of the blame. I think all partners in this future voyage of discovery into the nature of the reading process must move forward in humility, each recognizing the limitations of his own discipline honestly, but also ensuring that the wide avenues of educational epistemology are continually kept open.

In this discussion I have probably revealed my own ignorance more than enlightened yours and undoubtedly as Gary once wrote of the Eton College boys:

Thought would destroy their paradise
No more: where ignorance is bliss
'Tis folly to be wise.

No doubt it has been foolish wisdom to dally in this, the various sources of knowledge which might illumine the reading process.

Yet again, I am reminded of an appropriate section of Lewis Carroll's Through the Looking-Glass, a section favoured by philosophers.

"When I use a word," Humpty Dumpty said, in a rather scornful tone, "it means just what I choose it to mean, neither more nor less."

"The question is," said Alice, "whether you can make words mean so many different things."

"The question is," said Humpty Dumpty, "which is to be the master, that's all."

This passage is usually used to emphasize the intractability of language. In reading, the meanings of words, lexical, syntactical and structural, determine to a large extent what the reader can comprehend of the writer's ideas. Unless this is so, then the other Humpty Dumpty fable must ensue, and "We shall never put him together again".

REFERENCES

Abercrombie, D. O. Studies in Phonetics and Linguistics. Oxford: Oxford University Press, 1965.

Austin, J. L. How to Do Things with Words. (The William James Lectures at Harvard University in 1955.) (Edited by J. O. Urmson.) Oxford: Clarendon Press, 1962.

Ausubel, David Paul. Learning Theory and Classroom Practice. Toronto: Ontario Institute for Studies in Education, 1967. Bulletin No. 1.

Berylne, D. E. Structure and Direction in Thinking. New York: Wiley, 1965.

Black, N. Critical Thinking. Englewood Cliffs, New Jersey: Prentice-Hall, 1946.

Carroll, J. B. "An Operational Model for Language Behavior". Anthropological Linguistics 1:37-54, 1959.

Carroll, J. B. "Linguistics and the Psychology of Language". Review of Educational Research 34:119-126, April 1964.

Carroll, Lewis. Through the Looking-Glass. Oxford: Clarendon Press.

Chomsky, N. Cartesian Linguistics: A Chapter in the History of Rationalist Thought. New York: Harper and Row, 1966.

Cleland, D. L. "A Construct of Comprehension". Reading and Inquiry. (Edited by J. A. Figurel.) Conference Proceedings, Vol. 10. Newark, Delaware: International Reading Association, 1965, pp. 59-64.

Cooper, J. A. "Why the Monopoly in Epistemology?" Phi Delta Kappan 48:406, April 1967.

Dewey, John. How We Think. Boston: Heath, 1933.

Eastwood, G. R. "Uses of Models: Another Dimension". Alberta Journal of Educational Research 12:230, September 1966.

Findley, J. N. "The Teaching of Meaning". Thinking and Meaning. Entretiens d'Oxford, Organisés par l'Institute Internationale de Philosophie, Editions Nauwelaerts, Louvain, 1963.

George, F. H. Quoted in "Models in Education". Alberta Journal of Educational Research 12:168, September 1966.

Goodman, K. "A Linguistic Study of Cues and Miscues in Reading". Paper delivered at the American Educational Research Association, Chicago, February 21, 1964.

Gray, W. S. and Rogers, B. Maturity in Reading: Its Nature and Appraisal. Chicago: University of Chicago Press, 1956.

Gray, W. S. "The Major Aspects of Reading". Sequential Development of Reading Abilities. (Edited by H. M. Robinson.) Supplementary Education Monographs, No. 90. Chicago: University of Chicago Press, 1960, pp. 8-24.

Guilford, J. P. "Three Faces of Intellect". American Psychologist 14:469-79, August 1959.

Jenkinson, M. D. "Dispersed Mediations on Curriculum Evaluation". Paper presented at the Third International Curriculum Conference, Oxford, England, September 1967.

Jenkinson, M. D. "Reading: An Eternal Dynamic". Paper given at
the presentation of the N. S. S. E. Yearbook, April 1968, Innovation and Change in Reading Instruction.

Holmes, J. S. "Basic Assumptions Underlying the Sub-Strata
Factor". Reading Research Quarterly 1:4-28, Fall 1965.

Kingston, A. J. "A Conceptual Model of Reading Comprehension".
Phases of College and Other Reading Programs. (Edited by E. P.
Bliesmer and A. J. Kingston.) Milwaukee: National Reading Con-
ference, 1961, pp. 100-107.

Langer, S. K. Mind: An Essay on Human Feeling, Vol. 1. Baltimore:
Johns Hopkins Press, 1967.

Lefevre, C. A. "A Multidisciplinary Approach to Language and to
Reading: Some Projections". Detroit, Michigan: Wayne State University Press, 1968, pp. 289-312; 333-36.

Lefevre, C. A. Linguistics and the Teaching of Reading. New York:
McGraw-Hill, 1964.

Lyons, J. , and Wales, R. J. Psycho-Linguistic Papers. Edinburgh:
The University Press, 1966.

McCullough, C. M. "Balanced Reading Development". Innovation
and Change in Reading Instruction. N.S.S.E. Yearbook, Part II,
1968. Chicago: University of Chicago Press, 1968.

McLuhan, H. M. Understanding Media: The Extensions of Man.
New York: McGraw-Hill, 1964, p. 168.

Quine, W. V. "Ontological Relativity". The Dewey Lectures, 1968.
Journal of Philosophy 65:185-212, April 1968.

Quine, W. V. Word and Object. New York: John Wiley, 1960.

Robinson, R. Definition. Oxford: University Press, 1965.

Robinson, H. M. "The Major Aspects of Reading". Reading:
Seventy-Five Years of Progress. (Edited by H. Alan Robinson.)
Supplementary Educational Monographs, No. 96. Chicago: Uni-
versity of Chicago Press, 1966, pp. 22-32

Robinson, H. M. , ed. Innovation and Change in Reading Instruction
Sixty-Seventh Yearbook of the National Society for the Study of
Education. Chicago: National Society for the Study of Education,
1968.

Schopenhauer, G. The Art of Controversy. Oxford: University
Press, 1932.

Skinner, B. F. Verbal Behavior. New York: Appleton-Century-
Crofts, 1957.

Smith, D. E. Toward Better Reading by G. Spache. Champaigne
Garrard, 1963, pp. 67-72.

Spache, G. D. "Contributions of Allied Fields to the Teaching of
Reading." Innovation and Change in Reading Instruction. Sixty-
Seventh Yearbook of the National Society of the Study of Education.
(Edited by Helen M. Robinson.) Chicago: National Society for the
Study of Education, 1968, pp. 237-290.

Strang, R. The Reading Process and Its Ramifications. Invitational
Address. Newark, Delaware: International Reading Association,
1965, pp. 49-74.

Wardhaugh, R. "Recent Research in Linguistics". Paper delivered
at the 12th Annual Convention of the International Reading Association, 1968.

Wiener, M. , and Cromer, J. "Reading Difficulty: A Conceptual
Analysis". Harvard Educational Review 34:620-643, Fall 1967.
[Reprinted in the present volume, pages 136-162]

Wiseman, S. Curriculum Evaluation. Mimeograph, 1966, p. 21.

Wittgenstein, L. Philosophical Investigations. Oxford: Basil
Blackwell, 1958.

SOME LANGUAGE AND CULTURAL DIFFERENCES
IN A THEORY OF READING

by Roger W. Shuy

In this paper we will outline two basic areas in which linguistic research can help children with reading disabilities caused by behavioral mismatch with language phenomena as the focal point. Of the many areas of behavioral mismatch of materials to the child's culture, we will focus on two quite different dimensions, one having to do with his cultural environment, the other dealing with the way he proceeds to learn language symbolization. The former might be called positional; the latter processive.

Morton Wiener and Ward Cromer, in their article called "Reading and Reading Difficulty: A Conceptual Analysis", describe four different assumptions which are used to explain what is meant by the term "reading difficulty"[1]. Each assumption implies a kind of built-in model of remediation. Some researchers, for example, assume that reading difficulty involves a kind of malfunction, usually of the sensory-physiological type. Other investigators feel that reading difficulty involves a deficiency of some sort which must be corrected before adequate reading can take place. Still others attribute reading difficulty to certain things (bad method, anxiety, etc.) which are present but interfering, and which must be removed before good reading can take place. A fourth approach to "reading difficulty" is one in which the researchers assume that the child would read adequately if the material and method were consistent with his linguistic behavior patterns. The reader having difficulty is not necessarily defective physiologically. He does not lack something and he has no particular outside disruptive interference. His cultural operative system is simply different from that of the reading instruction. Investigators who work

Reprinted by permission from Kenneth S. Goodman and James T. Fleming (eds.), Psycholinguistics and the Teaching of Reading (Newark, Del.: International Reading Association, 1969), pp. 34-47.

under this assumption believe that in order to make the child read, either the material or the behavior patterns must be changed.

The abysmally slow process in the cross fertilization of the disciplines which are legitimately involved in the teaching of reading is a case in point. For several years now, it has been rightly assumed that linguistics has a major contribution to make to reading research. However, several situations have militated against such cross fertilization. For one thing, linguists are few in number and confronted with thousands of tasks. It is seldom difficult, for example, for a graduate student in linguistics to find a thesis topic. There are any number of things to do in linguistic theory and grammar writing, to say nothing of the many "hyphenated" disciplines such as psycholinguistics and sociolinguistics which have made recent though impressive appearances. With all of this theoretical, descriptive and relational work to do, applied linguistics does not hold high priority for the current generation of linguists. If the reason for this were simply that sound applications cannot be made until more adequate theory and descriptions are available, there would be little to complain about. There is some reason to suspect, however, that the failure of linguists to concern themselves about the various implications of their disciplines for pedagogy stems partly from the kind of academic snobbery that is pprdictable when a discipline is in the catbird seat. But for whatever reason, the application of linguistic knowledge to reading and language arts has been something less than satisfactory. A willing but linguistically unsophisticated educator is frequently at a loss to learn enough linguistics to help him with his tasks, because the style of thinking and writing in linguistics is as in-group oriented as any field in the curriculum. An educator who reads a linguistics textbook will probably have to slow down considerably and, even then, he will make errors and comprehend less than linguists.

Let us examine the educator's "reading difficulty" for a moment in light of the Wiener-Cromer taxonomy of research assumptions. We would be hard pressed to show that educators have sensory or physiological defects. They do not lack some function necessary to the reading process. Nor can we casually observe that an entire discipline is made up of scholars who have intrapsychic conflicts. Their reading difficulty seems, rather, to stem from a cultural difference characterized by a different view of life's problems, a different style of self presentation and a different orientation to the written page.

The educator's "reading problem" might easily be compared to that of a child from a culture which is in some way alien to the school processes[2] The systematic study of such cultural differences has not yet been completed, but there are several aspects of it

which are clear even at this early stage. We have already labeled
two dimensions of the problem as <u>positional</u> and <u>processive</u>. There
are undoubtedly many other aspects of the taxonomy and many other
examples of their membership. The following are meant to be
illustrative rather than exhaustive.

The Positional Dimension

In the past years linguists have been working diligently in different parts of the country to define the exact linguistic features which
characterize peoples of different social status. The work of the
Linguistic Atlas of the United States and Canada, begun in the
thirties, made some crude attempts at obtaining socially interesting information along with invaluable data which revealed important
historical and geographical insights. The rise of interest in urban
problems in the sixties, however, has called for an entirely new
strategy. As the interest of linguists shifted from historical and
geographical concerns to synchronic social matters, it became
increasingly difficult for them to hang on to older ways of operating.
They learned more about sampling design, about data gathering
techniques, about analytical procedures, about mechanical information retrieval, about statistics, and about social stratification.
Major linguistic research in urban areas has been conducted recently in New York, Chicago, Detroit, and Washington, D. C.
These research projects are just beginning to bear fruit to the
educators.

The Sociolinguistics Program of the Center for Applied Linguistics
in Washington, D. C., which now houses both the Washington, D. C.
and Detroit research projects, will be the source of what we have
to say about cultural position as a feature of reading difficulty.

Many linguists, although by no means in total agreement as to
the extent of the cultural contrast or as to its origins, have been
describing and analyzing the systematic language differences between social classes in America with a particular focus on urban
poor Negroes, Puerto-Ricans, and immigrants from impoverished
rural areas. How linguists have chosen to accomplish this focus
varies from project to project, but two major contrasts are apparent. One group feels that the proper way to study Negro speech
is to study only the speech of urban poor Negroes. In contrast,
the other group feels that in order to study Negro speech one must
study the speech of Negroes of all social classes as well as whites
of all social classes. In doing so, the latter group can be accused
of spending undue time and attention on the non-target audience.

In reply they assert that it is dangerous to talk about the speech of any group without carefully identifying it and without seeing it in relation to other contiguous social groups.

The Sociolinguistics Program at the Center for Applied Linguistics clearly focuses on the urban Negro, since research shows this group to be high in the school dropout rate and low in reading proficiency. Current research projects include studies of linguistic correlates of upward mobility among urban Negroes, various studies of social stratification as revealed through grammar and phonology, language attitude studies, linguistic age grading, culture studies, and preparation of classroom materials which stem from the basic research conducted in the program. Throughout the research, however, it should be clear that we are not dealing with sensory-physiological defects or disruptive psychological conflicts.

Nor are we involved in the study of phonetic or grammatical "deficiencies". That is, we are not saying that the child cannot learn to read because he does not know Standard English. We are saying, instead, that the linguistic system of the ghetto Negro is different in a number of identifiable features from that of Standard English. If this non-standard dialect is interfering with the acquisition of Standard English reading skills, we can take at least two courses. One is to adjust the child to suit the materials. Another is to adjust the materials to suit the child. If the end result is successful, it is a matter of indifference which system is used. Those who advocate that we teach the child Standard English before he learns to read assume that since it is a good thing to learn Standard English, he might as well learn it before he learns to read. Most linguists, on the other hand, realize that the complexity of language learning is such that this sort of engineering is too slow-moving to be effective. That is, the social value of learning Standard English is not worth the long delay it would cause in his learning to read. The simple truth is that speaking Standard English, however desirable it may be, is not as important as learning to read. (It would be extremely difficult, furthermore, to teach Standard English to children who have no Standard English speaking peers.)

In any case, the idea of changing the child to suit the materials seems educationally naive when one stops to give it careful consideration. The usual practice among educators has been to suit the materials to the child. It is hard to imagine how we ever got so sidetracked on this issue. But even assuming that it were desirable to first teach children Standard English, we have no research to show that children have any great conscious awareness of the fine distinctions of the social dimension of language. Of course they are quite able to use grammatical, phonological, and lexical forms in keeping with their own value systems, but these value systems are those of the unsophisticated child, who just may value the speech of a juvenile delinquent, a dope peddler or an athlete who lisps more than the speech of a teacher, an announcer or a judge. Furthermore, pre-adolescent children are relatively unable to articulate what they are doing when they adopt someone's linguistic norms. They can imitate someone's speech (without a mature value orientation) but they can't tell you what it is about the grammar or pronunciation that they are imitating[3] This is not suprising, since it is also difficult for adults, even language arts teachers, to identify these things. In her doctoral disserta-tion, Anne E. Hughes asked a random group of urban teachers of disadvantaged pre-school children to identify the language problems of their students[4] The teachers were first asked to talk about the characteristic linguistic problems. Then they were asked to listen to a tape recording of some of these children and identify the lin-guistic problems on that tape. The results showed a very low cor-relation of response to reality.

Eighty percent of the teachers observed that their students have a limited vocabulary. One teacher offered the following reason for this "handicap":

... the children came with a very meager vocabulary ... I think it's because of the background of the home and the lack of books at home, the lack of communication with the family, especially, if there are only one or two children in the family. Perhaps if there are more children in the family communication might be a bit better. They might have a few more words in their vocabu-lary.

Another teacher observed:

In the inner-city, the child's vocabulary is very limited. His experiences are very limited.

These comments are typical. Neither teacher gave any indication that the home environment might produce a different vocabulary. Both felt, on the contrary, that a lack of school vocabulary was equivalent to a lack of overall vocabulary. This reflects a widely-held but erroneous concept, in which the disadvantaged child is sometimes called non-verbal. Nothing in the current research on Washington, D.C. or Detroit Negroes supports this idea. The notion that children in disadvantaged homes are the products of language deprivation seem to mean only that the investigators proved to be such a cultural barrier to the interviewee that informants were too frightened and awed to talk freely, or that the investigators simply asked the wrong questions.

If the teachers' comments about vocabulary were unsophisticated, their descriptions of their childrens' pronunciation and grammar were even worse. Thirteen percent of the teachers observed that some students can not talk at all when they come to school; many felt that these children could not hear certain sounds, apparently on the assumption that because a child does not relate his sound system to printed symbols, he cannot hear these sounds. Yet such is the state of the profession. One-third of the teachers characterized their childrens' greatest grammatical failure as their inability to speak in sentences or complete thoughts.

This research showed clearly that one of the most important aspects of language development among disadvantaged children centers on imprecise descriptions of the problem, large-scale ignorance of how to make such a description, and the interference of pedagogical folklore which passes as knowledge about a conspicuously neglected and underprivileged group of human beings. If teachers have such trouble articulating whatever it is they are supposed to be doing about the disadvantaged child's language, how can we expect children to consciously manipulate their language toward an ill-defined Standard, especially with an as yet underdeveloped social value system?

The position of a Negro child in an urban ghetto is, then, that he has a functioning language system which does not necessarily match the language system of the school. This is further complicated by a conflict between the child's culture and that of the middle-class school system. Small boys in primer books often have white middle-class names like Jim and Chuck, whereas the preferred names of urban poor Negroes are James and Charles. Although this may seem like a minor matter, if it is important for children to identify with the characters in the primers, we must do more than color half the faces brown. Recent research on this problem has been done by Joan Baratz of the Center for Applied Linguistics, whose sentence repetition experiments clearly indicate that middle-class white children have as much difficulty repeating syntactical constructions commonly used by Washington, D. C. Negro children as the Negro children had in repeating the white middle-class syntactical forms. That is, if the systematic syntax of lower-class Negro children is used as a measure of middle-class white success, the white children will do poorly. The implications of this research point squarely to the fact that there is cultural mismatch between student and teaching materials.

The first major task for linguists is to describe and analyze this language system of the urban ghetto. In many ways it is similar to that of Standard English, but in several very important ways it is quite different. It differs basically in two ways: (1) the presence of some feature not found in Standard English or the absence of some feature found in Standard English; and (2) frequency distribu-

tion of a feature which is significantly different from that of Standard English.

A quite romantic picture of the differences between Standard
English and Inner-City Negro English would be to say that their
grammars and phonological systems are entirely different. Current research in New York, Detroit, and Washington, D.C., has
shown this to be a gross overstatement. If it were true, there
would be little mutual understanding between speakers of the different dialects. There are, however, significant contrasts that
are particularly evident when the verb systems of lower-class
and working-class Negroes are compared with those of middle-
class Negroes and with whites of all classes. The copula and
auxiliary have been the most fruitful areas of study so far, particularly with regard to a feature which is present in one social
group while absent in another.[5] There are many examples of
frequency distribution differences between racial and/or social
groups.[6] The most notable of these include recent studies of multiple negation, pronominal apposition, r-deletion, l-deletion,
consonant cluster reduction, devoicing of word-final stop consonants, among others.

The significance of this sort of research for beginning reading
instruction is of two kinds, depending on whether the feature is
phonological or grammatical.

Phonological features

A careful description of the phonology of disadvantaged classes
(in contrast to that of the middle classes) will be of more use to
teachers than to writers of classroom materials. The arbitrari-
ness of the symbolization process makes it rather unnecessary to
recast primers into graphemic series which delete the r in car
(cah), the l in help (hep), which substitute voiceless stops for
voiced ones in words like red (ret), and which show consonant-
cluster reductions in words like just (jus) and send (sen). Urban
disadvantaged Negroes should not find it difficult to discover that
/jəs/ is realized in print as just or that /kah/ is realized as car.
Their grapheme to phoneme rule would be ⟨st⟩→/s/ in final position. This is certainly no more unreasonable than other double
grapheme relations as single sounds such as ⟨th⟩→/θ/ in thin or
⟨mb⟩ → /m/ in thumb. That is, the decoding process of reading
is already imbued with such rules. One might also ask, however,
how different the problem is for urban poor Negroes than for, say,
middle-class whites. There is considerable evidence to show that

in some oral styles middle-class whites also reduce these consonant clusters, although not always as frequently as do Negroes.

In addition to cases in which the reduction of consonant clusters
occurs similarly for urban poor Negroes and Standard English
speakers, there are occasions in which the non-standard Negro
cluster reductions are different, depending on the surrounding
sounds, from Standard English. For example, if the Standard
English word ends in /st/ and the following word begins with /s/,
the /st/ cluster is frequently reduced to /s/, as in /wesayd/
(west side). However, in non-standard the cluster may be reduced
whether or not the following word begins with /s/, as in /wesindiyz/
(West Indies). The teacher will probably not correct the Standard
English speaking child when he says /wesayd/ but she may well
object to the non-standard speaker's /wesindiyz/.

As for the other phonological features, linguists can make good
cases for the systematic nature of the disadvantaged Negro's decoding process. For example, whereas a middle-class white or
Negro might decode ⟨time⟩ as /taym/, the ghetto Negro might
realize it as a front vowel, with a different glide segment, /tæhm/.
If the glide vowel is entirely absent, as it often is, the main vowel
is usually lengthened (in the sense of duration), thus producing
/tæ:m/. The rules[7] for these various realizations may be formulated as follows:

Standard	Non-Standard
Rule S 1 ⟨t⟩ → /t/	Rule NS 1 ⟨t⟩ → /t/
S 2 ⟨i...e⟩ → /ay/	NS 2 ⟨i...e⟩ → /æ:/~/æh/

Thus rules S 1 and NS 1 are identical. Rules S 2 and NS 2 have
different correspondent features but the same number of correspondences. That is, ⟨i⟩ followed by a non-contiguous ⟨e⟩
marker yields a glide /ay/ in Standard English of the North, whereas here it yields either a different glide, /æh/, or /æ/ plus a vowel
duration /:/ which may be said to replace or compensate for the
loss of the glide vowel.

All of this is meant to indicate that there is nothing irregular
about the phoneme-grapheme relationship of speakers of non-
standard. The correspondences are quite similar in quantity but
different in certain shapes. In terms of entire linguistic structures
these differences are actually very slight. They gain in importance
only as social groups assign values to them.

It is of utmost importance, however, that teachers be made
aware of these systematic decoding processes. A child who de-

codes ⟨time⟩ as /tæːm/ is not deficient in his ability to pronounce
the glide vowel most frequently heard in Standard English. Nor is
he misreading the word. Ironically, he is doing what any good
reader ought to be doing--taking printed symbols and translating
them into his own meaningful oral symbols. It might be said, in
fact, that learning to read has little or nothing to do with a child's
ability to handle Standard English phonology. But it is tremendously
important for the teacher to understand the child's phonological system in order to distinguish between reading difficulties and systematic features of the child's dialect. It is also important for the
teacher to understand the child's phonological system in order to
organize teaching materials into consistent groupings. For example, I once observed a teacher in a ghetto school tell beginning
readers that the vowels of fog, dog, hog, and log were all the
same. She then had the students repeat the words after her: /fag/,
/dɔg/, /hag/, /lɔg/. The students heard the difference. This
teacher never did. Learning the -og matrix is meaningful pedagogy
if there is consistency in the production of that matrix, /ɔ/ or /a/.
Either pattern is useful to the beginning reader who is being taught
on the basis of pattern.

Grammatical Features

   The analysis of the systematic grammatical structure of ghetto
English (the linguistic position of such speakers) has proved to be
a greater undertaking than one might suspect. Although we have
learned a great deal about the verb system, negation patterns,
question structures, possessives, pluralization, concord and other
things, relatively little of our knowledge has been translated into
materials for beginning readers. Because grammar and syntax
provide a different kind of decoding process than the phoneme-
grapheme relationships noted earlier, the task of the reading
teacher is more complicated. Such a sentence as "John asked if
Mary wore a coat" is frequently read by a ghetto child as "John
asked did Mary wear a coat". Likewise, "Mary jumps up and
down" is often read as "Mary jump up and down". In both instances,
the reader is decoding primer book grammar into his own grammatical system. In no way is he misreading did for if, wear for
wore and jump for jumps. As far as the reading process goes, he
has succeeded. If he fails to read these sentences adequately
(that is, in any of the above ways) he has failed. If, for example,
he were to read the first one as "John asked Mary if did she wear
a coat", or as "John asked Mary if she wear a coat", we might

consider this to be a reading difficulty. The failure would be evidence of interference from one grammatical system to a different grammatical system, all of which brings us back to the fourth assumption of Wiener and Cromer -- that a child would read adequately if the material and method were consistent with his linguistic behavior patterns.

If the major focus in the teaching of reading is on getting meaning from the printed page into the reader's consciousness, there should be no hesitation about developing materials which match the child's grammatical system[8]. Expanding or changing his grammatical system is not part of the reading process as such and, quite likely, ought to be introduced gradually in keeping with the child's general social awareness in other areas.

At this point then, we have indicated that some reading difficulties stem from a mismatch of teaching materials with the linguistic behavior of the learners. This has no bearing on the physiologically defective, or those who lack phonological or grammatical skills, or on the psychologically disrupted. It is a product of a cultural position which has its own system, its own problems, and its own beauty. This position must be understood much better if we are to do anything significant for those who hold it.

The Processive Dimension

We have briefly described the efforts of linguists to deal with the cultural position of a large portion of children with reading difficulties. Still another way in which linguists can be useful to reading teachers might be called processive. By this I mean that linguists think about language in process in ways which reading pedagogy may find useful. Studies in the language acquisition of children, of course, fall into this purview. The teaching of reading has not always accommodated itself to the natural progression of children's language acquisition and has been guilty of what I refer to, elsewhere, as aphasic teaching[9]. By this I mean that students, like victims of aphasia, are taught in the reverse order in which their learning can best take place. Teachers and textbooks too often view their task from their own, not the students', stage in the learning process. Teachers' manuals which discuss the "four sounds of a" well illustrate this principle. The child, by the age of six, has a pretty fair grasp of the sound system of English. He is likely to have little or no grasp of the symbols which represent these sounds on paper. If a beginning reader is taught that the letter a has four sounds, the teaching runs counter to the learn-

ing process. Fortunately, it is obvious to most teachers by now
that we should begin with a child where he is (with sounds) and
move toward where he is going (toward letters) than vice versa.
Yet there is still a great deal of work to be done before the teaching
of reading can reach the stage where aphasic teaching is overcome
and the processive dimension is well accounted for.

One such area is in syllabication. Annually thousands of third
grade children are set to work finding and counting the syllables
in their reading workbooks.

From the linguist's viewpoint there are at least three questions
in which reading instructions need clarification for the treatment
of syllabication to become maximally efficient. These questions
deal with the syllabic consonant, the identification of syllables in
general, and reasons for studying syllabication in the first place.
To say that reading instruction has been fuzzy in these areas is to
say the kindest thing imaginable.

The Syllabic Consonant

Until very recently a syllable was most commonly defined as
"...a part of a word in which we hear one vowel sound..." (Thorndike Barnhart Junior Dictionary, p. 35). It was on this basis that
my oldest son muddled his way through third grade syllabication.
Any audience of professional educators and researchers will appreciate the difficulty I had in confronting his teacher with the
fact that he was simply not hearing a vowel sound in the second
syllable of words like travel, weasel, and awful. Instead he heard
a phonetic /l/ and marked his work book accordingly. Of course,
the teachers' manual proved that he was wrong, and there was no
convincing the teacher that my son's ear was better than hers.

More recently, the Thorndike Barnhart Junior Dictionary has
added a statement about certain syllabic consonants: "For some
words of more than one syllable a vowel sound may not be heard
in an unaccented syllable. In such words the l sound or the n
sound takes the place of a vowel sound, and is called a syllabic
consonant" (p. 37). This dictionary, upon which many reading
texts rely, is consistent with syllabic l as long as the word is
spelled with a final -le (bundle, table, eagle). But in such words
as bushel and easel, there is apparent inconsistency (bush´əl)
and (ē´zl). Yet an investigation of this apparent inconsistency reveals, surprisingly enough, a deeper regularity.

When a syllable at the end of a word ends in /l/, it is possible
to predict whether or not this sound is preceded by the vowel /ə/.

If the final consonant sound in the penultimate syllable in such words as vigil, virile and bushel is /ǰ/, /č/, /r/, /š/, /ž/, or /l/, the schwa (/ə/) is present. If this consonant is any other sound, the final syllable is a syllabic /l/. In forming an /l/ after /č/, for example, a speaker must move the tip of his tongue sufficiently far enough to require the pronunciation of a vowel /ə/ between these two consonants. This is true only for the sounds /ǰ/, /č/, /r/, /š/, /ž/, and /l/ before /l/. As a result, syllabic /l/ is impossible in these syllables.[10]

This rule seems to be the implicit basis for syllabication in the case of /l/ employed by the Thorndike Barnhart Dictionary. Before this dictionary is given too much credit, however, it must be pointed out that this rule is violated in words which end in -ful. Thus, while sniffle is assigned a syllablic /l/ in conformity with the above principle, awful is inconsistently marked with a schwa before the /l/.[11]

We can see from these examples that a beginning reader who is learning syllabication may be handicapped by the very phonetic abilities he has been encouraged to develop, and by certain inconsistencies in dictionaries. Nor have current reading texts treated syllabication with consistency. They are not likely to make a great deal of progress until dictionaries begin to treat the subject more deeply.

The Identification of Syllables

A linguist, looking at syllabication, might approach the problem in several ways. He may choose to think in terms of both phonology and grammar. He may choose to think of syllables as some kind of voiced continuant peak with borders which are, somehow, not like peaks. The major problems in syllable division seem to be at these borders, naturally enough. Although the point may be argued, let us assume that the linguist feels that syllables should be, at the same time, true to the phonology, grammar and lexicon of the language. That is, they must satisfy criteria of the grammatical, lexical and phonological components of language. Grammatical components such as -ing or -ish should be preserved as syllables in complex constructions such as jump-ing and fool-ish rather than jum-ping and foo-lish. Monosyllabic lexical components such as some in something should be preserved as syllables, preventing either so-me-thing or so-mething. Since stop consonants so frequently form the borders of syllables, where medial consonant clusters exist, they may be the best place to mark syllable division.

Now, with these examples in mind, let me propose a series of semi-ordered syllabication rules.

Rule 1   (Lexical rule): Syllable division is marked at compounds which contain clearly marked monosyllabic segments (ink-well, not in-kwell).

Rule 2   (Grammatical rule): Syllable division is marked at inflections and/or affixes (love-ly, slopp-y, drumm-er, etc.). Note here that doubled spellings are irrelevant (syllables are not based on spellings).[12]

Rule 3   (Phonological rule 1): When syllable borders are ambiguous grammatically, they can be split at medial consonant clusters (of differing consonants) if such clusters are present (tar-get, sil-ver, win-dow).

Rule 4   (Phonological rule 2): When syllable borders are ambiguous grammatically and when they do not have consonant-cluster borders, the syllabication should follow the pattern of monosyllabic words in English. That is, the phonological restrictions of English monosyllabic words may be applied to syllables which appear as parts of polysyllabic words. Thus, tiger and spider (with glided, unchecked vowels which can appear word finally, as in buy and high) are split ti-ger and spi-der. On the other hand, shadow, lemon and lizard (with unglided, checked vowels which cannot appear finally (/æ, e, i/), are split shad-ow, lem-on, and liz-ard.

Rule 5   (Phonological rule 3): When a voiced continuant such as /l/, /r/, /m/, or /n/ can be heard as the nucleus of the syllable (a syllabic consonant), it is marked as a separate syllable. Thus, poodle is pood-le, dimp-le, and pupil is pup-il.

I introduced these five rules as "semi-ordered" primarily because the phonological rules are fairly equal, and rules 3, 4, and 5 may apply in any order. The most significant thing here is that the lexical rule takes precedence over the grammatical rule which, in turn, takes precedence over all the phonogical rules. It should also be noted here that these rules constitute a beginning toward a linguistic theory of syllabication. They do not account for all English words, although they handle a significantly large majority with a consistency hitherto absent from dictionaries and introductory reading materials.

It must also be noted here that these five rules can apply to both the syllables of sound and the syllables of writing. Past syllabication has been based on the printed word entirely, even though claims were made for the usefulness of such activity in word attack. Past "rules" for end-line word splitting have accounted for the lexical rule in a non-rigorous fashion (I know of no restraint on <u>something</u> being split <u>so</u>-<u>me</u>-<u>thing</u>). Past rules have rather carefully accommodated the grammatical rule. The phonological rules have been only partially observed, naturally enough for an orthographical orientation. Rules 4 and 5 were unformulated, and there was no notion of a hierarchical order.

The Reason for Studying Syllabication

The usefulness of syllabication for word attack may be seriously called into question in the traditional sense of the meaning of word attack. It is quite apparent, if the preceding semi-ordered rules are accepted, that a child must know a great deal about phoneme-grapheme relationships and morphophonemic spelling and a great deal about grammatical inflections and derivational affixes before he can become a successful syllable finder. In short, the solution to a well-defined theory of syllabication tells us that this feature of language seems to have less to do with initial reading skill than it does with general skill in the language arts. In order to find the proper syllable divisions, the child must already know the things he needs to know in order to be a successful beginning reader. On the other hand, by focusing on syllable identification, the teacher can determine whether or not the child has mastered these rules. That is, his ability to find syllables is really a test of his reading ability and, like all good tests, it should <u>teach</u>, perhaps by calling attention to what has been happening all along. In any case, it can be safely affirmed that if a child has mastered these five rules and can find syllables adequately, he should be able to meet new words, even nonsense words, with confidence. A child who syllabifies <u>unflurbly</u> as <u>un</u>-<u>flurb</u>-<u>ly</u> or <u>camip</u> as <u>cam</u>-<u>ip</u> evidences word-attack skills which surely reflect sophistication, whether it is called reading or language arts.

In the processive dimension of reading, then, linguists ask questions about language acquisition and how teaching processes match or mismatch with it. One example of past cultural mismatch has been in the aphasic teaching associated with syllabication. Children are asked to do a task which is supposedly helpful in developing reading ability but which requires skills that evidence

<u>developed</u> reading abilities. We have been giving a test, thinking that it was the homework. This is one aspect of the processive dimension which interests linguists. Another aspect is the semi-ordered rules themselves. With the advent of contemporary linguistics has come the notion of ordered rules in grammatical analysis. We are content not simply with finding rules but with seeing how they sequence. It seems clear, in the case of syllabication, that linguistic rule ordering is a very useful feature.

From this analysis, it should be clear that developers of reading materials and dictionary makers must rethink their entire approach to syllabication and the reading process. Students have been plagued by inconsistent dictionary practice with respect to syllabic consonants, inadequate instruction in how to identify syllables, dictionary syllabication which is not faithful to the lexicon, grammar, and phonology of the language, and an inadequate theory of pedagogical sequencing which does not distinguish between developing and developed skills. One by-product of such a situation ought to be embarrassment over the artificial separation between reading and the language arts. One might hope that future elementary textbooks will find it so difficult to distinguish the reading lessons from the language arts lessons that these hitherto separate subjects will merge into a more sensible unitary body.

Here, then, we have two general areas in which linguistic research can help children with reading difficulties caused by mismatch of specific child culture to pedagogical materials. The positional dimension and the processive dimension are both legitimate fields in which linguists may provide many insights in the near future.

NOTES

1. Morton Wiener and Ward Cromer, "Reading and Reading Difficulty: A Conceptual Analysis, "Harvard Educational Review, XXXVII (1967), Number 4, 620-643. [Reprinted in the present volume, pages 136-162.]
2. It must be realized, however, that the educator's reading problem does not stem from a different grammatical system, as does the difficulty of the urban child.
3. Occasionally, however, they can cite lexical matters which they think have social consequence.
4. Anne E. Hughes, An Investigation of Certain Socio-linguistic Phenomena in the Vocabulary, Pronunciation and Grammar of Disadvantaged Pre-School Children, Their Parents and Their

Teachers in the Detroit Public Schools (unpublished Ph.D. diss., Michigan State Universtiy, 1967). For a summary, see Roger W. Shuy, Walter A. Wolfram, and William K. Riley, <u>Linguistic Correlates of Social Stratification in Detroit Speech,</u> Final Report, Cooperative Research Project 6-1347, U.S. Office of Education, IV, 1-10.

5. See Marvin Loflin, <u>On the Structure of the Verb in a Dialect of American Negro English,</u> Office of Naval Research Group Psychology Branch, Technical Report No. 26, Center for Research in Social Behavior, University of Missouri; and Ralph W. Fasold, "Tense and the Form <u>Be</u> in Black English", in Roger W. Shuy and Ralph W. Fasold, (eds.), <u>Current Viewpoints Toward Non-Standard "Be"</u> (Washington, D.C.: Center for Applied Linguistics, forthcoming).

6. See, for example, William Labov, <u>The Social Stratification of English in New York City</u> (Washington, D.C.: Center for Applied Linguistics, 1966); and Shuy, Wolfram, and Riley, <u>op, cit.</u>

7. The term "rule" is not used here in the current sense in which it is found in theoretical linguistics. That is, we are not referring to derivational history. From the linguist's viewpoint, a more accurate term might be "correspondence".

8. Such materials are, in fact, being developed by Joan C. Baratz and William A. Stewart at the Center for Applied Linguistics, Washington, D.C.

9. Roger W. Shuy, <u>Four Dimensions of Language in the Classroom</u> (Dodd-Mead, forthcoming).

10. A small set of such rules will also account for syllabic /n/, /r/, and /m/. Research on this problem is currently being carried out by the author.

11. Many of these problems with syllabic consonants disappear if phoneme-grapheme correspondences are not insisted upon but, instead, written forms are assumed to reflect the organization of sounds at the morphophonemic level.

12. Rules 1 and 2 can be said to be two cases of the same principle. That is, phonological material which can be shown to belong to one morpheme should not be assigned to another in syllabication. These cases are presented separately here for purposes of clarity and pedagogical sequencing.

SOME CONDITIONS FOR DEVELOPING BEGINNING
READING MATERIALS FOR GHETTO CHILDREN

by Roger W. Shuy

In previous paper, I described what I called the "positional"
dimension of the linguists' approach to reading difficulties caused
by behavioral mismatch[1] It was emphasized at that time that I had
reference to reading difficulties caused by behavioral mismatch of
extant beginning reading materials to the synchronic cultural position of certain inner-city Negro children, and that I had nothing to
say about reading difficulties caused by physiological malfunction-
ing, educational deficiency or psychological interference. I discussed, further, the relative merits of suiting teaching materials
to the child or changing the child to suit the materials. Advocates
of the latter seem unaware of the cultural difficulties involved in
trying to get children to speak standard English when they have few
or no peers who use it. I ventured to say that it is more important
to learn to read than to learn to speak standard English and that
since the traditional theory in education has been to suit materials
to the child, I see no reason why this should not be done for non-
standard beginning readers.

Specially developed beginning reading materials which avoid
linguistic mismatch of the child's oral language and the written
text may draw on three levels of data: lexical, phonological and
grammatical.

A great deal of the consideration given to speakers of non-
standard varieties of English in the past has been in lexical matters.
The educational world has generally thought of language as lexicon
and it is not suprising that they would equate cultural adjustment
to the words of the city, the inner-city in particular. Most linguists would maintain, however, that people of all types are more
tolerant of different, even mismatched, vocabulary than they are
of variant pronunciations or grammar. Some linguists further

Reprinted by permission from the Journal of Reading Behavior
1:2.33-43, (Spring 1969).

maintain that these same people are more tolerant of pronunciation differences than they are of matters of grammar. The conclusion drawn from my preceding paper is that if special materials are developed for beginning readers whose major language contact and use is the non-standard variety found in urban Negro ghettos, these materials should focus on avoiding grammatical mismatch rather than on lexical or phonological matters.

If phonological considerations appear to be of no great consequence to the development of such materials, one might legitimately ask what importance to attach to grammatical considerations. In order to do this, we might do well to suggest some principles upon which such considerations are based. Such principles can be expected to be broadly relevant for judging the effectiveness of such materials but they should also serve as judgment categories in reading generally, whether it be for non-standard readers, standard readers, speed readers, literature readers and readers of any other sort. Three such principles suggest themselves:

1. The grammatical choices should not provide extraneous data. In the case of beginning reading materials for non-standard speakers, the text should help the child by avoiding forms which are not realized by him in his spoken language (third singular verb inflections, for example).

2. The grammatical choices should provide adequate data. In the case of beginning reading materials for non-standard speakers, grammatical forms which occur in non-standard but not in standard should be inserted where they appear natural within the non-standard system (the be in "All the time he be happy", and the to in "Make him to do it", for example).

3. The grammatical choices should provide sequentially relevant data. In the case of beginning reading materials for non-standard speakers, syntactic constructions such as adverbial phrases should be reduced to their derivative nominalized forms where it is natural to do so on the dialect (the as a janitor in the sentence, "Samuel's brother is working as a janitor", for example, reduced to "Samuel brother, he a janitor").

At this point, the domino theory of research catches up with us, for the reading theorists have not adequately defined just exactly what reading is and, subsequently, what reading problems really are. This puts the linguist at a disadvantage, to say the least. But even if we can't define reading, we can at least talk about some of its characteristics and perhaps see how the interference of one grammatical system on another may contribute some problems therein.

If we are willing to say that some of the characteristics of reading include the reader's discovering meaning from certain

visual symbols with the aid of some unexplainable help from his
knowledge of semantic, phonological, grammatical probabilities
and non-linguistic context, then we can proceed along the following
lines. It seems likely that these characteristics of the reading
process may operate (with considerable oversimplification) according to the chart below.

A Schematic Chart of the Child's Dependence on Some
Characteristics of the Reading Process

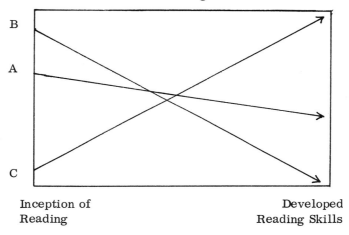

Inception of   Developed
Reading   Reading Skills

Key:
A: Sound-Symbol Relationship
B: Visual Discrimination
C: Underlying Language Structure

If this schematization in anyway reflects reality, it is obvious
that the characteristics necessary for the beginning reader may be
called upon in progressively different degrees as he moves toward
more mature reading abilities. That is, the child must call on
visual discrimination (B) and sound-symbol relationships (A) quite
heavily at the beginning stages and he must rely on them less and
less as he reads faster and better. His underlying language structure (C) however, though called upon throughout the reading process,
is used increasingly as A and B diminish.

The importance of underlying language structure in the reading
process cannot be overestimated although very little has been said
about it in the literature of reading. By underlying structure here
I mean that ability which even beginning readers have which enables

them to avoid misreading via any manner other than by the phonological, and grammatical rules of their native language. Thus they
do not render cat as cta (an impossible phonological realization in
English) although they quite possibly could realize it as cet or cep
or any other sequence of sounds allowable in English. Such ability
also prevents grammatical misreadings of sentences like The man
chased the cat as The man the chase cated or Man the the chased
cat. If the reader is going to err, he will err within the framework
of possible variants in phonology and grammar, although not necessarily within the framework of standard English (e. g. The man done
chased the cat). Some linguists would say that a child has some
innate capacity for language learning which accelerates such apparently learned characteristics, or that this underlying structure
undergirds all types of linguistic performance and that, in reading,
a person perceives in relationship to such an underlying system.
The blind can learn to read despite absent visual discrimination (B)
and the deaf can become literate despite an absent sound-symbol
relationship (A). The fact that many children learn to read in spite
of the inadequacies of reading theory and teaching today may be a
silent tribute to the magnificence of the human brain and the marvels
of underlying language structure.
        Certain kinds of supposed reading errors, then, can be said to
result from differing surface realizations of similar underlying
language structures. A child who reads He is John's freind as He
John friend may be evidencing exactly the same underlying structure
of the writer with only surface differences.
        The real questions from these realizations and with others like
them are:
    1. What kind and how much interference is caused by the absence
       of non-standard grammatical features in standard English
       texts ?
    2. What kind and how much interference is caused by the presence
       of standard English features in the text which are not used by
       non-standard speakers ?
    3. What kind and how much interference is caused by syntactic
       variations between non-standard and standard English features ?
All of these questions relate to grammatical matters in which the
underlying structures of standard English and non-standard are
equivalent but in which the surface realizations vary. It goes without saying that where both performance and the underlying structure
fail to match or, worse yet, where performance is identical and
where the underlying structures are not equivalent, there are
bound to be reading problems.
        It might appear, in fact, that there is no more to worry about in
terms of potential cross-dialectal interference for many gram-

matical matters than there is to concern us with cross-dialectal
interference in phonological features. In an effort to determine
potential reading interference caused by the conflict in performance realizations between non-standard speakers and standard text,
let us list some of the understanding characteristics of non-standard
as they appear in most American Negro ghettos.

Written Expression	Linguistic Feature	Oral Expression
1. John's house	possession	John house
2. John runs	3rd. sing. pres.	John run
3. ten cents	plurality	ten cent
4. He jumped	past	He jump
5. She is a cook	copula	She a cook
6. He doesn't have any toys	negation	He ain't got no toys
		He don't have no toys
		He don't got no toys
7. He asked if I came	past conditional question	He asked did I come
8. Every day when I come he isn't here	negative + be	Every day when I come he don't be here

In the first five items, sound-symbol relationships and visual
discrimination have little if any effect on the non-standard reader's
realization of the written standard text. These realization rules
may be stated as follows:

	Standard	Non-Standard
1. possession	→ -'s	→ ∅
2. 3rd singular verb	→ -s	→ ∅
3. plurality	→ -s	→ ∅
4. past tense	→ -ed	→ ∅
5 copula	→ is	→ ∅

If the non-standard reader has no reason to supply an oral sound
for the standard written representation of possession, 3rd singular,
plurality, past tense, and the copula, we can safely say that the
sound-symbol relationship plays little or no part in his reading
ability in these instances. He is perfectly able to produce non-
inflectional word-final sounds which are identical to those above

(e.g. mis<u>s</u>, hi<u>s</u>, bu<u>zz</u>, <u>b</u>et, etc.), discounting the possibility that
he has a speech production problem. As he reads, he must be in-
fluenced by his grammatical system which, as indeed is the case,
contains a differently marked possession, 3rd singular verb, plurality, past tense and copula. He must become wary of certain
morphemes just as he must become wary of such graphemes as the
<u>l</u> in <u>could</u> and the <u>s</u> in <u>island</u>. Most likely the sound-symbol rela-
tionship has been submerged by reading skills provided by his
underlying language structure (C) which in turn leads him to produce language performance consonant with his dialect even though
the visual symbols might argue otherwise.

Sentences 6 through 8 provide somewhat different kinds of
problems.

6. <u>Negation</u>
   Standard: do + neg + have + any

   Non-Standard:

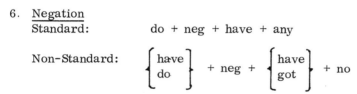

7. <u>Past conditional question</u>
   Standard: if + S + V (past)
   Non-Standard: do (past) + S + V
8. <u>Negative + be</u>
   Standard: be + neg
   Non-Standard: do + neg + be

In each of the above cases there are sufficiently different sound-
symbol relationships between the written standard and the oral non-
standard to suggest that this aspect of the reading act is called
upon scarcely at all in these instances. Instead, the non-standard
speaker who converts the standard text into non-standard grammatical patterns seems to be more influenced by what seems
"natural" to him than by what is found on the printed page.

Research into reading errors produced by speakers of non-
standard is still in its infancy but already several things have become clear. Children in the intermediate grades have fewer
reading problems of the sort noted in sentences 6 through 8 and
produce more "errors" of the sort found in sentences 1 through
5. This seems to indicate that the more basic the difference
between standard and non-standard grammatical items, the more
likely the intermediate child is to have developed an ability to read

it successfully aloud. Conversely, the less basic the difference, the less importance it appears to make to this child, a fact which seems to support the notion that sound-symbol relationships are ultimately deemed less basic than grammatical features, since the readers appear to work harder at grosser differences and ignore smaller ones.

These conclusions, like all conclusions derived from the study of reading errors, are drawn from the oral reading experiences of children who develop sufficient reading skills to read aloud. What is unfortunate about such conclusions, of course, is that children who can't read well enough to risk exposing their ignorance cannot be studied in this way and their performance cannot be measured. It is just possible that one aspect of their reading failure can be attributed to their inability to cope with the grosser differences of the sort noted in sentences 6 through 8, where currently available reading pedagogy with its emphasis on phonics and word method only confuses the matter. William A. Stewart has referred to the grammatical plight of the non-standard ghetto resident as that of a quasi-foreign language situation,[2] which, if true, would indicate that we have a far more complicated situation to deal with than normally faces the reading teacher. The situation is further complicated by the fact that the many similarities between the standard and non-standard grammatical patterns obscure the few but crucial differences. One can legitimately wonder, however, how irrational it might seem to a beginning reader to be told in essence that there is a regular sound-symbol relationship involved in reading but that in some instances there are words or parts of words attached which are not pronunced in his own language, some words or parts of words in his own language which are not written in standard English, and occasionally the written words are in a different order from the way he says them. Perhaps this is discouragement enough to prevent him from going any further in this irrational and unrealistic world of the classroom.

If the processes of learning to read and learning to speak standard English are somewhat separate entities (as many linguists believe), and if the suggested model of reading acquisition skills noted earlier is accurate, we can reasonably say that beginning readers with their heavy leaning on sound-symbol clues to reading, ought to be protected as much as possible from the mismatch between their social dialect and the written text, in the following ways:

1. Include in the beginning reading materials the grammatical forms which occur in non-standard even though they may be absent in standard English (e.g. sentences 6 through 8).

2. Exclude from the beginning reading materials the grammatical forms which occur in standard but do not occur in non-standard (e.g. sentences 1 through 5).

3. Write beginning reading materials in such a way that the syntactic structures of the written text reflect the syntactic structures of the reader's oral language experience in a way that is consistent with the task at hand--learning to read (e.g. sentences 6 and 7).

It is point number 3 which requires explanation at this time, for we have said very little about syntactic presentation. A major consideration ought to be that sentences in beginning reading materials be well organized, in order to show the clearest possible relationship between constituent elements. For beginning readers, less concern needs to be shown for problems of monotony than for obscurity or ambiguity. Such obscurity can be seen in the following sentences: "Larry went to the movies. 'At the movies we had fun,' said Larry". Beginning readers from all social classes are apt to stumble on the prepositional phrase beginning the second sentence. The experience of our research shows that children tie it to the first sentence, probably because such prepositional phrases seldom are found in sentence-initial position in their oral language. Perhaps writers of beginning reading materials should take certain clues from translators of materials for the new literate or for the only slightly educated readers. William Wonderly suggests the following techniques like the following:[3]

1. Avoid complex or derived constructions and stick to simple or kernel constructions. Use verbal rather than nominal constructions and active rather than passive verbs.

Although it is important for children to eventually develop an ability to vary sentence structure by using derived constructions (such as nominalizations) and passive voice verbs, there is practically no need for such variation in beginning reading materials. To illustrate his contention that complex derived sentences provide excessive embedding for the beginning reader, Wonderly uses the sentence <u>John told George to tell Mary to bring her sister,</u> which has at least four base sentences:

John told George (something).
George told Mary (something).
Mary had a sister.
Mary brought the sister.[4]

Several psycholinguists have suggested that such complex sentences tend to be stored in the human memory in the form of their underived, "kernel" constructions (along with their rules for embedding).[5] If this is true, then the reading of embedded sentences might be considered to be a kind of pre-storage disembedding process. It also suggests that beginning readers (of any social class) should be provided materials in kernel or near-kernel form, even at the expense of monotony (a less decisive factor for those who have not become over-familiar with the printed page).

2. Avoid structural ambiguity. This is, of course, good advice for beginning reading materials for any class or dialect-speaking group. Some of the more humorous sayings of small children stem from unrealized ambiguities such as:

> Mother: Sally, go see how old Mrs. Jones is today.
> Sally: Mrs. Jones, how old are you today?

Such unintentional ambiguities pose unnecessary additional burdens on the beginning reader. The dangers of potential ambiguities for beginning ghetto children are painfully apparent in the following sentences:

Standard	Potential "Reading" by Non-Standard Speaker
1. She arose.	She is a rose.
2. We jump into the water.	We jumped into the water.
3. He sat on the bank.	He sat on top of the bank. (First National)
4. The policeman is my friend.	?
5. Flying planes can be dangerous.	The flying planes... or, Flying the planes...
6. They took the bus to Akron.	They "rode" the bus... or, they "brought" the bus...

Sentences 1 and 2 are ambiguous as a result of the differing grammatical systems between the child's oral language and that of the printed page. Sentences 3 and 4 stem from cultural contrasts in the ghetto child's oral language practice. We may decide to include such so-called redundant features as multiple negatives and pronominal apposition in the beginning reading materials:

> He don't have no baseball bat.
> My brother John, he struck out.

If redundancy is reinforcing to the language learner (in this case, the aspiring literate), one must use the inventory of available redundancies.

If beginning reading materials for ghetto children are to relate to the oral language of the learners, these considerations must be reflected in the primers. The matter of the reader's language sense must be given considerable emphasis in these primers, particularly where there is mismatch of standard and non-standard grammatical phenomena. There is considerable room for improvement in the construction of beginning reading material for children of all social classes and races, but there is drastic need for adjustment of such materials for the Negro non-standard speaker, whose grammatical system is sufficiently different from standard English to hinder his learning to relate his oral language to the grammatical forms of the primer.

The problems of producing overcomplex or derived constructions, ambiguous readings, and under-redundant material for standard English speaking readers has by no means been solved, but it is even multiplied for non-standard speaking children, whose derivations, systematic ambiguities, and redundancies have only begun to be observed, much less utilized in reading materials.

NOTES

1. Roger W. Shuy, "Some Language and Cultural Differences in a Theory of Reading", in Kenneth S. Goodman and James T. Fleming (eds.), Psycholinguistics and the Teaching of Reading (Newark, Del.: International Reading Association, 1969), pp. 34-47. [Reprinted in the present volume, pages 72-87.]
2. William A. Stewart, "Foreign Language Teaching Methods In Quasi-Foreign Language Situations", in William A. Stewart (ed.), Non-Standard Speech and the Teaching of English (Washington, D.C.: Center for Applied Linguistics, 1964), pp. 1-15.
3. William Wonderly, Bible Translations for Popular Use (New York: American Bible Society, 1968).
4. Ibid., pp. 150-151.
5. See, for example, G.A. Miller, "Some Psychological Studies of Grammar", American Psychologist 17 (1962), pp. 748-762; and E.B. Coleman, "Learning of Prose Written in Four Grammatical Transformations", Journal of Applied Psychology 49 (1965), pp. 332-341.

A GLANCE AT THE LINGUISTIC ORGANIZATION
OF ELEMENTARY READING TEXTBOOKS

by David W. Reed

The textbooks most commonly used to teach beginning reading may be classified, from the point of view of linguistics, under four headings: (1) the basal series, which increasingly have phonic supplements; (2) the language-experience series; (3) the phonic readers; and (4) the linguistic readers.

The principal characteristics of the basal series that serve to distinguish them from other types of beginning reading textbooks are, first, rigid control of the introduction of new vocabulary items, and, second, the view that the process of reading and the use of reading are essentially one and the same thing, so that reading becomes a developmental skill to be taught from first grade through high school. Both of these characteristics deserve careful scrutiny.

The vocabulary of basal readers has been frequently studied. In fact, in a quite circular fashion, the word lists employed in earlier basal readers form the basis of the vocabulary introduced in the newer series. Moreover, the usual tests of reading achievement are based on these word lists, so that a child who is learning to read by some other method may be unfairly penalized by the tests in his early stages of mastering the process. What the original basis of such word lists may have been is by no means clear. There has been no study of the oral vocabulary common to most children at the time they enter school since that of Madeleine Horn in the 1920's[1] and such a study, to parallel Ruth Strickland's more recent research in oral grammatical structures known to first grade children,[2] is desperately needed. The authors of basal readers have not recognized this need, because they do not view reading as a two-stage process: first, acquiring the skill to recognize written language that is already familiar to the child in oral form and, second, applying this skill to expanding one's control of the language, including its vocabulary. As long as the number of new words introduced per page is strictly limited, the basal series have no concern with the question of whether the words are already part of the child's oral vocabulary. The only gesture they make in this direction is to concentrate on short words in the early stages of teaching reading.

The notion that reading consists of "getting meaning from the printed page", coupled with rigid control of new vocabulary items, has a number of serious consequences in the reading materials themselves. First, the child is encouraged to make use of every possible clue -- linguistic and non-linguistic -- in identifying the words he is supposed to read. These clues range from pictures (if the caption under a picture of a boy jumping is "The boy is jumping", it would be unreasonable to read jumping as "standing") through words shapes (jumping hangs down below the line at the beginning, in the middle, and at the end, whereas standing sticks up above the line just after the beginning and again in the middle, but hangs down below the line at the end) to general language context (if one has identified "The boy is . . .", he should know that the last word cannot be jumps). The emphasis on employing every clue available discourages the child from making generalizations in terms of the linguistic structure of the material he is reading. Reading becomes a process of memorization, and the child who might have difficulty in making generalizations under the most favorable circumstances usually becomes a remedial reading problem when the capacity of his memory is reached at around the fourth grade level.

A second consequence of the word-oriented approach of the basal readers is that the authors are tempted to compose sentences like, "Oh, oh, oh! Look, look, look!" which, if not flatly ungrammatical in English, are at best deviant from the normal grammar with which the child is familiar in his oral language. The child is bewildered, because the material he sees on the printed page has little or nothing to do with the language he has learned orally. A common reaction among the more perceptive children is "Nobody talks that way."

A third consequence of rigid vocabulary control is that it makes it difficult or impossible to write material that will arouse the child's interest. The authors of basal reading series have not, by and large, been persons of great literary talent. Lacking such abilities and hampered by the severely limited vocabulary of the early books, they have produced boring materials that not only fail to motivate children to learn to read, but may actually produce in them a strong aversion toward the written language.

Turning to the second major characteristic of the basal series-- that of teaching the process and uses of reading concurrently from first grade through high school -- we can identify two-fold serious consequences: First, failure to recognize that the process of reading consists of the ability to identify from the printed symbolizations all those linguistic forms that one knows from their spoken symbolizations, and failure to isolate and teach this ability thoroughly in the initial stages of reading instruction produces children who are still struggling to master the process, even into their secondary school years. Such children are incapable of using reading to expand their knowledge of the world, themselves, and their relation to their environment. Second, the segregation of reading instruction into a special class period from third grade through high school seems to confer upon it the status of a subject matter and to absolve teachers of social studies, science, mathematics, and the fine arts of the responsibility for teaching students how to read in their special subject-matter areas. A common result of this approach is that the child who has mastered the mechanics of mathematics at his particular level so that he can solve most problems that have been set up in numbers for him, is utterly frustrated if faced with a "word problem" that must be converted into figures before it can be solved. If there were no reading classes above second grade, perhaps teachers in the genuine subject matter areas would come to recognize their obligation to teach students to deal with the logic, rhetoric, and composition of the language typically used in expounding their particular disciplines. The teacher who formerly taught reading would also be freed to concentrate on his proper concern -- that of teaching children to deal with the very special organizations of language inherent in those artistic uses of it that we call literature.

Before leaving the basal series of elementary reading textbooks, I should say a word about the phonic supplements to these series, that are becoming so popular. When I turn to the third general type of reading series, those based on phonics, I shall have several points to make about their general inadequacies. All of these criticisms apply equally to the phonic supplements to the basal series. In addition, these supplements suffer from another shortcoming. The severely limited vocabularies of the basal readers provide, by the end of the second-year book, relatively few examples of the most useful phonic generalizations. Unless the introductory vocabulary has been selected with sound-letter correspondences in mind, phonic generalizations will appear to the child to be totally unrelated to the process of reading.

In summary, given the nature of the English language and of the writing system that has been devised to represent it, the approach to teaching reading that is incorporated in the basal series has many apparent shortcomings and disadvantages. It is consequently tragic that the basal series have become the most widely used method of teaching reading in the United States.

In discussing the second general classification of elementary reading textbooks, the language-experience approach to teaching reading, I shall have to confess that my comments are based more on discussions I have had with persons who have been engaged in

teaching and studying the process of reading by this method than on
a detailed examination of the materials themselves.

The language-experience method shares with the basal approach
a rather strict limitation of vocabulary. It is more realistic than
the basal reader, however, in concentrating on vocabulary that is
already largely familiar to the child through oral sources. The
language-experience approach is, in fact, an approach to the total
reading and language training of the child rather than to reading
alone. In a typical language-experience classroom, the teacher
may bring in several fertilized hen's eggs that have been incubated
near the point of hatching. The children watch the eggs as they are
kept under heat until they hatch. The students are encouraged at
all times during this period to talk about what they are observing.
Their sentences are written down by the teacher, who aids the
children in reading the sentences, copying them in writing, and
composing original written sentences about the same events.

Such an approach, while more realistic in terms of the psychology
of learning, seems completely unstructured as far as language and
writing are concerned. The approach, like that of the basal readers,
is word-oriented. One cannot easily control the sound-letter correspondence of words that occur spontaneously in children's speech
nor the grammatical structure of children's sentences. Furthermore, this approach to reading does not permit distinction between
the process and the uses of reading, which is crucial in the phonic
and linguistic approaches to the same problem. In the language-
experience curriculum, children are simultaneously learning to
read forms that are already in their oral control of the language
and forming new concepts that are represented by new language
forms in their oral and written language.

In summary, the language-experience approach to beginning
instruction in reading and writing has much to recommend it from
the point of view of the psychology of learning. It does not suffer
some of the severe disabilities inherent in the method of the basal
readers. Whether this second approach to the teaching of reading
can be meaningfully combined with a scientific view of the structure
of the English language and of the nature of the English writing
system remains to be seen.

If the basal readers and the language-experience approach to
reading and writing are essentially word-oriented, the third major
classification of reading textbooks may be said to be sound- and
letter-oriented. It seems to me that phonics materials should be
viewed as belonging to one of two subtypes, which I shall call "pure"
phonics and phonics through gimmickry.

The two original hallmarks of phonics readers that served to distinguish them from the other three major types were, first, em-

phasis on "sounding out" words letter by letter, and, second, emphasis on memorization of rules of sound-letter correspondence as an aid to recognition of the underlying regularities of the spelling system. There are several problems with both of these procedures. In order to sound out a word, a child must be able to isolate the sounds of which the word is made up. This calls for analytical abilities of a high order that are sometimes lacking even in graduate students when they approach the study of phonetics for the first time. Assuming, however, that many children will be able to isolate sounds in this manner, the next problem is to pronounce the sound in isolation. At this point the procedure becomes highly artificial because no sound pronounced in isolation is identical to any sound pronounced in the normal stream of speech. The artificiality is especially apparent with stop consonants, where the normal tendency of a native speaker of English is to add a neutral vowel, so as to form a pronounceable syllable. ⟨t⟩ thus becomes [tə]. Some phonics series emphasize that pupils should not be permitted to add this vowel when sounding out words, but if a teacher were successful in preventing the vowel addition, the voiceless stops would be inaudible in most cases. If a child has been successful in following the procedure to this point and has sounded out ⟨tip⟩ as [təi pə], he is then told to "blend" the sounds into a word. This process is a mysterious one in which the child is given no direction. Presumably he is to omit the extraneous [ə] vowels and syllable junctures and convert the pitch patterns of [tə i pə], which is read with three intonation contours, into a single intonation phrase. If he can accomplish all this, he will then read the word correctly as /tip/.

My criticisms of this procedure up to now have dealt with its artificiality, in terms of the way a phonological system really works, and its difficulty -- perhaps even impossibility -- for some children to acquire. We ought to consider now whether the procedure of sounding out words may have any positively harmful effects at a later stage in the child's reading. It has been charged that since phonically regular words that are not in the child's oral language are often introduced at an early stage of reading, the child is encouraged to think that he has learned to read if he can produce the proper sounds, even though he has no idea what the words mean. In this regard, the phonics readers share with the basal readers the fault of making no distinction between the process and the uses of reading. If there were an adequate study of children's oral vocabulary, this defect in the phonic readers could be remedied by vocabulary control within the range of phonically regular words.

A second shortcoming may not be so easily remedied. Since phonic methods never consider sounds in any larger environment than the word, students taught by such methods often develop the habit of reading sentences as if they were lists of isolated words. Being unaware of the function of English intonation in identifying the grammatical structure of sentences, the phonically oriented teacher is likely to identify this problem as one of elocution, on which he has no better advice to give than "Try to read naturally." (The teachers who prefer a basal series, when confronted with this same problem, are likely to assume that the child has not understood the meaning of the sentences, an analysis that is probably closer to the mark. But then they will give the potentially harmful advice to "think what the words mean as you read them," which, if it has any effect, can only make the child's oral reading more halting).

A third harmful effect that is often attributed to phonics methods of reading instruction is that the excessive attention to individual sounds at the beginning stages inhibits the development of reading fluency, so that some children never get past the stage of lip movement in silent reading, while others continue subvocal activity that can be detected by physiological study with delicate enough instruments. I know of no empirical findings that definitely identify phonics as the causative agent in such types of reading disability, but there are a priori reasons to suppose that there may be such a link.

Turning to the second major emphasis of the phonics materials -- that on memorization of rules of sound-letter correspondence -- we can recognize at least two potential objections. First, with the exception of a very few rules of high utility, most phonic generalizations, if they are in a form simple enough to be helpful to a child, are grossly inaccurate and misleading. Theodore Clymer has shown that some of the most frequently quoted phonic rules apply in less than half the instances to which they refer.[3] The research of Paul Hanna and others at Stanford shows very well the extreme complexity and proliferation of rules necessary to account for only 90 percent of a 17,000 word vocabulary.[4] Second, even if the rules had greater generality, there is no evidence to suggest that memorizing them has any appreciable transfer value to reading and writing. Many children seem to be incapable of acquiring a skill through such a process of deduction, and efforts based on such procedures may prove a waste of time.

The criticisms that have been made, up to this point, apply equally to the "pure" and "gimmicked" varieties of phonic materials. I shall next discuss briefly some of the principal gimmicks that have been advanced to support phonic methods. The first of these is "Reading through Writing", in which close coordination is attempted between learning to write and to read the letters that rep-

resent particular sounds, as they are introduced. It is reasonable
to suppose that reading and writing are mutually reinforcing, and
to that extent this method ought to be superior to pure phonics.

A second kind of gimmick is "Words in Color", which uses special colors for different letters to reinforce the child's discrimination of them in the early stages of reading. Again it seems reasonable to assume that providing a child with extra clues at the beginning of the learning process may assist him in getting started. It
is not so clear, however, whether such clues may not become for
some children the primary means of identifying letters and words.
If this situation should arise, can the extra clues be gradually
withdrawn, without producing a disruption of the learning process?

The same question must be asked about the last of the approaches
that I have classified as phonics with a gimmick -- namely, i.t.a.
First, I should say that it may not be entirely fair to put the initial
teaching alphabet in this classification. Certainly those who devised this method of reading instruction had a far better grasp of
the morphophonemic structure of English than do the authors of
most phonic series. As a result, the alphabet they devised is by
no means a simple phonetic or phonemic alphabet. If an alphabet
of one of the latter types were used for initial reading instruction,
it would have to be actively unlearned when the child turned to
ordinary English spelling, and considerable interference from the
first alphabet could be anticipated. The makers of i.t.a., however,
have given considerable thought to the shape of each of their special
letters, so that while they contain additional clues not found in
traditional orthography, they also bear a maximum resemblance
to traditional letters, so that the transfer from i.t.a. to traditional
orthography ought to be accomplished with minimum difficulty.
Whether the transfer can be so easily accomplished has to remain
the principal question about i.t.a. As with Words in Color, is it
possible that with some children the extra clues in i.t.a. become
primary and inhibit a smooth transfer to traditional orthography?

The fourth classification of readers, the linguistic series, differs from the first three types in that they are neither word-
oriented nor sound- and letter-oriented. Language is viewed by
most linguists, regardless of minor differences in analysis, as an
abstract system that mediates between the meanings one wishes to
express and some more concrete system of representation such as
speech or writing. Any stretch of language, whether spoken or
written, represents meaning, has an underlying syntactic
structure, and a surface form of spoken or written symbols -- all
simultaneously. The word-oriented approaches to reading instruction emphasize meaning, but in doing so preclude any apprehension
of the structure of surface forms. The phonic readers, in con-

centrating on the relationship between two systems of surface representation, speech and writing, tend to ignore linguistic forms
and their associated meanings. From the point of view of linguistics,
meaning, language forms, and spoken or written symbolizations
must all be dealt with simultaneously, since this is the way they
occur in speech or writing and since the child has already learned
to perform such simultaneous analysis when he learned to talk.
How can reading courses be organized so as to aid the child in
making a total response to written material? To most linguists
who have constructed reading materials, the answer seems to lie
in rigorous control of the introduction of new spelling patterns and
new grammatical constructions. As for vocabulary control, after
the first few lessons when the child is still becoming accustomed
to the fact that there is such a thing as reading, only three restraints
ought to be exercised: (1) new items, with very few exceptions,
should conform to spelling patterns that have been or are being
introduced; (2) new items should not require departure from the
schedule of introducing new grammatical constructions; and (3) new
items introduced while the child is still mastering the process of
reading ought to be limited to words with which the child is already
familiar in his oral language. Unfortunately, since there is no up-
to-date study of first graders' oral vocabulary, the linguistic series
are hardly better off than other reading materials with respect to
this last goal. The important thing at this stage of our knowledge
is that they do recognize the third point as a real goal.

Although the child is confronted simultaneously in the linguistic
readers with the problems of identifying what spelling patterns
represent and how grammatical forms signal meaning, he is given
only a restricted task in each of these areas and is confronted only
with linguistic forms whose meanings he should know from his oral
use of the language.

Among the readers that qualify as linguistic according to these
criteria there is still considerable range and latitude, because
linguistics does not prescribe the exact organization of reading
materials, but only their general outlines. One dimension along
which the readers vary markedly from one another is the extent to
which they exclude other types of material in favor of purely linguistic organization. Books like Bloomfield and Barnhart, Let's
Read,[5] and the series by Charles C. Fries et al.[6] are based on the
assumption that illustrations and story line distract the child from
his primary task -- that of learning to decode written symbols.
These authors maintain that if reading is approached as a puzzle
to be solved, children will enjoy the task and will be quite well
motivated to read isolated words and sentences until they are prepared to take on longer passages of connected discourse.

Toward the opposite end of this scale are the materials of Henry Lee Smith, Jr. et al[7] and the Miami Linguistic Readers[8] These books try to maintain all the traditional values that reading teachers have recognized and that do not seem to be in basic conflict with principles of linguistic organization. Thus both series have attractive illustrations and seek to motivate the child through interesting story lines. Connected discourse is read from the outset. At present, there seems to be no empirical evidence favoring or opposing the use of pictures and stories in connection with linguistically organized readers.

In conclusion, there are several aspects of the organization of reading textbooks in which basic research is needed. It is to be hoped that linguists and more particularly psychologists will address themselves to some of those problems about which everyone makes assumptions but about which little solid evidence has been collected.

NOTES

1.   Madeleine Horn, A Study of the Vocabulary of Children Before Entering First Grade, International Kindergarten Union, 1928.
2.   Ruth Strickland, The Contribution of Structural Linguistics to the Teaching of Reading, Writing, and Grammar in the Elementary School, Indiana University School of Education Bulletin, Vol. 40, No. 1, January 1964.
3.   Theodore Clymer, "The Utility of Phonic Generalizations in the Primary Grades", The Reading Teacher 16.252-258 (January 1963).
4.   Paul R. Hanna, Jean S. Hanna, Richard E. Hodges, and Edwin H. Rudord, Jr., Phoneme-Grapheme Correspondences as Cues to Spelling Improvement, U.S. Department of Health, Education, and Welfare, Office of Education, 1966.
5.   Leonard Bloomfield, and Clarence L. Barnhart, Let's Read, Detroit: Wayne State University Press, 1961.
6.   Charles C. Fries, Rosemary Green Wilson, and Mildred K. Rudolph, Merrill Linguistic Readers, Columbus, Ohio: Charles E. Merrill, 1966.
7.   Henry Lee Smith, Jr., and Clara Stratemeyer, The Linguistic Readers, New York: Harper and Row, 1963-1967.
8.   Miami Linguistic Readers, Ralph F. Robinette, Production Director, Boston: D.C. Heath, 1964-1967.

READING: A PSYCHOLINGUISTIC GUESSING GAME

by Kenneth S. Goodman

As scientific understanding develops in any field of study, pre-existing, naive, common sense notions must give way. Such out-moded beliefs clutter the literature dealing with the process of reading. They interfere with the application of modern scientific concepts of language and thought to research in reading. They confuse the attempts at application of such concepts to solution of problems involved in the teaching and learning of reading. The very fact that such naive beliefs are based on common sense explains their persistent and recurrent nature. To the casual and unsophisticated observer they appear to explain, even predict, a set of phenomena in reading. This paper will deal with one such key misconception and offer a more viable scientific alternative.

Simply stated, the common sense notion I seek here to refute is this: "Reading is a precise process. It involves exact, detailed, sequential perception and identification of letters, words, spelling patterns and larger language units."

In phonic-centered approaches to reading, the preoccupation is with precise letter identification. In word-centered approaches, the focus is on word identification. Known words are sight words, precisely named in any setting.

This is not to say that those who have worked diligently in the field of reading are not aware that reading is more than precise, sequential identification. But, the common sense notion, though not adequate, continues to permeate thinking about reading.

Spache presents a word version of this common sense view: "Thus, in its simplest form, reading may be considered a series of word perceptions."[1]

The teacher's manual of the Lippincott <u>Basic Reading</u> incorporates a letter-by-letter variant in the justification of its reading approach: "In short, following this program the child learns from the

Reprinted by permission from the <u>Journal of the Reading Specialist</u> 4. 126-135 (May 1967).

the beginning to see words exactly as the most skillful readers
see them . . . as whole images of complete words with all their
letters. "[2]

In place of this misconception, I offer this: "Reading is a selective process. It involves partial use of available minimal language
cues selected from perceptual input on the basis of the reader's
expectation. As this partial information is processed, tentative
decisions are made, to be confirmed, rejected or refined as reading progresses. "

More simply stated, reading is a psycholinguistic guessing game.
It involves an interaction between thought and language. Efficient
reading does not result from precise perception and identification
of all elements, but from skill in selecting the fewest, most productive cues necessary to produce guesses which are right the first
time. The ability to anticipate that which has not been seen, of
course, is vital in reading, just as the ability to anticipate what has
not yet been heard is vital in listening.

Consider this actual sample of a relatively proficient child reading orally. The reader is a fourth grade child reading the opening
paragraphs of a story from a sixth grade basal reader:[3]

"If it bothers you to think of it as baby sitting, " my father said,

"then don't think of it as baby sitting. Think of it as homework.

Part of your education. You just happen to do your studying in the

room where ~~your~~ ^{the} baby brother is sleeping, that's all. " He helped

my mother with her coat, and then they were gone.

                                  hoped .. opened a
So education it was! I ~~opened the~~ dictionary and picked out a

               s   Phil/ōso/phi/cal he
word that sound~~ed~~ good. "Philosophical!" ~~I~~ yelled. Might as well

      what it means   Phizo .. Phizo/sophicly
study ~~word meanings first~~. "~~Philosophical~~: showing calmness and

         his   fort .. future .. futshion
courage in ~~the~~ face of ill ~~fortune.~~ " I mean I really yelled it. I

guess a fellow has to work off steam once in a while.

He has not seen the story before. It is, by intention, slightly
difficult for him. The insights into his reading process come primarily from his errors, which I choose to call miscues in order to
avoid value implications. His expected responses mask the process

of their attainment, but his unexpected responses have been achieved through the same process, albeit less successfully applied. The ways that they deviate from the expected reveal this process.

In the common sense view that I am rejecting, all deviations must be treated as errors. Furthermore, it must be assumed in this view that an error either indicates that the reader does not know something or that he has been "careless" in the application of his knowledge.

For example, his substitution of the for your in the first paragraph of the sample must mean that he was careless, since he has already read your and the correctly in the very same sentence. The implication is that we must teach him to be more careful, that is, to be more precise in identifying each word or letter.

But now let's take the view that I have suggested. What sort of information could have led to tentatively deciding on the in this situation and not rejecting or refining this decision? There obviously is no graphic relationship between your and the. It may be, of course, that he picked up the in the periphery of his visual field. But, there is an important non-graphic relationship between the and your. They both have the same grammatical function: they are, in my terminology, noun markers. Either the reader anticipated a noun marker and supplied one, paying no attention to graphic information, or he used your as a grammatical signal, ignoring its graphic shape. Since the tentative choice the disturbs neither the meaning nor the grammar of the passage, there is no reason to reject and correct it. This explanation appears to be confirmed by two similar miscues in the next paragraph. A and his are both substituted for the. Neither are corrected. Though the substitution of his changes the meaning, the peculiar idiom used in this dictionary definition, "in the face of ill fortune", apparently has little meaning to this reader anyway.

The conclusion this time is that he is using noun markers for grammatical, as well as graphic, information in reaching his tentative conclusions. All together in reading this ten-page story, he made twenty noun marker substitutions, six omissions and two insertions. He corrected four of his substitutions and one omission. Similar miscues involved other function words (auxiliary verbs and prepositions, for example). These miscues appear to have little effect on the meaning of what he is reading. In spite of their frequency, their elimination would not substantially improve the child's reading. Insistence on more precise identification of each word might cause this reader to stop seeking grammatical information and use only graphic information.

The substitution of hoped for opened could again be regarded as careless or imprecise identification of letters. But, if we dig beyond this common sense explanation, we find (a) both are verbs, and (b) the words have <u>key</u> graphic similarites. Further, there may be evidence of the reader's bilingual French-Canadian background here, as there is in subsequent miscues (<u>harms</u> for <u>arms</u>, <u>shuckled</u> for <u>chuckled</u>, <u>shoose</u> for <u>choose</u>, <u>shair</u> for <u>chair</u>). The correction of this miscue may involve an immediate rejection of the tentative choice made on the basis of a review of the graphic stimulus, or it may result from recognizing that it cannot lead to the rest of the sentence, i.e. "I hoped a dictionary ..." does not make sense. (It isn't decodable.) In any case, the reader has demonstrated the process by which he constantly tests his guesses, or tentative choices, if you prefer.

<u>Sounds</u> is substituted for <u>sounded</u>, but the two differ in ending only. Common sense might lead to the conclusion that the child does not pay attention to word endings, slurs the ends, or is otherwise careless. But, there is no consistent similar occurrence in other word endings. Actually, the child has substituted one inflectional ending for another. In doing so he has revealed (a) his ability to separate base and inflectional suffix, and (b) his use of inflectional endings as grammatical signals or markers. Again he has not corrected a miscue that is both grammatically and semantically acceptable.

<u>He</u> for <u>I</u> is a pronoun-for-pronoun substitution that results in a meaning change, though the antecedent is a bit vague, and the inconsistency of meaning is not easily apparent.

When we examine what the reader did with the sentence "Might as well study word meanings first", we see how poorly the model of precise sequential identification fits the reading process. Essentially this reader has decoded graphic input for meaning and then encoded meaning in oral output with transformed grammar and changed vocabulary, but with the basic meaning retained. Perhaps as he encoded his output, he was already working at the list word which followed, but the tentative choice was good enough and was not corrected.

There are two examples, in this sample, of the reader working at unknown words. He reveals a fair picture of his strategies and abilities in these miscues, though in neither is he successful. In his several attempts at <u>philosophical,</u> his first attempt comes closest. Incidentally, he reveals here that he can use a phonic letter-sound strategy when he wants to. In subsequent attempts he moves away from this sounding out, trying other possibilities, as if trying to find something which at least will sound familiar. Interestingly, here he has a definition of sorts, but no context to work with. <u>Philosophical</u> occurs as a list word a number of times in the story. In subsequent attempts, the child tried <u>physica,</u> <u>physicacol,</u>

physical, philosoviqul, phizzlesoviqul, phizzo soriqul, philazophgul.
He appears to move in concentric circles around the phonic information he has, trying deviations and variations. His three unsuc-
cessful attempts at fortune illustrate this same process. Both
words are apparently unknown to the reader. He can never really
identify a word he has not heard. In such cases, unless the context
or contexts sufficiently delimit the word's meaning, the reader is
not able to get meaning from the words. In some instances, of
course, the reader may form a fairly accurate definition of the
word, even if he never recognizes it (that is, matches it with a
known oral equivelent) or pronounces it correctly. This reader
achieved that with the word typical, which occurred many times
in the story. Throughout his reading he said topical. When he
finished reading, a check of his comprehension indicated that he
knew quite well the meaning of the word. This phenomenon is
familiar to any adult reader. Each of us has many well-defined
words in our reading vocabulary which we either mispronounce or
do not use orally.

I've used the example of this youngster's oral reading not because what he's done is typical of all readers or even of readers
his age, but because his miscues suggest how he carries out the
psycholinguistic guessing game in reading. The miscues of other
readers show similarities and differences, but all point to a selective, tentative, anticipatory process quite unlike the process of
precise, sequential identification commonly assumed.

Let's take a closer look now at the components the reader ma-
nipulates in this psycholinguistic guessing game.

At any point in time, of course, the reader has available to him
and brings to his reading the sum total of his experience and his
language and thought development. This self-evident fact needs to
be stated because what appears to be intuitive in any guessing is
actually the result of knowledge so well learned that the process
of its application requires little conscious effort. Most language
use has reached this automatic, intuitive level. Most of us are
quite unable to describe the use we make of grammar in encoding
and decoding speech, yet all language users demonstrate a high
degree of skill and mastery over the syntax of language, even in
our humblest and most informal uses of speech.

Chomsky[4] has suggested a model of sentence production by
speakers of a language (Fig. 1) and a model structure of the
listener's sentence interpretation (Fig. 2).

Thus, in Chomsky's view, encoding of speech reaches a more
or less precise level and the signal which results is fully formed.
But in decoding, a sampling process aims at approximating the
message, and any matching or coded signal which results is a
kind of by-product.

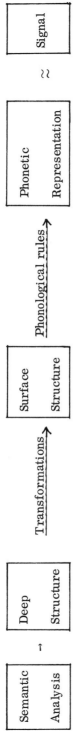

Fig. 1. Model of Speaker's Sentence Production.

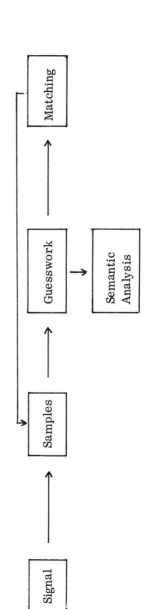

Fig. 2. Model of Listener's Sentence Interpretation.

In oral reading, the reader must perform two tasks at the same time. He must produce an oral language equivalent of the graphic input which is the signal in reading, and he must also reconstruct the meaning of what he is reading. The matching in Chomsky's interpretation model is largely what I prefer to call a recoding operation. The reader recodes the coded graphic input as phonological or oral output. Meaning is not normally involved to any extent. This recoding can even be learned by someone who doesn't speak the language at all, for example, the bar mitzvah boy may learn to recode Hebrew script as chanted oral Hebrew with no ability to understand what he is chanting; but when the reader engages in semantic analysis to reconstruct the meaning of the writer, only then is he decoding.

In oral reading there are three logical possible arrangements of these two operations. The reader may recode graphic input as oral language and then decode it. He may recode and decode simultaneously. Or, he may decode first and then encode the meaning as oral output.

On the basis of my research to date, it appears that readers who have achieved some degree of proficiency decode directly from the graphic stimulus in a process similar to Chomsky's sampling model and then encode from the deep structure, as illustrated in Chomsky's model of sentence production. Their oral output is not directly related to the graphic stimulus and may involve transformation in vocabulary and syntax, even if meaning is retained. If their comprehension is inaccurate, they will encode this changed or incomplete meaning as oral output.

The common misconception is that graphic input is precisely and sequentially recoded as phonological input and then decoded bit by bit. Meaning is cumulative, built up a piece at a time, in this view. This view appears to be supported by studies of visual perception that indicate that only a very narrow span of print on either side of the point of fixation is in sharp focus at any time. We might dub this the "end of the nose" view, since it assumes that input in reading is that which lies in sharp focus in a straight line from the end of the nose. Speed and efficiency are assumed to come from widening the span taken in on either side of the nose, moving the nose more rapidly or avoiding backward movements of the eyes and nose, which of course must cut down on efficiency.

This view cannot possibly explain the speed with which the average adult reads, or a myriad of other constantly occurring phenomena in reading. How can it explain, for example, a highly proficient adult reader reading and rereading a paper he's written and always missing the same misprints. Or how can it explain our fourth grader seeing "Study word meanings first", and saying, "Study what it means"?

No, the "end of the nose" view of reading will not work. The reader is not confined to information he receives from a half inch of print in clear focus. Studies, in fact, indicate that children with severe visual handicaps are able to learn to read as well as normal children. Readers utilize not one, but three kinds of information simultaneously. Certainly without graphic input there would be no reading. But, the reader uses syntactic and semantic information as well. He predicts and anticipates on the basis of this information, sampling from the print just enough to confirm his guess of what's coming, to cue more semantic and syntactic information. Redundancy and sequential constraints in language, which the reader reacts to, make this prediction possible. Even the blurred and shadowy images he picks up in the peripheral area of his visual field may help to trigger or confirm guesses.

Skill in reading involves not greater precision, but more accurate first guesses based on better sampling techniques, greater control over language structure, broadened experiences, and increased conceptual development. As the child develops reading skill and speed, he uses increasingly fewer graphic cues. Silent reading can then become a more rapid and efficient process than oral reading, for two reasons: (1) the reader's attention is not divided between decoding and recoding or encoding as oral output, and (2) his speed is not restricted to the speed of speech production. Reading becomes a more efficient and rapid process than listening, in fact, since listening is normally limited to the speed of the speaker. (Recent studies with speeded up electronic recordings where distortion of pitch is avoided have demonstrated that listening can be made more rapid without impairing comprehension, too.)

Though the beginning reader obviously needs more graphic information in decoding and, therefore, needs to be more precise than skilled readers, evidence from a study of first graders by Yetta Goodman[5] indicates that they begin to sample and draw on syntactic and semantic information almost from the beginning, if they are reading material which is fully formed language.

RIDE IN[6]

Run
~~Ride~~ in, Sue.

Run
~~Ride~~ in here.

Come   here
~~Here~~ I ~~come~~, Jimmy.

Can Come
~~And here~~ I ~~stop~~.

STOP AND GO[7]

Jimmy said, "Come here, Sue,

      too
Look at my ~~toy~~ train.

See it go.

        toy
Look at my little ~~train~~ go."

         toy
Sue said, "Stop the ~~train~~.

    come
Stop it ~~here~~, Jimmy."

            toy
Jimmy said, "I can stop the ~~train~~.

   toy
See the ~~train~~ stop."

          too
Sue said, "Look at my ~~toy~~.

    toy
It is in the ~~train~~.

       too
See my little red ~~toy~~, Jimmy.

      toy
It can ride in the ~~train~~."

        toy
Jimmy said, "See the ~~train~~ go.

Look at it go."

  Suzie   too
~~Sue~~ said, "Look at my little red ~~toy~~.

      toy
See it go for a ~~train~~ ride."

  Suzie   too
~~Sue~~ said, "My little red ~~toy~~!

    said too
Jimmy, my ~~toy~~ is not here.

       toy
It is not in the ~~train~~.

    toy
Stop the ~~train~~, Jimmy.

        too
Stop it and look for my ~~toy~~."

Here are excerpts from two primer stories as they were read by a first grade child at the same session. Ostensibly (and by intent of the authors) the first, from a second pre-primer, should be much easier than the second, from a third pre-primer. Yet she encountered problems to the point of total confusion with the first and was able to handle exactly the same elements in the second.

Note, for example, the confusion of <u>come</u> and <u>here</u> in "Ride In." This represents a habitual association in evidence in early reading of this child. Both <u>come</u> and <u>here</u> as graphic shapes are likely to be identified as <u>come</u> or <u>here</u>. In "Stop and Go" the difficulty does not occur when the words are sequential. She also substitutes <u>can</u> for <u>and</u> in the first story, but encounters no problem with either later. <u>Stop</u> stops her completely in "Ride In", a difficulty that she doesn't seem to know she has when she reads "Stop and Go" a few minutes later. Similarly, she calls ⟨ ride ⟩ <u>run</u> in the first story, but gets it right in the latter one.

Though there are miscues in the second story, there is a very important difference. In the first story she seems to be playing a game of name the word. She is recoding graphic shapes as phonological ones. Each word is apparently a separate problem. But in "Stop and Go" what she says, including her miscues, in almost all instances makes sense and is grammatically acceptable. Notice that as Sue becomes better known she becomes <u>Suzie</u> to our now confident reader.

A semantic association exists between <u>train</u> and <u>toy</u>. Though the child makes the same substitution many times, nothing causes her to reject her guess. It works well each time. Having called ⟨ train ⟩ <u>toy</u>, she calls ⟨toy⟩ <u>too</u> (actually it's an airplane in the pictures), not once, but consistently throughout the story. That doesn't seem to make sense. That's what the researcher thought too, until the child spoke of a "little red <u>too</u>" later in retelling the story. "What's a 'little red too'?" asked the researcher. "An airplane," she replied calmly. So a train is <u>toy</u> and a plane is a <u>too</u>. Why not? But, notice that when <u>toy</u> occurred preceding <u>train</u>, she could attempt nothing for <u>train</u>. There appears to be a problem for many first graders when nouns are used as adjectives.

Common sense says go back and drill her on <u>come</u>, <u>here</u>, <u>can</u>, <u>stop</u>, <u>ride</u>, <u>and</u>; don't let her go to the next book which she is obviously not ready to read.

But the more advanced story, with its stronger syntax, more fully formed language and increased load of meaning makes it possible for the child to use her graphic cues more effectively and supplement them with semantic and syntactic information. Teaching for more precise perception with lists and phonics charts may actually impede this child's reading development. Please notice, before we leave the passage, the effect of immediate experience on anticipation. Every one of the paragraphs in the sample starts with "Jimmy said" or "Sue said." When the reader comes to a line starting <u>Jimmy</u>, she assumes that it will be followed by <u>said</u>, and it is not until her expectation is contradicted by subsequent input that she regresses and corrects her miscue.

Since children must learn to play the psycholinguistic guessing game as they develop reading ability, effective methods and materials, used by teachers who understand the rules of the game, must help them to select the most productive cues, to use their knowledge of language structure, to draw on their experiences and concepts. They must be helped to discriminate between more and less useful available information. Fortunately, this parallels the processes they have used in developing the ability to comprehend spoken language. George Miller has suggested that "... psycholinguists should try to formulate performance models that will incorporate ... hypothetical information storage and information processing components that can simulate the actual behavior of language users."[8]

I'd like to present now my model of this psycholinguistic guessing game we call reading English. Please understand that the steps do not necessarily take place in the sequential or stretched out form they are shown here.

1. The reader scans along a line of print from left to right and down the page, line by line.
2. He fixes at a point to permit eye focus. Some print will be central and in focus, some will be peripheral; perhaps his perceptual field is a flattened circle.
3. Now begins the selection process. He picks up graphic cues, guided by constraints set up through prior choices, his language knowledge, his cognitive styles, and strategies he has learned.
4. He forms a perceptual image using these cues and his anticipated cues. This image then is partly what he sees and partly what he expected to see.
5. Now he searches his memory for related syntactic, semantic, and phonological cues. This may lead to selection of more graphic cues and to reforming the perceptual image.
6. At this point, he makes a guess or tentative choice consistent with graphic cues. Semantic analysis leads to partial decoding as far as possible. This meaning is stored in short-term memory as he proceeds.
7. If no guess is possible, he checks the recalled perceptual input and tries again. If a guess is still not possible, he takes another look at the text to gather more graphic cues.

8. If he can make a decodable choice, he tests it for semantic and grammatical acceptability in the context developed by prior choices and decoding.

9. If the tentative choice is not acceptable semantically or syntactically, then he regresses, scanning from right to left along the line and up the page to locate a point of semantic or syntactic inconsistency. When such a point is found, he starts over at that point. If no inconsistency can be identified, he reads on seeking some cue which will make it possible to reconcile the anomalous situation.

10. If the choice is acceptable, decoding is extended, meaning is assimilated with prior meaning, and prior meaning is accommodated, if necessary. Expectations are formed about input and meaning that lies ahead.

11. Then the cycle continues.

Throughout the process there is constant use of long- and short-term memory.

I offer no apologies for the complexity of this model. Its faults lie, not in its complexity, but in the fact that it is not yet complex enough to fully account for the complex phenomena in the actual behavior of readers. But such is man's destiny in his quest for knowledge. Simplistic folklore must give way to complexity as we come to know.

REFERENCES

1. George Spache, Reading in the Elementary School (Boston: Allyn and Bacon, 1964), p. 12.

2. Glenn McCracken and Charles C. Walcutt, Basic Reading, Teacher's Edition for the Pre-Primer and Primer (Philadelphia: B. Lippincott, 1963), p. vii.

3. William D. Hayes, "My Brother is a Genius", in Adventures Now and Then, Book 6, Betts Basic Readers, 3rd ed., Emmett A. Betts and Carolyn M. Welch (New York: American Book Company, 1963), p. 246.

4. Noam Chomsky, lecture at Project Literacy, Cornell University, June 18, 1965.

5. Yetta M. Goodman, College of Education, Wayne State University, Doctoral Study of development of reading in first grade children, in progress.

6. "Ride In", <u>Time to Play</u>, Second Pre-Primer, Betts Basic
    Readers, 3rd ed., Language Arts Series (New York: American
    Book Company, 1963).

7. Emmett A. Betts and Carolyn M. Welch, "Stop and Go", <u>All
    in a Day</u>, Third Pre-Primer, Betts Basic Readers (New York:
    American Book Company, 1963).

8. George A. Miller, "Some Preliminaries to Psycholinguistics",
    <u>American Psychologist</u>, Vol. 20 (1965), p. 18.

II. READING RESEARCH

READING RESEARCH: WHAT, WHY, AND FOR WHOM?

by Harry Levin

When one looks at the research on reading over the past half
century, the sheer volume of the literature and the welter of topics
and findings (and lack of findings) is incredible[1] Yet, we are sore
put to name even a few trustworthy generalizations or research
based guides to educational practice. Fries recently surveyed the
claims of procedures presumably grounded in research and with
Olympian detachment says, "I have not been able to find the evidence to justify the assertion that the published findings of recent
educational research (since 1916) have provided the basis of most
of the modern reforms in reading instruction."[2] There is no doubt
that teaching procedures have succeeded one another with some
rapidity and that there is usually some redundancy in new procedures. With the mass of writing about how to teach reading, it is
no surprise to find that every "new" idea has been at least hinted at
in the past. The claims for a research base to new procedures and
the frequent inadequacy of this base are not unique to reading. Most
new curricula of the past decade may be faulted on the same grounds.
It is not difficult to find sociological reasons for these conditions.
Dewey and Thorndike established research as an important value in
education. At the same time, educational practice has been responsive to the momentary, practical demands of the schools.

Apparently, the practicalities have been most influential. Yet
the values for research have been given at least lip homage, but
since it has followed practice it has been, at least in the last two
decades, argumentative research.

It is fashionable, we know, to dismiss past wisdom in educational
research and practice. This would be a foolhardy tack in reading
research. Procedures have usually been based on at least implicit
theory which when formulated often provides interesting and useful
hypotheses. For example, we have found that words are not recog-

Reprinted by permission from Elementary English 43:2. 138-147
(February 1966).

nized as "wholes" but that children follow a consistent sequence of
basing their recognition on first letters and if these are inadequate
cues, on terminal letters, and finally, on medial letters.[3] To take
another example, the "linguistic approach" of training on regular
sound-to-spelling correspondences has been found to be less than
optimal for transfer.[4]

   Reading is a skill rather than a body of curricular content. When
we compare the development of a curriculum for acquiring this skill,
the problems are different than the construction of a curriculum
in biology or history, for example. When the curriculum concerns
a circumscribed corpus of information, expert opinion decides what
should be presented and the research issue revolves around the
optimal display of the chosen materials. In teaching children to
read we have no information to present, as such, but must devise
exercises and materials for the most efficient development of a
complex perceptual and cognitive skill. The aim is to make the
skill as automatic as walking so that the reader may use the skill
for a host of purposes. Such training can be based only on knowledge about the nature of the process and its acquisition.
   To think of reading as a complex skill is to borrow an analogy
from the research on other skill-learnings in which the total process is analysed into component parts. When a standard reading
test is used to appraise reading skills, the score may be due to
uneven mastery of the various subcomponents. Since some of the
skills form a natural hierarchy, in that mastery of successive steps
is limited by degree of competence in earlier ones, a global appraisal of reading skill in uninformative.
   Let me illustrate my first approximation to the major component
skills in reading by several anecdotes. A man received a letter in
a foreign language that he spoke fluently but cound not read. He had
a friend who could make the sounds indicated by the writing, but who
understood nary a ward. (This, incidentally, is not strange to those
who have learned the ritual use of Hebrew or Latin.) The man who
received the letter took it to his friend, who said the words that
gave joy to the recipient of the missive. Which one was reading?
   If you will bear with a personal story, I would like to tell you an
episode about my son, who, until recently, was a very poor reader.
One afternoon when we were exploring Rome, we passed a building
with the huge sign, Ministero di Telecommunicazione. Incidentally,
my son read it, with proper stress and intonation. When I reminded
him that he would not have tried an English legend so long and complicated, he said, "Yes, but it always works in Italian."

In Italy I also queried first grade teachers about their teaching children to read. They averred, and I know it was true, that after three months all children could read anything presented to them. I wrote some nonsense materials following the rules for Italian spelling, and every child in the group that I called on could "read" the materials. I have made such informal inquiries in other countries whose languages and writing systems have uncomplicated relationships to each other, with the same results.

Therefore, I suggest that, as a first approximation, reading may be broken into two broad sub-skills. The first is the skill of decoding the writing system to its associated language. English orthography is an impressive and complicated representation of the sounds of the language, about which I shall have more to say shortly. In one form or another, the child must learn this code. Most importantly, teaching must be oriented to making access to the code completely automatic--to make the code transparent.

The second rubric of component skills in reading concerns the use of the code--the written version of the language--for the many uses to which reading may be put. This category includes comprehension, reading for different levels of meaning, reading for pleasure, and so forth. By dividing the process of reading into these two very broad categories, I am not implying that one is more important than the other or that emphasizing one skill excludes the other. I am frankly at a loss to understand the furor that this essentially bland statement arouses. To say that reading is really comprehension is like saying that ice skating is really performing "figure eights".

On the basis of some preliminary research evidence, we know that mastery of the code and comprehension of what the code signals are intertwined. We have asked children to read words and pseudo-words which follow the spelling rules of English. Theoretically, both forms on the basis of spelling-to-sound correspondences alone should be equally difficult. The fact is that the children read the real words more rapidly and with fewer errors. This implies that before decoding, the readers scan the word before reading it aloud.

In other words, to look at two logical components of the skill of reading is not to imply that one is more important than the other. It does imply that the acquisition of the two kinds of skills may follow different rules. Further, it raises important questions about the sequencing of the subskills. Should one precede the other? How much mastery in one before the second is introduced? Should they be simultaneously introduced to the child, as is usually done now in reading instruction? These and similar questions can be answered only by empirical means, by research, and not by polemics. Yet even these research questions are in the form of second order questions.

I shall trace the implications of the prior question in terms of
that new meteor in the galaxy of methods of teaching reading, the
so-called "Linguistic Method". I choose this method not because
of partiality but because of its newness and potential influence. It
provides a kind of case study in process. Linguists' concern with
reading was stated programmatically by Bloomfield in his influential book, Language, in 1932[5] The implications were drawn for
practical use in his massive tome with Barnhart, Let's Read[6]
More recently, Fries's Linguistic and Reading[7] provides a good
statement of what pedagogical procedures a scholar highly trained
in linguistics would suggest.

The postulates in this system are deceptively simple; the implications are profound and only partially verfied. I find in discussing
this approach that the arguments over the assumptions should be
reserved instead for the implications which are indeed controversial
and only partially realized in any linguistic curriculum. Basically,
the linguists are saying that the writing system is a rendition or a
code for the spoken language. We cannot quarrel with this obvious
fact. In English the code, as we all know, is a very complicated
one. The first task of learning to read, say these theorists, is to
teach the child to decode the written version to its language equivalents. So much, so good! However, there are no guides implicit
in the theory which tell us how such correspondences may most effectively be taught.

Here we must face the definition of reading. If the aim is to teach
the child to decode groups of letters into equivalent sounds, one procedure may be most efficient. If, the other hand, our criteria are
the efficiency of decoding new instances, novel combinations of previously learned units, if you will, other instructional techniques are
reasonable. On this point my students and I have done a number of
studies.

Bloomfield provided our jumping off point. His advice is straight
forward: teach the child the regular correspondences and then introduce the other possible values: mat, cat, rat, sat before mate, rate,
hate, etc. The advice is fine, if only the English language would
cooperate. Unfortunately, when one reads prose of any complexity,
the correspondences do not order themselves in one form and then
another. On psychological grounds, it seemed reasonable to simultaneously learn more than one associated sound to letters or letter
groups. The consequence we predicted would be greater flexibility
in trying out sounds when the child met new instances.

Our experiments were reasonably simple. In artificial, laboratory
tasks the child learned either one sound associated with a letter, in
the context of a meaningful word, or more than one associated sound
to a letter. For example, that c may have the value of /s/ or /k/.

The results are clear that (1) dual associations are more difficult to acquire, and (2) that once acquired, they facilitate the child's learning to read new words containing these letters and associated sounds.

I cite this experimentation mainly to point out that a reasonable linguistic analysis of the task is not necessarily the optimal presentation to the learner. The answers will come only when the approaches are combined.

The Linguistic Method makes further assumptions about acquisition processes. Usually, regular spelling patterns are presented in the context of whole words, with the notion that children will form at least functional rules on the basis of these regular instances. The rule to be derived from the instances, sit, hit, bit, etc., is obvious. And if children were reasonable, it would seem obvious that they would induce this obvious consistency. However, the whole problem of the relationships between rules and instances is open to experimental investigation. Should the rule be explicitly stated before the children are exposed to the examples? Should the rule be verbalized after the instances? What is the function of a negative instance? Such simple rules as the terminal it group will not take one far in learning to read English. Rather, the most highly generative rules involve contingencies of various kinds. The value of the initial c depends on immediately following letters; of medial vowels, on terminal e (mate); of consonant groups, on whether they cross syllable boundaries, etc. Certain words, such as homographs, depend for their decoding on cues outside of the word itself. Unfortunately, there is little evidence about the acquisition and use of such complex rules, although the investigations would benefit basic theory as well as the practicalities of learning to read. That children are able to behave according to exceedingly complex rules at very young ages is apparent when they learn to talk, but here too the mechanisms are obscure.

I have been perplexed by the apparent ease with which children learn to operate according to complex rules in natural situations, like the classroom, and the apparent difficulty of such learning in the laboratory. Take, for example, the two words sit and lap where the task is to recombine the consituent sounds into lit and sap. Silberman[8] has found that this is a devilishly difficult chore for young children, taking about ten hours of training on a brief list. Yet, I have seen first grade children quickly form the insight in the classroom.

Two other research areas which are implied by the Linguistic Method have intrigued us. Since the decoding process depends on the reader's language, we should in the design of reading materials

bring to bear our knowledge of the child's language. Most reading
systems do not even approximate the richness of the six-year-old's
language. But the influence is not one way. We suspect that learning to read creates changes in the form of spoken language. I will
have some information on this below. On the other hand, the influence is not as profound as it might be. Prof. Labov[9] of Columbia
University has been carrying out some exciting research on urban
dialects. His informants talk under both formal and spontaneous
conditions and they also read lists of words and a narrative. The
non-standard characteristics of their speech are most evident in
spontaneous discourse and less in reading and still less in reading
lists. It is as though the speakers of non-standard dialects are
bidialectal, using one form for reading and another for speaking.
If we knew how to create a mutual influence between the two we
would be well on the way to language change, which is increasingly
concerning us among the disadvantaged segments of our population.

The final issues raised by the Linguistic Method concern purely
linguistic analysis. Reading materials and exercises are based on
the mapping of the correspondences between the language and writing
system. At what level, however, do we search for these relationships? To this point, the analyses have been between letters and
letter groups and associated sounds, i.e. grapheme-to-phoneme
relationships. The designers of teaching programs have relied on
informal analyses. More recently, Prof. Hockett, at Cornell, and
Richard Venezky, who is now at Stanfors, analysed a complete dictionary with the aid of a computer. We now have the sound values
for all letters and letter groups and the context in which the letters
occur. Even at this level, there are more regularities than we
anticipated and the materials are potentially useful for program-
ming reading instruction. The existing reading programs operate
at this grapheme-phoneme level because until now that has been the
state of our knowledge.

We may, however, search for consistencies at more complex
linguistic levels. We would agree that democratic and democracy
are basically the same, except for the suffixes. Yet our pronunciation and a spelling system matching each letter to each sound obscure the underlying sameness. The traditional spelling system,
however, maintains the underlying identity: the words look the
same. Linguists--Weir, Hockett, Chomsky--are trying to isolate
the level of our language where pairs like geography, geographical,
society, social, subject, subject are the same and to reveal how
the actual pronunciation of a member of one such pair is systematically related to the other.

Although I have not thought them through the pedagogical implications of these analyses may be profound. The teaching program
will be designed to maximize correspondences. In some instances

the most useful relationships will be between letters and sounds and for others the unit will be morphemes or words. In the latter cases, I can imagine that teaching may emphasize recognition of whole words. It does sound as though we are back to an eclectic method, but this is only apparent because the current analyses will prescribe which forms to treat one way and which another.

I have dwelled on the Linguistic Method to show the kinds of issues that arise when one concentrates on the process rather than on the efficacy of the method. Similar analyses could be carried out for any teaching method. To my mind, the potential of the Linguistic Method is far from realized. I have indicated that the method as we know it now is a first approximation which represents, after all, our present state of knowledge. A serious linguistic approach would have implications not only for reading but for the total language arts curriculum.

The question What is reading? implies a model of research distinctively different from our previous data gathering methods. More than any other, the empirical design for reading research, and for all of educational research, for that matter, has been the comparison of two or more teaching methods. These designs are contentious, costly, and uninformative. We should relegate them to a minor part in our research armamentarium.

Perusal of the research literature shows that for every study in which method A was superior to method B, we can unearth one that shows contrary or equivocal findings. As you know, the design has been to equate groups on prior measures, subject the groups to different treatments, make some post experimental outcome measures, and then start a post hoc brief to explain any finding. This preoccupation with which is better can be faulted on a number of grounds, all familiar to you. Were the groups equated on relevant variables? Did the treatments follow their prescriptions? Were the teachers equally competent and enthusiastic? Are the outcome measures reasonable in terms of the experimental variations? And so forth.

Historically, our preoccupation with this research design stems from the assumption that the curriculum is set and we have only to show its efficacy. This may be good advertising copy but it certainly is not science. For our purposes, the most serious indictment of the Method A vs. Method B design is that it is useless for curriculum design and revision. What are the alternatives?

Data should come from a fine-grained analysis of the learner with the curriculum. The time intervals in which we gather data should be as small as practicable: from a minute to a day, but certainly no more gross than that. The data must include the con-

ditions--teacher behavior and materials--and the learners' responses
to them, and, in turn, the teachers' behavior, because the stream
of influence is certainly continuous. In the early stages of curriculum development we should be free enough from the tyranny of statistics to make the observations informal. Opportunities might be
taken to tinker with the curriculum in situ. If some presentation
does not work, immediate modifications are really hypothesis tests
about the teaching-learning sequence. Successful outcomes are the
guidelines for how the curriculum must be modified. At early stages
of curriculum development, these observations performed by skilled
researchers might be devoted to the accumulation of wisdom. Later,
the observations may become more formal and precise. The outcomes will be massive information about the learning process with
specific guides for revision and again revision. Unfortunately, the
outcome is not likely to be a publishable manuscript. We will have
to be content with a first-rate curriculum. And if at this point we
must go back to argumentative research, I shall be prepared to put
a curriculum so designed into the lists against any other.

Obviously, these steps are followed in many curiculum projects,
but in an informal, uncommunicable fashion. We do have the
methods to carry out intensive observational research fashioned
from social and experimental psychology. There is much experience in formal classroom observation which can be brought to
bear, provided that we change our focus from the socio-emotional
aspects of the classroom to cognitive, learning variables. To summarize, I would suggest that the steps in curriculum development
go in this way: a first approximation to the curriculum; informal
observation and tinkering; revision followed by more formal,
category-directed observations; again revision and large-scale
testing. This final stage should again include classroom observations, detailed individual measurements of children's performance,
as well as outcome measures.

The order is a large one. Larger masses of data will be ac-
cumulated and they will have to be ordered and condensed. Clear
specification of short- and long- term criteria are involved. Our
greatest block is the dearth of educational researchers who are
equipped to use the many techniques which such curriculum development entails and to move competently between the laboratory,
the classroom, and the classroom, and the computer. I am urging
my students who are preparing to work in the area of reading to
gain skills in experimental and social psychology, curriculum, and
linguistics. The major training competencies will obviously come
from apprenticeship to modern curriculum development projects.
And I would make the same recommendations for the design of math,
social studies, and science curricula.

   The interest in detailed observation of children acquiring cur-
ricul
a led Suppes and his co-workers at Stanford to build an elaborate computer-based instructional system. The nature and sequencing of displays to the learner can be precisely regulated and
response-by-response behavior recorded and collated.
   At Cornell, we have started to apply the model for curriculum
analysis to a first grade classroom, which we have organized for
a variety of purposes. The team consists of a first grade teacher,
a psychologist, and a linguist, who are present through the whole
school day. The endeavor is a search for hypotheses about the
nature of reading as well as an opportunity to try out observation
schemes and teaching ideas. Detailed records are kept of the
teacher's actions, the curricular materials, and the children's behavior. As ideas occur to the team they are able to implement
them immediately so that each day gives us the test of hypotheses.
We systematically record each child's reading and have some notions about the quantification of oral reading to yield objective indices of reading skill. We are ascertaining through standardized
interviews the home experiences vis-à-vis reading. In general,
this is the first step in the model of curriculum development that
I mentioned earlier.

   Of many insights from this classroom, two problems intrigue me
and merit intensive laboratory experimentation. There is an interesting feedback of reading on language. We noticed soon after the
beginning of the year that the children developed a "literary style."
Their storytelling, especially those to be written down, took on
qualities that were different in many respects from their spontaneous speech. It is difficult to describe without a tape recording.
The "literary style," I think, is less rapid than spontaneous speech,
more staccato, equal spaces between words, grammatically simple
sentences, etc. Now that the teacher is having the child read
"spontaneously" we expect the literary style to change.
   Another interesting series of research issues came up from our
classroom observations. We reasoned that if the child is forming
spelling-to-sound associations the units in his spoken language
should be perceptually distinct. We have tested children's ability
to segment words into constituent sounds and devised techniques
for giving children facility in such behavior. There is much more
that we have to learn on this issue and there is, incidentally, sug-
gestive research from educational research laboratories in Russia.
   Our plan, you see, is to create an interplay between the classroom
and the laboratory. There are many basic findings which have implications for reading instruction. Likewise, the observation of

classrooms is a fount of problems which can profitably be abstracted
from the school and investigated under the controlled conditions of
the laboratory. Ideally, this is a self-generating cycle. Two circumstances stand in the way of an immediate realization of these
research ideals: appropriately trained personnel and efficient ecological arrangements. Very few people have been trained to trace
the implications of basic research for educational practice. The
tasks are something like a design engineer's. Secondly, though not
absolutely essential, it would be nice to have laboratories and classrooms in physical proximity. Teachers could see the laboratory
operations, could leaven the basic research with their experiences,
and the researcher would have the class at hand for observation and
tryouts. Such arrangements are commonplace in medical research
but have usually been only visions for research in education.

Obviously, the empirical program that I have outlined would be
overwhelming for a lone investigator or even for a single laboratory.
Consequently, with funds from the U.S. Office of Education, we
organized Project Literacy, whose general purpose is to instigate
and coordinate research on reading. Project Literacy represents
an ideal in educational research. The criteria of its accomplish-
ments, however, will be visible: the development of curricula and
instructional procedures for teaching children, and adults, to read.
The specific aims of the Project are the following:

1. To instigate basic and applied research on topics which directly
    or indirectly will increase our knowledge of the process of
    learning to read.
2. To bring these findings to bear on the development of materials
    and methods for instruction in reading.
3. To involve in research those productive investigators who
    have not heretofore worked on education-related problems
    but whose research indicates their potential contributions to
    understanding the reading process.
4. To attract talented younger scientists and graduate students
    to educational research.
5. To provide a model of a research-based curriculum which
    may have implications for curriculum development in various
    content areas.

Project Literacy has taken a broad view about relevant research.
For example, we found that we needed more information about the
development of the perception of graphic materials by children, and
have solicited such research. Also, since there is the obvious relationship between reading and language, we have encouraged potentially relevant research on children's language. Linguistic analysis

of the relationships between spoken and written forms of the language seemed essential. The basis for inference about the nature of correspondences between spelling and sound invited research on the nature of instances and rules. Social class differences in reading skill pointed to necessary work on these problems, including the efficacy of compensatory pre-reading programs for very young children. To cite one final example, some exciting research has been started on the relationships between non-standard dialects and reading.

The brief citation of some research that has been planned shows that we have taken a "long view" of relevance. The eventual payoff for educational practice seems reasonable but at this point is clearly faith. On the other hand, if it is successful we will have a model for educational research which synthesizes basic and applied research. On one point our initial planning was naive and has been modified. We had thought to wait for an accumulation of basic research results before starting classroom observation and experimental curricula. Currently, classroom work and approximations to curricula are being started at the same time as the laboratory research. The two approaches form an organic program in this way: the developmental aspects will be modified by the laboratory findings and the issues which arise in the classroom are communicated to the laboratory for rigorous investigation.

Ultimately, the basic faith of Project Literacy lies in the talents of the scientists and teachers who are carrying out the program. Hence, we have searched for imaginative and productive people who might bring fresh approaches to their work. At the same time, we realize that research personnel are scarce and we have devised schemes for attracting young people to educational research. So far, this has been one of our more successful activities.

The first activity of Project Literacy was to conduct an informal survey and to compile a roster of scientists whose work was conceivably relevant to understanding the process of reading. We visited most of the potential affiliates of the Project to discuss their work and their interest in educational research. Almost without exception, the response was enthusiastic. A selected number of the researchers were invited to one of four research planning conferences. Since we were aware of the scarcity of talent for research and because of our commitment to training new people, every senior investigator was asked to bring an able graduate student to the planning sessions. In retrospect, this was one of the more inspired ideas in the organization of Project Literacy.

The four conferences covered the following topics:
1. Psychological bases of reading skill.
2. Linguistic and psycholinguistic disciplines and their relationships to reading.

3. Motivational and sociological factors in reading.

4. Curriculum development and techniques of instruction.

To date, these four meetings formed the focus of activities of Project Literacy. Approximately 75 researchers from 25 different universities and research centers presented their research plans. Our impressions are that the meetings accomplished their purposes adequately. The research plans were generally of high scientific caliber and generated interest among the participants. There were many instances where collaborative research grew out of the discussion. Graduate students were inspired to undertake research which meshed with the work in other laboratories. Perhaps the most important consequence was that the participants developed loyalties to the conception of Project Literacy and are prepared to devote their efforts to both basic and applied research germane to literacy. In other words, we have succeeded in forming a research consortium. Our primary task now is to maintain this viable affiliation and to bring their coordinated efforts to fruition in curriculum revision.

We cannot emphasize too strongly the need to bring the research activities to bear on the development and testing of curricula. We plan, therefore, to hold two curriculum writing seminars during the summers of 1965 and 1966. The members of the seminar will be affiliates of Project Literacy together with experienced teachers and curriculum writers. The task will be to state the research knowledge which must be taken into account in teaching young children to read. At this early stage of the activities of Project Literacy, it is clear that the curriculum will be only an approximation. Nevertheless, it will point out the gaps in our knowledge which should, in turn, influence some of the subsequent research activities of members of the consortium. Another consequence of the seminar will be to train people in the important but now almost non-existent skills of translating laboratory research into educational practice.

During the academic year, 1965-66, the curriculum will be informally tested in two first grade classrooms. The try-out will be directed by a research associate who is a competent teacher as well as a skilled researcher. A research assistant will be assigned to each classroom for intensive observation. After the year's experience, we plan to convene the second seminar during the summer, 1966. Curriculum revisions at this point will be based on the results of the try-out as well as on the accumulation of new research findings.

Again, the revised curriculum will be tried out in two classrooms. On the basis of two years' experiences we expect to go into a large-scale curriculum development and testing program.

To summarize, I have discussed what I think is the fundamental question in reading research: What is the process of reading? This formulation of the problem leads us to an organic interplay between basic and applied research and suggests empirical and organizational devices which are not ordinary. I am aware that in our research field, pure discovery without some rediscovery is rare. This does not discourage me, however, because the history of science is full of examples where rediscovered ideas, previously dormant, blossomed in new intellectual climates. We do not have a crash program. We are prepared to wait for answers. I can say that my colleagues and I are vitalized by these complex issues. We hope in time that school learners will benefit from our excitement.

NOTES

1. Talk delivered to National Conference on Research in English. AERA Annual Meetings, Chicago, Illinois, February 12, 1965.

2. C.C. Fries, Linguistics and Reading, New York: Holt, Rinehart and Winston, 1963, p. 29.

3. Gabrielle E. Marchbank and H. Levin, "The Cues by Which Children Recognize Words," Journal of Educational Psychology 56 (1965) 57-61.

4. H. Levin and J. Watson, "The Learning of Variable Grapheme-to-Phoneme Correspondences," In H. Levin et al., A Basic Research Program on Reading, Final Report, Coop. Res. Project No. 639.

5. L. Bloomfield, Language, New York: Holt, Rinehart and Winston, 1933.

6. L. Bloomfield and C.L. Barnhart, Let's Read, Detroit: Wayne State University Press, 1961.

7. Fries, Linguistics and Reading.

8. H. Silberman and J. Coulson, Systems Development Corporation, Report TM-895/200/00, June 29, 1964.

9. W. Labov, "A Proposed Study of Negro and Puerto-Rican Speech in New York City," Project Literacy Reports, No. 2, September 1964, Cornell University, Ithaca, N.Y.

READING AND READING DIFFICULTY:
A CONCEPTUAL ANALYSIS

by Morton Wiener and Ward Cromer

In trying to impose some coordinating conceptual framework upon the phenomena subsumed under reading and reading difficulty, we believe with T. L. Harris (1962) that "the real issues arise from different conceptions of the nature of the reading process itself and of the learning processes, sets and principles to be stressed" (p. 5). In the present paper we will specify and discuss a number of issues which we believe must be considered to develop a more adequate conceptual framework. The issues are derived from an analysis of the diversity of definitions of reading and the variety of explanations offered to account for reading difficulty. Once the issues are clearly defined, a coordinating framework may be possible. We will spell out what we think to be one such conceptualization of reading and reading difficulty.

An Analysis of Reading Definitions

Four interrelated issues emerge from an examination of the many definitions of reading. Discussion of these issues may help clarify some of the present ambiguity and confusion about reading.

Identification versus Comprehension. The first issue is, what behaviors define reading? Some definitions focus primarily on the identification of the stimulus configurations (letters, letter patterns, words, clauses, sentences) appearing on the printed page, while others emphasize the comprehension of the material. When identification skills are emphasized, the defining attribute of reading is the correct "saying" of the word. Comprehension, on the other hand, implies the derivation of some form of meaning and the relating of this meaning to other experiences or ideas.

Reprinted by permission from the Harvard Educational Review 37:4. 620-643 (Fall 1967). Copyright 1967 by the President and Fellows of Harvard College.

The assessment of identification is restricted to some evaluation of what and how words are "said." (How the word is to be pronounced and the variability permitted are both based on some implicit consensus.) Comprehension, on the other hand, is assessed by such criteria as the ability of the reader to paraphrase, to abstract the contents, to answer questions about the material, or to deal critically with the contents. Comprehension can also be inferred partly from the relative quality of identifications, i.e., by the tone, inflection, and phrasing of the identifications. However, the inability to demonstrate comprehension in any of these ways may be a function of restricted language, restricted experience, limited intelligence, or combinations of these three, rather than a function of a reading difficulty. If comprehension is used as the criterial behavior of reading, then these other possible antecedents of noncomprehension must be ruled out before the problem can be called a "reading difficulty."

When both kinds of behaviors are included in definitions of reading, the question arises whether these are solely a matter of emphasis on two parts of one process, or whether different activities are implied? At first glance, it would appear that these differences are matters of emphasis only. For those holding a single process view, identification can be considered a necessary antecedent to comprehension. Closer examination of the relationships between identification and comprehension shows, however, that rather than this one relationship, several are possible.

Although both identification and comprehension require some discrimination process (i.e. to identify or comprehend the reader must be able to distinguish among words), comprehension and identification do not necessarily imply each other. One example of the occurrence of identification without comprehension is the child who may be able to read (i.e. "say") the words printed in a scientific journal with some facility without having any notion of the meaning of the words. Another example is an American or a Frenchman who, with only a limited amount of training, can pronounce most words in Italian (a language which has a high relationship between spelling and sound), without knowing the meanings of the words. Whether these instances are considered reading depends upon the definition. We recognize that there may be differences between the saying aloud of material by individuals who do not comprehend and by those who do. Comprehension can sometimes be inferred from inflections, tone, and pauses, all of which may be derived from the context of the material read rather than from the sentence construction. These differences, when present, are often both subtle and difficult to denote reliably.

The occurrence of comprehension without identification, on the other hand, is less evident and examples are somewhat more difficult to cite. The best single example is given by Geschwind (1962) in his work with aphasics. He finds that some aphasic patients are able to respond appropriately to the meanings of a written communication, but apparently are unable to identify the words, i.e. to say them. As we understand it, some aphasics may be able to follow printed instructions without being able to "say" them aloud. A more subtle example can be found in "speed reading" which appears to exemplify nonidentification in that the very speed required makes identification unlikely. To acquire speed reading the individual must learn to eliminate persisting identification patterns. We hold, first, that the behavior occurring in speed reading is similar to that of more typical fast readers and, second, that in the advanced stages of reading, the presence of certain identification activities may interfere with the speed of reading and may result in less than maximum comprehension. Once reading skills have been acquired, reading may go from the discrimination of stimuli directly to comprehension without concomitant identification. Futher, in good readers identification occurs primarily for novel or difficult material where there is an attempt to achieve some auditory or other discriminations which can be the basis for comprehension[1] (e.g. by sounding out an unfamiliar word).

Acquisition versus Accomplished Reading. A second issue emerging from comparisons of definitions of reading is, does reading refer to the behavior occurring during acquisition of skills or to the behavior manifested after these "skills" have been achieved? Investigators who define reading in terms of accomplished reading often imply that certain other skills are present without spelling them out. Those who emphasize the acquisition of reading give definitions which focus on the skills that need to be mastered, often without stating what constitutes the end-product[2].

Definitions of reading generally associate acquisition with identification behavior on the one hand, and comprehension with accomplished reading on the other. An emphasis on problems associated with the acquisition of skills most often implies a focus on identification skills, while a focus on accomplished reading often implies a stress on comprehension activities.

The failure to distinguish between acquisition and accomplished reading in definitions partially accounts for the confusion about the relationship between identification and comprehension. In the acquisition of reading skills, identification may be a necessary antecedent to comprehension (as we will discuss in more detail below, word meanings are typically available to the child primarily in auditory form). But identification, which is essential in the acquisition phase for comprehension, may be irrelevant for the skilled reader who already has meaning associated with the visual forms and who may go directly from the written forms to the meaning without identification: that is, without an intermediary "verbal-auditory" transformation. Put another way, although some form of identification (saying a word either aloud or subvocally) may be essential for comprehension during acquisition, its nonoccurrence is not a problem for an experienced reader. Thus, the final product of reading need not include components that went into its acquisition. To draw an analogy, many of the components that go into the acquisition of good driving skill disappear as the driver becomes more proficient. In early learning there is much more cognitive behavior associated with the sensory-motor behavior, while in the later phases operating a car is almost totally sensory-motor.

Relative versus Absolute Criteria. Another source of ambiguity for conceptualizing reading is the different implicit criteria used for designating "good" reading. Sometimes, reading skill (and reading difficulty) is defined in terms of absolute or ideal criteria, but more often in terms of relative criteria. Both approaches present problems. When absolute or ideal criteria are used, a good reader is typically specified as someone able to read a certain number of words at a given rate with some particular level of comprehension. Insofar as ideal criteria are arbitrary, standards can be designated which include differing proportions of the reading population. Using absolute criteria, children during the acquisition of reading skill would not be considered good readers.

A relative definition of reading skill invokes criteria which specify, either implicitly or explicitly, some normative group. The implication of a relative criterion is that the same kind or level of skill may be called "good or bad reading" depending on who is doing what and when. For example, a second-grade child who has difficulties in phonetic skills (such as blending of sounds into words, which may be a necessary precursor of auditory comprehension) is not considered a reading problem when relative criteria are used, while a child in the sixth grade who lacks this skill is labeled as having a reading difficulty. In both instances, the same skill is missing. In this context, a sixth-grader may be defined as a poor reader, yet a third-grader behaving the same way (as far as we can determine) might be considered a good reader. It becomes evident that very little information can be communicated by statements about good or poor readers unless they are accompanied by clear specifications of the normative group's behaviors. Further, unless the relative criteria are made explicit, there can be no basis for comparing two "poor readers" since they might have been defined as such by different criteria.

The most important problem raised by a relative point of view is that very different behaviors may be given the same label. Having been given the same label, these different behaviors may later be treated as if they were the same phenomenon. The reading-research literature given evidence that this danger is real in that poor reading is used as a generic term, apparently without the recognition that different investigators may be talking about very different forms of behaviors.

Research approaches and inferences are influenced by whether a relative or an absolute point of view is assumed. These different viewpoints implicitly specify the groups to be studied (those who are taken to be poor readers) and, more importantly, what is considered to be the appropriate control group for the study (the normative baseline against which the experimental group is to be compared). If the criteria are not made explicit, inappropriate control groups may often be established. For example, if a third-grader with an IQ of 75 is compared with other third-graders, he may be defined as a poor reader. Yet if he is compared with other children with IQ's of 75 in the third grade, he may be labeled a good reader by some relative criterion. In the former case, what is at issue may be relevant to intelligence, not to reading.

It may be more useful to specify the "ideal" case of reading and what its components or essential behaviors are. Having spelled out the ideal case, different people can be compared in terms of the presence or absence of these specifications, independent of distinctions between a person learning to read and an accomplished reader, and independent of evaluative statements as to how "good" the reading is.

Reading versus Language Skills. Investigators vary in the extent to which they emphasize the role of already present auditory language (i.e. knowledge of word meaning and the availability of grammatical forms) either as a separate skill or as one included in reading. There may be little or no concern with previously acquired auditory language capabilities when reading is considered as identification. When reading is considered as comprehension, some investigators (Fries, 1962; Lefevre, 1964; Bloomfield, 1961) deal explicitly with the role of language in reading. The majority of research is less explicit, even though comprehension implies the utilization of meanings already available in some other (usually auditory) form. In studying reading difficulty, Milner (1951) explicitly notes the differential experience with verbal language skills in children from middle and lower socioeconomic backgrounds and its relationship to reading skill. Bereiter and Engelmann (1966) also consider this issue a major one as evidenced by their attempt to train culturally deprived children in language skills before introducing reading. A failure to be explicit about the relationship between reading and previously acquired auditory language often leads to ambiguities as to whether a particular difficulty is a reading problem, language problem, or both.

Examination of Specific Definitions. Having noted some issues, we can now examine specific definitions [3] of reading in order to demonstrate their varying degrees of emphasis on: (a) discrimination, identification, and comprehension; (b) acquisition versus the final product of accomplished reading; (c) absolute versus relative criteria for good reading; and (d) the relation of language skills to reading skills.

The first definition reveals an emphasis on the acquisition of reading skills without specification of the attributes of an accomplished reader. More particularly, it focuses on the development of identification processes with comprehension skills noted only incidentally:

> There are several ways of characterizing the behavior we call reading. It is receiving communication; it is making discriminative responses to graphic symbols; it is decoding graphic symbols to speech; and it is getting meaning from the printed page. A child in the early stages of acquiring reading skill may not be doing all these things; however, some aspects of reading must be mastered before others and have an essential function in a sequence of development of the final skill. The average child, when he begins learning to read, has already mastered to a marvelous extent the art of communication. He can speak and understand his own language in a fairly complex way, employing units of language organized in a hierarchy and with a grammatical structure. Since a writing system must correspond to the spoken one, and since speech is prior to writing, the framework and unit structure of speech will determine more or less the structure of the writing system, though the rules of correspondence vary for different languages and writing systems....
>
> Once a child begins his progression from spoken language to written language, there are, I think, three phases of learning to be considered. They present three different kinds of learning tasks, and they are roughly sequential, though there must be considerable overlapping. These three phases are: learning to differentiate graphic symbols; learning to decode letters to sounds ("map" the letters into sounds); and using progressively higher-order units of structure. (Gibson, 1965, pp. 1-2)

In that the above definition focuses on acquisition, we can infer that a relative scale would be used for designating individuals who are not progressing adequately. What is most noteworthy is that

there is also some ambiguity in this definition as to whether the development of language skills is part of reading or prior to and/or
independent of reading.

In contrast to Gibson, Geschwind (1962, p. 116) working with
aphasics, offers a definition which focuses only on the accomplished
reader and comprehension and which makes no reference to identification behaviors or processes in acquisition of reading:

> The word read is used in the narrow sense of "ability to com-
> prehend language presented visually" and not at all in the sense
> of "ability to read aloud."

By this definition, any reading without comprehension would be designated either as non-reading or as a reading problem, though it
does not require "saying" for "reading" to occur. The definition
makes no reference to the role of discrimination of the printed
stimuli, which we assume must occur in order for comprehension
to take place. Further, no explicit statement is made about either
the relative or the absolute amount of comprehension which must
be present for an individual to be designated a good or poor reader.

The following definition is ambiguous about the relationship of
identification to comprehension:

> ... reading involves... the recognition of printed or written
> symbols which serve as stimuli for a recall of meanings built
> up through the reader's past experience. New meanings are
> derived through manipulation of concepts already in his pos-
> session. The organization of these meanings is governed by
> the clearly defined purposes of the reader. In short, the read-
> ing process involves both the acquisition of the meanings in-
> tended by the writer and the reader's own contributions in the
> form of interpretation, evaluation, and reflection about these
> meanings. (Bond & Tinker, 1957, p. 19)

The word "recognition," as used here can be taken to mean either
discrimination or identification; both usages are incidental to the
role of comprehension. Further, this definition refers almost exclusively to the activities of the accomplished reader without apparent concern for the activities necessary for acquiring reading
skills (other than the acquisition of meaning). By this definition,
most children could be designated as having reading difficulties
in that they have not yet acquired the "recognitions" nor the "meanings intended by the writer." This definition also makes little distinction between reading and language skills, thereby making it
possible to confuse a language deficiency with a reading difficulty.

In contrast, the next definition makes an explicit distinction between language use and reading

> The first stage in learning the reading process is the "trans-
> fer" stage. It is the period during which the child is learning to

transfer from the auditory signs for language signals, which he has already learned, to a set of visual signs for the same signals. This process of transfer is not the learning of the language code or a new language code; it is not the learning of a new or different set of language signals. It is not the learning of new "words," or of new grammatical structures, or of new meanings. These are all matters of the language signals which he has on the whole already learned so well that he is not conscious of their use. This first stage is complete when within his narrow linguistic experience the child can respond rapidly and accurately to the visual patterns that represent the language signals in this limited field, as he does to the auditory patterns that they replace.

The second stage covers the period during which the responses to the visual patterns become habits so automatic that the graphic shapes themselves sink below the threshold of attention, and the cumulative comprehension of the meanings signalled enables the reader to supply those portions of the signals which are not in graphic representation themselves.

The third stage begins when the reading process itself is so automatic that the reading is used equally with or even more than live language in the acquiring and developing of experience --when reading stimulates the vivid imaginative realization of vicarious experience. (Fries, 1962, p. 132)

This definition is also more explicit than most in distinguishing between acquisition and the accomplished reader, the relation of identification to comprehension, and the difference between language skills and reading skills. It does not, however, specify the forms of behaviors which would constitute reading difficulty, except those skills necessary for adequate "transfer" to occur.

The next definition focuses on the sequential development of reading from identification to comprehension. It does not make explicit the role identification plays in the skills which develop later. It also exemplifies the relativity of definitions of reading when it states that what constitutes reading skill depends upon the level of the learner as he progresses from acquisition to accomplished reading.

We may define reading as the act of responding appropriately to printed symbols. For the beginner, reading is largely concerned with learning to recognize the symbols which represent spoken words. As proficiency in reading increases, the individual learns to adapt and vary his method of reading in accordance with his purpose for reading and the restrictions imposed by the nature of the material. As the learner achieves skill in the recognition side of reading, the reasoning side of

reading becomes increasingly important. The nature of the
reading task, therefore, changes as the learner progresses
from less mature to more mature levels; reading is not one
skill, but a large number of interrelated skills which develop
gradually over a period of many years. (Harris, A.J., 1948,
p. 9)

These examples should make evident the diversity of emphases,
the ambiguity and confusion in definitions of reading. Further,
this discussion has shown that investigators, with few exceptions
(e.g. Fries), have not made distinctions between reading activities
and language activities, or if so, they have been ambiguous as to
the independence or interdependence of language and reading. All
definitions that focus on meaning or comprehension imply language
as an antecedent, but do not necessarily offer a basis for identifying
poor reading as a reading difficulty rather than as a language
difficulty.

An Analysis of Reading Difficulty

The issues raised thus far have been related to different usages
of the term "reading." Other issues emerge when the term "reading difficulty" is examined. An analysis of the usages of the term
"reading difficulty" indicates that four different assumptions are
used to account for reading difficulty and its etiology. Each of the
four models implies particular kinds of remediation.

The Assumption of Defect. Investigators who hold that reading
difficulty is attributable to some malfunction, i.e., something is
not operating appropriately in the person so that he cannot benefit
from his experiences, exemplify what we call a defect model. This
approach generally implies that this impairment is considered to
be relatively permanent. Defect explanations typically involve
sensory-physiological factors. For example, Reitan (1964) discusses "reading impairment... and its relationship to damage of
the left cerebral hemisphere" (p. 104). Some investigators appear to assume a defect whenever there is a reading difficulty.
We hold that while an assumption of defect may be appropriate for
some instances (e.g. cases of visual, hearing or other sensory
impairment) there is no evidence that an assumption of defect accounts for all reading difficulties. Further, investigators holding
a defect view often do not distinguish between the implications of
a defect during acquisition of reading skill and after acquisition
has taken place (e.g. blindness, brain damage). This type of explanation also implies that for "normal" reading to occur in indi-

viduals with a defect, change must occur (e.g. brain surgery) relatively independent of reading, or a different sequence in the acquisition must be utilized (e.g. teaching a blind person to read
through the use of the tactual modality).

The Assumption of Deficiency. Other investigators have argued
that reading difficulty is attributable to the absence of some function,
i.e. a particular factor or process is absent and must be added
before adequate reading can occur. Most attempts at remedial
reading instruction are based on this interpretation of reading
difficulties. The child must learn something he has not yet learned
(e.g. phonetic skills, language skills, etc.) in order to make up
his deficiency. In contrast to the defect explanation of reading difficulty, reversibility is almost always assumed.

The Assumption of Disruption. A third type of model used to
account for reading difficulty assumes that the difficulty is attributable to something which is present but is interfering with reading
and must be removed before reading will occur. For example, if
a child is "anxious," "hyperemotional," or has "intrapsychic conflicts," he may be unable to learn to read (cf., Koff, 1961). An
assumption of disruption is implicit in investigations of so-called
neurotic learning disabilities. It is also implicit in any approach
which maintains that using the wrong methods to teach reading will
disrupt and interfere with the learning that takes place when the
correct teaching method is used. Occasionally the assumption of
disruption operates jointly with the deficiency assumption, the
notion being that first the interference must be removed and then
the missing components must be added.

The Assumption of Difference. Lastly, various researchers
assume that reading difficulty is attributable to differences or
mismatches between the typical mode of responding and that which
is more appropriate, and thus has the best payoff in a particular
situation. This model assumes that the individual would read
adequately if the material were consistent with his behavior patterns;
thus a change in either the material or in his patterns of verbalization is a prerequisite for better reading.

Cromer and Wiener (1966) posit that poor readers have evolved
different response patterns; i.e. they elaborate "cues" in a manner different from that of good readers. Within their framework,
both good and poor readers "scan" and derive partial information
from the printed stimuli; the specific difference between the good
and poor readers is that poor readers generally elaborate these
cues by responding more idiosyncratically than do good readers,
either because they have not learned consensual response patterns
or because they have learned idiosyncratic patterns too well. In
this framework, reading difficulty is expected to occur when there

is a mismatch between the material being read and the response
patterns of the reader.

An example of a mismatch is when auditorally- and visually-
presented languages are discrepant, as might be the case for a
lower-class child who speaks a neighborhood "slang". The child
may not be able to elaborate the cues in "formal language patterns".
He does not read well because he does not draw from the same
language experiences as does the middle-class child for whom a
typical reading test is written; there is a mismatch between the
reading material and his typical pattern of responding. If, however, the material were presented in the same form as his spoken
language, we posit that he would then be able to read more adequately. This child would not be considered a reading problem but
rather a language problem in that he does not draw from the same
language experiences as the middle-class child for whom a typical
reading text is written.

Still another example of a mismatch involves the reading of highly
technical material. An individual may have difficulty because he
(in contrast to an expert in the same area) has sequences which are
less likely to match the reading input. A psychologist reading a
physics book or a physicist reading a psychology book would be
slowed down, would show more errors in his reading, and would
have less comprehension than when each reads in his own field.
In this instance, there are differences in reading abilities, depending on the material being read. It does not seem meaningful, however, to consider these differences in skill as reading problems.
Thus no pathology is posited for a "reading difficulty" stemming
from a mismatch.

Associated with each of the assumption models are implicit differences in the kinds of factors--sensory-perceptual (physiological),
experiential-learning, and personality-emotional (psychological)--
assumed to account for reading difficulty. Pointing to physiological
factors generally implies a defect; i.e. something other than the
behaviors involved in reading must be changed or in some way
dealt with before improved reading can occur. When the focus is
on experience or learning, either a deficiency or a difference is
implied; i.e. the individual has not learned a particular skill or
has learned a different one. On the other hand, explanations that
focus on psychological factors imply a disruption and/or a deficiency.
In sum, not only are there different assumptions to account for
reading difficulty but in addition, each assumption model implies a
particular set of operative factors and a particular form of intervention or remediation.

Models for Conceptualizing Reading Difficulty: Antecedent-
Consequent Relationships. Another source of confusion in the

literature is the form of explanation offered to account for "reading problems." Some investigators refer to single "causes" of reading difficulty while others state that multiple "causes" need to be invoked. Applying a formal or logical analysis to these kinds of explanatory statements reveals additional conceptual problems. This task can be facilitated by reformulating and extending a model developed by Handlon (1960) to spell out possible forms for explaining schizophrenia.[4] We have substituted the term "reading difficulty" where in Handlon's original application the term schizophrenia appears. We will try to "explain" reading difficulties by relating the variables associated with reading (antecedents) to the variables associated with reading difficulties (consequents).

   1. Model One (in Handlon's form of explanation states that reading difficulty "is a class with a single member, this member having a single radical cause." In our conditional form, Model One is "If A, then X," where A is a single specific antecedent and X is a class ("reading difficulty") in which each instance of a reading difficulty is considered equivalent.

   An example of Model One is Carrigan's (1959) synaptic transmission (chemical) theory of reading disability. She maintains that disabled readers are part of a population of slow learners characterized by atypical production of two chemicals, ACh (acetycholine) and ChE (cholinesterase). Although the balance and concentration level of these chemicals is affected by environmental (anxiety producing) factors, it is the chemical factor itself which is seen to underly reading disability, that is, reading disability is presented also as if it were a single member class. Another example of Model One, Delacato's (1959) theory of "central neurological organization," attributes reading difficulty to a lack of cerebral cortical dominance.

   Although logically possible, Model One does not seem very promising. Most investigators reject both the notion that a single antecedent accounts for all reading difficulties, and the notion that reading difficulty is in fact a class with only a single member.

   2. Model Two states that reading difficulty is "a class with a member, that member having multiple factors constituting the radical cause."[5] In our conditional form, Model Two is "If A or B or C..., then X," where A, B, etc. are particular and independent[6] antecedents, and, as in Model One, X is a class with a single member called "reading difficulty."

   Rabinovitch (1959) appears to use a Model Two form of explanation. He defines reading retardation as reading achievement two or more years below the mental age obtained on performance tests and then goes on to list three subclasses of antecedents of reading difficulty (exogenous, i.e. cultural and emotional factors; congenital brain damage; and endogenous, i.e. biological or neurological distrubances). Similarly, Roswell and Natchez (1964) in their treatment of reading disability argue for a multi-causal model and describe a series of antecedents that can "cause" reading difficulty (e.g. intellectual, physical, emotional, environmental, educational, and growth factors). Investigators using this model might <u>consider</u> reading difficulty as different for the different "causes," but they do not <u>specify</u> nor delineate these differences; that is, they seem to treat reading difficulty as if it were a single-member class.

Although this form of explanation may also be logically tenable, we are convinced that the assumption that reading difficulty is a class with a single member is unacceptable. Our belief is that reading difficulty is a multiple-member class and that Model Two forms of statements might better be changed to "If A, then X_1"; If B, then X_2"; "If C, then X_3" where X_1, X_2, X_3 are particular and independent manifestations within the class reading difficulty (Model Five, see below). We maintain that if an investigator looks carefully enough, he will find different members within the class X which might better meet the criteria of a class with a single member associated with a particular antecedent, and that it is incumbent on investigators to explore their "single consequent" in a multiple-antecedent/single-consequent model to determine whether the consequent is in fact a class with only a single member.

3. <u>Model Three</u> states that reading difficulty "is a class with several members, all members having the same single...cause." This statement can be represented in the following form: "If A, then X_1 or X_2 or X_3..." where A is a particular antecedent and X_1, X_2, etc. are particular members of the class called "reading difficulty." To the extent that investigators have not labeled the specific forms of reading difficulty (that is, different members of the class reading difficulty), then they would be unlikely to apply a model using a single antecedent and multiple consequents. In fact, no appropriate examples of Model Three were located in the literature. Those that appeared at first to be examples of Model Three were found to be more appropriately assigned to Model One, which treats the consequent as a single-member class.

4. <u>Model Four</u> states that reading difficulty "is a class with several members, each having single or multiple causes that are not necessarily unique to that member." In other words, there are many antecedent variables and many manifestations of reading difficulty (consequents) and the relationships between these antecedents and consequents are unspecified or unspecifiable. This model can be represented in the form; "If A and/or B and/or C..., then X_1, or X_2, or X_3..."

This form of explanation appears to be most popular in the current literature; for examples one can turn to almost any comprehensive book on the "diagnostic teaching of reading" (e.g. Strang, 1964; Bond and Tinker, 1957; Bryant, 1963). These textbook approaches list all the possible "causes" of reading difficulty and then discuss techniques for remedial instruction. The relationships between the many antecedents and the many consequents are never clearly specified. The problems inherent in this approach are exemplified most clearly in a study reported by Goltz (1966). Working with "individual remedial reading for boys in trouble," he advocates the simultaneous use of five basic approaches to the teaching of reading (sight word, phonics, combination, linguistic, experiential) in the hope that one will work (he draws the analogy of shotgun pellets). The results of this approach were "some astounding successes and remarkable failures." The need for a theoretical rationale for relating possible difficulties and specific types of intervention is obvious. Again, we argue that it is incumbent on investigators to attempt to locate the particular antecedent and its relationship to a particular consequent.

5. Model Five appears to be the most acceptable form for explaining the phenomenon called reading difficulty. It states that reading difficulty is "a class with several members, each member having a single, unique cause. This statement can be represented in the form: "If A, then X_1; or if B, then X_2; or if C, then X_3 ... " where the X's represent different particular patterns of less-than-ideal reading. This model says that there are many antecedent variables and many manifestations under a general rubric "reading difficulty"; and the relationships between the antecedents and the consequents are, at least in theory, specifiable. Both Model Five and Model Four have multiple antecedents and multiple consequents. Model Five, however, associates a different antecedent with a specific consequent. For example, de Hirsch (1963) attempts to distinguish between two groups of adolescents with language disorders by suggesting that the etiology of each is different. Kinsbourne and Warrington (1963) note that two syndromes of developmental cerebral deficit seem to be associated with different forms of reading difficulty.

6. Model Five assumes that each of the manifestations of reading difficulty (i.e. the X's) is a member of the general class called reading difficulty and that each of these forms is independent. It may be, however, more meaningful to conceptualize the manifestations within the class, reading difficulty, in a model which includes a notion of sequence. This kind of model is not considered by Handlon; we will elaborate it as Model Six. This model can be represented in the following form: "If A, then X_1 " and "If X_1 , then

B" and "If B, then X_2 , " and "If X_2 , then C" and "If C, then X_3
...X_n ." If, for example, C does not occur nor does X_3 , then X_n ,
the particular form of behavior defined as reading, would not be
expected to develop (X_n being defined as a class with a single member, a particular form of reading which is the end-product of the
sequence and can be considered as an indicator on an absolute
scale). Model Six explicitly includes the notion of an ordinal series
and implies that if any member of the sequence were missing, further evolution of the sequence would not be expected, or at least
not in the acquisition phase of learning to read. If the sequence
has already evolved and there is a disruption, then depending on
the point in the sequence where disruption occurs later forms of
reading may be present, even though some or all earlier forms
are absent. This kind of formulation can account for differences
in the kinds of reading difficulties noted when a disruption is
present during acquisition or occurs in an accomplished reader
(e. g. the reading of brain-damaged adults who were previously
good readers versus the reading of brain-damaged children during
the acquisition phase). Another implication is that the arbitrarily
designated end point of a sequence specifies the antecedents and
prior sequences to be included.

A Conceptualization of Reading and Reading Difficulty

We pointed out earlier that some investigators treat reading as
identification while others treat it as comprehension and that this
difference has implications for what was defined as reading difficulty. In an effort to integrate these seemingly disparate approaches, reading will be conceptualized and discussed as a two-
step process involving first identification and then comprehension.
During the discussion, the antecedents for identification will be
considered first and then comprehension will be considered.

Identification. Identification will be used to mean "word-naming,"
in the context of a transformation of stimuli.[7] In the discussion that
follows, our formulation comes from an analysis of visual-to-
auditory transformation; similar analyses could be derived for
other transformations. We assume a physiological substrate which
is adequate for "normal" functioning to occur.

"Discrimination" constitutes one set of antecedents to identification. Prior to discrimination, however, a child must attend to the
stimulus to make sensory input possible. Given sensory input, the
child must then be able to make form discriminations. By discrimination, we mean the ability to make proper focal adjustments;

to distinguish figure-ground, brightness, lines, curves, and angles; and to respond to differences in the amount of white space surrounding the forms (this latter discrimination is involved in the delineation of word units). These forms of discrimination are antecedents of identification.

Given the ability to discriminate, the child can begin to identify by distinguishing on the basis of angles and curves ("man" from "dog") or word length ("dog" from "good"), by responding to variations in relations among letter sequences ("on" vs. "no"), and by responding to spatial orientations of visual stimuli (left/right and up/down). These antecedents not only make possible new identifications but also make earlier forms of identification easier because the reader can respond to more of the available and co-occurring cues. For example, "dog" and "good" can be discriminated on the basis of word length, and the orientation of the first and last letters.

Using discriminations among sequences and general configurations, the child can now learn to identify a relatively large number of words solely by discriminating the first and last letters in an otherwise similar configuration (e.g. length, round vs. angled, internal letters, etc.). Although this discrimination may be adequate in the early stages of reading acquisition, the child must later learn to discriminate other components in the word such as internal letters ("bat" vs. "but" vs. "bet" vs. "bit"), sequence of letters ("there" vs. "three"), additions of letters ("smile" vs. "simile"), etc. In these cases, to increase speed, it would appear that the child has to learn to respond to the variety of available cues and the order of their importance as the basis of discrimination of words within his language.

Antecedents for the identification of words in isolation are not sufficient for reading words in a sequence such as a phrase or a sentence; the individual must learn to say the words in the order given, although he does not necessarily have to "look" at them in that order. A knowledge of language and language sequences will facilitate the discrimination of words in a sequence insofar as the co-occurrences of words can become an additional basis for discrimination, e.g. "the horse's mane" vs. "the horse's mine."

The antecedents discussed thus far are associated with learning to read using the "look-say" approach, which is essentially how one learns to read an ideographic language. Both this approach and languages requiring its use present special difficulties in that the reader must maintain a great many specific forms in his memory. Although he can discriminate new from old words and even among new words, he has no readily available way of identifying ("saying") the new words. If it were possible for a child to have a source of identifying words the first time he encountered them (e.g. via

another person reading it or a speaking typewriter), and if he had
the ability to store and recover the words as presented and as said,
then the "look-say" method would be sufficient for reading. However, if new or novel words occur and there is no external source
for initial identification, then a skill for identifying by oneself is
required.

There are at least three different ways in which identification of
new words occurs. They can be ordered by degree of explicitness
for relating visual to sound forms. First, the individual may respond to some similarities among graphic forms, and he may also
respond to some of the patterns of similarity among associated auditory forms. For example, the word "mat" looks like "man" and
"hat," such that one approximation of the sound of "mat" could be
the combination of the first part of "man" and the last part of "hat."
The first sound approximated might not have exactly the same form
as if it were emitted in the presence of the object. It could be corrected, however, by the reader's recognizing that the word as said
sounds like some other word he had said at some other time.

The second way is like the first in that the reader uses similarities
among graphic forms to aid his identification. In the first case,
however, this response to similarity is incidental; in the second,
it is systematic. An example of a systematic approach is the use
of what linguists (such as Fries, 1962) call "spelling patterns."
The individual is taught to look for similarities among visual and
auditory forms by systematic exposure to various types of possible
patterns, their variations, and their associated sounds. For example, if the individual learns to identify the words "man," "ban,"
"hat," and "fat," he will be able to identify the word "mat." Other
examples of spelling patterns are mane/bane/hate/fate; and mean/
bean/heat/feat. Thus, the possible similarities among visual forms,
among auditory forms, and between visual and auditory forms are
made somewhat more explicit by example.

In contrast to these two ways where similarity among graphic configurations is the basis for identifying new configurations, the third
way requires the reader to know more explicit rules for transforming
specific visual configurations into specific sounds, i.e. phonetics, to
use Fries' terminology. For example, there is a "rule" that says
when there is only one vowel in a word and it comes at the beginning
or middle of a word it is usually short ("hat," "and," "bed," "end").
These rules also include the notion that various locations and combinations of letters are associated with different sounds. One example
is the "rule" that a vowel when followed by an "r" is neither long nor
short, but is controlled by the "r"; e.g. "fur," "bird," "term."[8] One
major difference between the phonetics approach and the other two is
that identification of new words does not require previous experience

with similar old words. However, the use of phonetics requires one additional ability, that of ordering letters from the beginning through to the end of a word. This skill, called "scanning," involves systematic eye movements from left to right and an organization of the input in that order.

Knowledge of co-occurrence of letters and words within a language will increase the rate of reading. Because not every word can come at a particular point in a sequence, the individual can identify words or groups of words rapidly even from very brief scanning of the material. Thus, "knowledge" of language or word sequences independent of visual input will reduce the amount of information required from scanning for identification to occur. At later stages, the reader may even be able to skip some of the words in a particular sequence, yet respond adequately with this decreased information. We propose that the ability to respond to this partial information, that is, the "elaboration" of these cues, can be based on learned patterns of sequential occurrences or what has been called "previously learned co-occurrence probabilities" (Kempler and Wiener, 1963). Differences among readers in their ability to identify a sequence correctly may be explained by differences in response availabilities rather than by differences in visual inputs. Since response patterns may be differentially available among individuals, given specific reading materials, a reader may "respond" to the same material with differing degrees of adequacy depending upon the availability of appropriate response patterns, even assuming the "same" input.

Comprehension. If comprehension[9] is now included in the definition of reading, additional antecedents must be considered. In our usage, comprehension refers to the addition of some form of meaning associated with the identifications or discriminations, i.e. the words elicit shared associations, or consensual indicator responses to or about the referent, or a synonymous response. At least during acquisition, comprehension can occur and be examined at any point at which identification can occur; once the visual forms are transformed to auditory forms, there is a possibility of comprehension, given the presence of appropriate language skills. These language skills can be learned either before or along with the acquisition of identification skills. Language can include not only meaning but also those subjects typically dealt with by linguists (patterns, grammar, sequences, meaningful units, and so on). To the extent that these structural components are critical for meaning, these forms must also have been mastered or, alternatively, they must be learned during the acquisition phase.

It has been implied that meaning is available primarily through language as it occurs in the auditory form. We also have assumed

implicitly that once there is a transformation from the visual to the
auditory form, comprehension would follow. It the reader's auditory
transformation (identification) corresponds to his already available
auditory language forms, then meaning can be associated with the
visual forms. For example, if a child in his identification says the
word "ball" in the same way as he has heard it or as he says it in
the presence of the referent object, then meaning can be transferred
to the visual form. The assumed sequence has been: discriminations
among input forms and output forms; transformation; identification;
comprehension--all of these being required.

In all of the discussion thus far, individual differences may be
highly relevant in accounting for differences in forms of discrimination, identification, or comprehension. For example, individuals
with low intelligence or with restricted language skills or restricted
experiences might better be considered as having "problems" in
these particular areas rather than in reading per se. Similarly,
there are other instances of non-reading which might better be attributed to the conditions under which reading occurs, the content
of the material being read, or the "motivation" of the individual
reader and his interest in the material. In these instances, a
reading problem cannot be assessed until learning has been tried
under more "ideal" conditions with materials of more significance
to the reader.

We can now note some instances: (a) where auditory transformations may not lead to comprehension although the reader ostensibly
uses the same language as is used in the printed material; and (b)
where comprehension facilitates or even makes possible identification which would not otherwise occur.

A first instance of an identification without comprehension is
when the reader has had either insufficient or no previous experience
with the referent so that it is not part of his meaning-vocabulary.
For example, a story about children playing with a kite may elicit
no referent (and no meaning) in an individual in a subculture where
no one plays with kites. A second instance of identification without
comprehension can occur in individuals who have had experience
with the referent, but in circumstances where these referents are
typically communicated in nonverbal forms such as gesture or tone.
This problem is likely to occur in individuals who use what is sometimes called "expressive language" or nonverbal rather than verbal
language. For example, a child could point and say "ball" in a
particular tone as a substitute for saying, "I want this ball!" or
"May I please have the ball?" or "Give me the ball" (cf. Bereiter
and Engelmann, 1966; Bernstein, 1965; Deutsch, 1962). For comprehension to occur in these instances, the individual must be
taught to use verbal language or at least to recognize that the "mes-

sage" he communicated gesturally can also be communicated through words. A third way identification can occur without comprehension is when the sounds of the words as read are different from the sounds of the words as they occur in the reader's vocabulary. For some rural Southern children "y'all" may be the commonly heard and said form of "you." If a reader identifies (says) the word "you," he may not transfer the sound "you" to the meaning of "y'all." Another example is a child from a lower-class background who may not "say" the words in the same way or in the same sequence as his middle-class teacher; and therefore, if he makes his tranformations into the teacher's language, comprehension may not occur. A fourth instance of identification without appropriate comprehension is when there is a lack of correspondence between the reader's auditory language and that of the material being read. For example, note how difficult it is to read and comprehend the following passage, which is a description of Harlem.

On school: "Everyone shouting and screaming and nobody care about what they is going on. But at least it somewhere to stay away from when they make you go." And on the purpose of fighting gangs: "In this bizness you got have a place of your own and a chain of command and all that. Everything go by the book. Then you get a name. And when you get the name maybe you can stay live a while. Thas why most men get in gangs. To stay live. Thas why the gangs form in the first place."
(Time Magazine, February 24, 1967, p. 96)

In the third and fourth examples, there is a discrepancy between the language of the material being read and the reader's own language. This discrepancy can be resolved either by "correcting" the reader's language so that it matches the written form or by modifying the written material to correspond to his language patterns. As Labov (1967) notes, however, if the teacher is to locate the source of the difficulty and take appropriate remedial steps, he should "know" the child's nonstandard language. Labov spells out in some detail the possible discrepancies between the disadvantaged students and their teachers in their pronunciations and uses of grammar. He also discusses some of the implications of such discrepancies in the teaching of children who speak a nonstandard dialect.

One further way in which identification can occur without comprehension is when the particular meaning of the graphic material is different from the meaning typically elicited in the individual (e. g. slang, idiomatic expressions, and poetry), all of which depend on less consensual meanings. An example is a foreigner trying to read a popular detective story which uses slang and colloquialisms. Another example would be an accomplished reader reading James Joyce, where the words have highly personalized referents.

On the other hand, comprehension can facilitate identification if the reader has highly advanced language skills available, e.g. vocabulary, sequences, appropriate generating grammar (in Chomsky's, 1957, sense). To the extent that each of these skills facilitates identification by decreasing the range of possibilities of what is likely to occur in the written material, less information is necessary from the visual input to elicit the whole sequence. Thus, there are a number of ways in which knowledge of language in terms of both meaning and structure may aid identification and even make possible specific identifications which otherwise would not occur. First, the context and meaning of the material already read may generate and/or limit new forms of identification via the individual's understanding and elaboration of the material being read. For example, all other factors being constant, two scientists will differ in the rate and understanding of specific scientific material if they have a different familiarity with the subject matter. A second way in which language aids identification is through the structure of the language which limits the possible types of words or sequences which can occur at any given point. Further, comprehension may make possible identifications which otherwise might not occur. A beginning reader who has not learned phonics but who has a good vocabulary and uses language as it typically occurs in written form may be able to "guess" a word he has not previously identified. He can identify the word on the basis of his comprehension of the context, or familiarity with the structure of the language, or both. To exemplify how the structure and context contribute to identification, all one needs to do is to remove words randomly from a story (Cloze technique, Taylor, 1953) and note the limited number and types of word insertions which occur. Third, extensive language experience facilitates speed of reading. Having learned (and being familar with) possible elaborations, the reader requires fewer cues for a particular response to occur; the assumption here is that the requirement of fewer cues is associated with more rapid scanning, e.g. speed reading of familiar material. Fourth, comprehension facilitates the recognition of errors in reading when there is a mismatch between any of the three possible sources of information mentioned above and the identification as "said." For example, when the word elaborated from the cues is not congruent with later elaborations-- it does not fit the content, context, or sequences as previously experienced--the reader will experience the possibility of an error and "check" the input for more cues.

Once reading is defined as comprehension (which we hold can occur only after basic identification and language skills have been mastered), then identification becomes secondary and may eventually be eliminated except for identifying new words. As noted earlier, an individual with good language (meaning and structure) skills can, in the case of speed reading, go directly from the discrimination to the meaning without the intermediate step of (auditory) identification. Typically, readers use identification in "reading" (here "reading" is being defined in terms of comprehension) in the following ways: first, to make the words auditorally overt (i. e. saying the words aloud so they can be understood); second, to make the words covertly auditory (i. e. lip moving); then, implicit identification (i. e. the reader experiences the words as if they were said aloud but there is no evidence of overt saying); and, finally, identification is eliminated when the reader goes directly from the visual configurations--without experiencing the words as auditory forms--to their associated meaning, e. g. speed reading. Theoretically, at least, identification (in contrast to discrimination) is not necessary and, in fact, may not occur in the accomplished reader. It is even possible that a method could be devised for teaching reading (i. e. comprehension) without the intermediate step of auditory identification. If, for example, we could evolve principles for understanding how a child learns his original language--which includes the transformation of the experience of objects into words in auditory form--we might begin to understand how a child might learn to go from an original visual form directly to meaning without an intermediate auditory "naming."

We hope this attempt to impose some order on the diversity of phenomena included under reading or reading difficulty will be of heuristic value to other investigators. Recognizing that we have only touched on the complexities of reading behavior, we hope others will bring to bear other coordinating principles to this area of investigation.[10]

NOTES

1.   We will attempt later to make a distinction between visual and auditory comprehension as components in the acquisition of reading.

2.   The research literature on reading difficulties reflects these same differences in emphasis. Some researchers focus on difficulties that can be considered as problems of acquisition, e.g. difficulty with word recognition or phonetics, etc. (Budoff, 1964; Elkind, 1965; Goens, 1958; Robeck, 1963; Goetzinger, 1960; Marchbanks, 1965). Others focus on difficulties that occur after acquisition is relatively complete, e.g. advancement of comprehension skills, critical reading,

or enhancement of experiences (Robinson, 1965; Woestehoff, 1960; Chapman, 1965; Emans, 1965; Gray, 1960).

3.   The particular definitions offered here are not meant to be exhaustive but were chosen primarily because they appear to exemplify the different emphases with which we are concerned.

4.   Handlon, in his model called Single-Multiple Causal Factors uses the terms "cause" and "effect"; with our philosophical bias we prefer the terms "antecedent" and "consequent." These terms will be used here in a conditional ("If, then") rather than a causal form. The conditional statement is not meant to imply either a spatial or temporal relationship, but a relationship in a formal-logical sense. We thank Dr. Roger Bibace who brought this artical to our attention.

5.   We will consider this statement only in the form "If A or B or C, then X" rather than the form "If A and B and C, then X," since the latter is logically reducible to "If A, then X," where A stands for a conjunctive category.

6.   By using the symbols A, B, C... and X_1, X_2, X_3, etc., there is a possible implication that these symbols may be treated as an ordinal series, with the later implying the earlier. In each model except for Model Six, these symbols are used only in the sense of a nominal scale (Stevens, 1951) and could be written in the form "If alpha, then X_{alpha}; if aleph, then X_{aleph}; etc.

7.   Identification presupposes a discrimination of one graphic symbol from others, discrimination of auditory symbols from others, and a transformation of these symbols from one form (usually visual) to a second form (usually auditory). The original visual forms and the transformed auditory forms are considered to be equivalent, differing only in that the referents are represented in different modalities. The two symbol forms are considered equivalent in that they contain the same information for members of a communication group. Essentially, then, the major critical antecedents of identification are the discriminations among the original symbols, the discriminations among the transformed symbols, and a "knowledge" of the principles of transformation from one form to the other. Implicit in this conceptualization is that the transformed symbols (i.e. words as said aloud) can become an input for another individual. Implied also is that there is some consensual basis to assess the adequacy of the identification, with consensus meaning only that there is agreement within the group using the particular language or dialect.

8.   In this context, ITA, (cf., Downing, 1964; Downing, 1965) is seen as a procedure for simplifying acquisition; that is, for

decreasing the number of "rules" the child must learn during acquisition of reading.

9. A concern with the definition of comprehension and meaning would take us too far afield, even if we were competent to deal with this complex problem.

10. The authors wish to thank Dr. Joachim F. Wohlwill, Dr. James M. Coffee, and the other colleagues and students who read the manuscropt in one or more of its revisions and who made helpful suggestions and criticisms. The time to write this paper was made possible in part by Grant M-3860 from the National Institute of Mental Health, United States Public Health Service.

REFERENCES

Bereiter, C. & Engelmann, S. Teaching disadvantaged children in the preschool. New York: Prentice-Hall, 1966.

Bernstein, B. A socio-linguistic approach to social learning. In J. Gould (Ed.), Social science survey. New York: Pelican, 1965.

Bloomfield, L. & Barnhart, C. L. Let's read. Detroit: Wayne State Univer. Press, 1961.

Bond, G. & Tinker, M. Reading difficulties: their diagnosis and correction. New York: Appleton-Century-Crofts, 1957.

Bryant, N. D. Learning disabilities in reading. Mimeo.

Budoff, M & Quinlan, D. Reading readiness as related to efficiency of visual and aural learning in the primary grades. J. educ. Psychol., 1964, 55 (5), 247-252.

Carrigan, Patricia. Broader implications of a chemical theory of reading disability. Paper presented at Amer. Psychol. Assn. Meeting, 1959.

Chapman, Carita. Meeting current reading needs in adult literacy programs. In H. A. Robinson (Ed.), Recent developments in reading. Supplementary educ. Monogr., Univer. of Chicago Press, 1965, No. 95.

Chomsky, N. Syntactic structures. The Hague: Mouton & Company, 1957.

Cromer, W. & Wiener, M. Idiosyncratic response patterns among good and poor readers. J. consult. Psychol., 1966, 30 (1), 1-10.

De Hirsch, Katrina. Two categories of learning difficulties in adolescents. Amer. J. Orthopsychiat., 1963, 33, 87-91.

Delacato, C.H. The treatment and prevention of reading problems. Springfield: Charles C Thomas, 1959.

Deutsch, M. The disadvantaged child and the learning process: some social, psychological and developmental considerations. Paper prepared for the Ford Foundation "Work Conference on Curriculum and Teaching in Depressed Urban Areas." New York: Columbia Univ., 1962.

Downing, J.A. The initial teaching alphabet. New York: Macmillan, 1964.

Downing, J.A. The i.t.a. reading experiment. Chicago: Scott, Foresman, 1965.

Elkind, D., Larson, Margaret, & Van Doorninck, W. Perceptual decentration learning and performance in slow and average readers. J. educ. Psychol., 1965, 56 (1).

Emans, R. Meeting current reading needs in grades four through eight. In H.A. Robinson (Ed.), Recent developments in reading. Suppl. educ. Monogr., Univer. of Chicago Press, 1965, No. 95.

Fries, C.C. Linguistics and reading. New York: Holt, Rinehart, and Winston, 1962.

Geschwind, N. The anatomy of acquired disorders of reading disability. In J. Money (Ed.), Progress and research needs in dyslexia. Baltimore: John Hopkins Press, 1962.

Gibson, E.J. Learning to read. Science, 1965, 148, 1066-1072.

Goens, Jean T. Visual perceptual abilities and early reading progress. Suppl. educ. Monogr., Univer. of Chicago Press, 1958, No. 87.

Goetzinger, C. P., Dirks, D. D., & Baer, C. J. Auditory discrimination and visual perception in good and poor readers. Annals of Otology, Rhinology, and Laryngology, March 1960, 121-136.

Goltz, C. Individual remedial reading for boys in trouble. Reading Teacher, 19 (5).

Gray, W. S. The major aspects of reading. In H. A. Robinson (Ed.), Recent developments in reading. Suppl. educ. Monogr., Univer. of Chicago Press, 1965, No. 95.

Handlon, J. A metatheoretical view of assumptions regarding the etiology of schizophrenia. AMA Archives of gen. Psychiat., January 1960, 43-60.

Harris, A. J. How to increase reading ability. London: Longmans, Green, 1948.

Harris, T. L. Some issues in beginning reading instruction, J. educ. Res., 1962, 56 (1).

Kempler, B. & Wiener, M. Personality and perception in the recognition threshold paradigm. Psychol. Rev., 1964, 70, 349-356.

Kinsbourne, M. & Warrington, E. K. Developmental factors in reading and writing backwardness. Brit. J. Psychol., 1963, 54, 145-156.

Koff, R. H. Panel on: Learning difficulties in childhood. Reported by E. A. Anthony, J. Amer. Psychiatric Assn., 1961, 9.

Labov, W. Some sources of reading problems for Negro speakers of nonstandard English. In A. Frazier (Ed.), New directions in elementary English, Nat. Council of Teachers of English 1967.

Lefevre, C. A. Linguistics and the teaching of reading. New York: McGraw-Hill, 1964.

Marchbanks, Gabrielle & Levin, H. Cues by which children recognize words. J. educ. Psychol., 1965, 56 (2), 57-61.

Milner, Esther. A study of the relationship between reading readiness in grade-one schoolchildren and patterns of parent-child interaction. Child Devel., 1951, 22 (2), 95-112.

Rabinovitch, R. D. Reading and learning disabilities. In S. Arieti (Ed.), American handbook of psychiatry. New York: Basic Books, 1959.

Reitan, R. Relationships between neurological and psychological variables and their implications for reading instruction. In H.A. Robinson (Ed.), Meeting individual differences in reading. Suppl. educ. Monogr., Univer. of Chicago Press, 1964, No. 94.

Robeck, Mildred. Readers who lacked word analysis skills: a group diagnosis. J. educ. Res., 1963, 56, 432-434.

Robinson, Helen M. Looking ahead in reading. In H.A. Robinson (Ed.), Recent developments in reading. Suppl. educ. Monogr., Univer. of Chicago Press, 1965, No. 95.

Roswell, Florence & Natchez, Gladys. Reading disability: diagnosis and treatment. New York: Basic Books, 1964.

Strang, Ruth. Diagnostic teaching of reading. New York: McGraw-Hill, 1964.

Stevens, S. S. (Ed.) Handbook of experimental psychology. New York: John Wiley and Sons, 1951.

Taylor, W. "Cloze procedure": a new tool for measuring readability, Journ. Quart., 1953, 30, 415-433.

Woestehoff, E. Methods and materials for teaching comprehension--in corrective and remedial classes. In Helen Robinson (Ed.), Sequential development of reading abilities. Suppl. educ. Monogr., Univer. of Chicago Press, 1960, No. 9.

PERCEPTUAL TRAINING AND READING ACHIEVEMENT
IN DISADVANTAGED CHILDREN

by David Elkind and Jo Ann Deblinger

Reading is probably the most extensively researched problem in education, so that a certain temerity is needed to initiate still another project in this domain. Despite the wealth of research, however, considerable disagreement remains as to the best methods of teaching reading and as to the major cause of reading retardation (which has been linked with everything from emotional disturbance to mixed dominance). The lack of clarity in the field may be due in part to the fact that most of the research appears to be pragmatic rather than guided by theoretical considerations. There are signs, however, that this situation is changing and that, as Holmes and Singer (1964) noted in their review of reading research, a new theoretical orientation is emerging in research on reading. Such a theoretical orientation, namely, the theory of perceptual development propounded by Piaget (1961), is the starting point for the study described here. Since the path from the theory to the actual research is somewhat winding, a brief recapitulation of the theory and of our previous research in probably in order.

According to Piaget the perception of the young child is <u>centered,</u> in the sense that it is caught and held by the dominant aspects of the visual field. In each case, the dominant aspects of the field are determined by Gestalt-like aspects of the configuration—such as continuity, proximity, and closure—which Piaget terms "field effects". With increasing age, however, and the development of perceptual regulations (internalized actions), the child's perception becomes increasingly <u>decentered</u>, in the sense that it is progressively freed from the constraints imposed by field effects. The perceptual activities which underlie decentration are multiple and include: visual exploration, transport (comparisons of visual

Reprinted by permission from <u>Child Development</u> 40:1. 11-19 (March 1969).

stimuli separated by space or time), reorganization (as in figure-
ground reversal), schematization (as in part-whole combinations),
and set or anticipation. While the Piagetian analysis of perception
would seem to have relevance for a variety of perceptual phenomena,
he and his colleagues have limited themselves almost exclusively
to the study of visual illusions. For our part, we have been concerned with testing out the Piagetian notions as these apply to the
perception of figurative materials.

To this end, we devised figurative tests for assessing the development of the different types of perceptual activities described by
Piaget. Results of administering these tests to children at different
age levels indicated that the various perceptual activities described
by Piaget did indeed improve with age. For example, the tendencies
to reverse figure and ground (Elkind & Scott, 1962), to schematize
part-whole relations (Elkind, Koegler & Go, 1964), and to explore
arrays in systematic fashion (Elkind & Weiss, 1967) increase regu-
larly with age during the early elementary school years. One by-
product of these studies was the observation that children who performed well on the tests were also better readers than those children who had performed poorly. This suggested that there might be
a relation between decentration activities and reading and that the
heretofore purely developmental research might have some practical applications.

In order to test the relation between decentration activities and
reading, a variety of dencentration and reading achievement tests
were given to a large group of elementary school children. A
factor analysis of the results did indicate that a "decentration
factor" was common to both the figural and verbal perceptual tasks
(Elkind, Horn & Schneider, 1965). To insure that this common
perceptual factor was not general intelligence in disguise, a second
experiment was carried out with slow and average readers matched
for IQ. Results showed that, in comparison with the average
readers, the slow readers performed less well on the tests of
perceptual activity and were less able to profit from perceptual
training than were their average reading peers (Elkind, Larson &
Van Doorninck, 1965). A reasonable case could thus be made for
perceptual activity as playing at least a part in successful reading.

The rationale for the relation between perceptual activity and
reading is straightforward. We may assume that to read well the
child must be able systematically to explore or scan the printed
page and to schematize the letters as words, and words as phrases
and sentences. In addition, he must be able to recognize that one
and the same letter can have different sounds in different contexts
and that the same sound can be represented by different letters.
The latter ability would seem to be comparable to the ability to

recognize that one and the same contour line--when associated with different areas- can give rise to different forms, as in reversible figures such as the Rubin vase profile. Finally, in order to comprehend a text, it would seem that the child would have to transport and anticipate meanings among words and sentences.

In view of the foregoing empirical and theoretical considerations, and in view of the finding that perceptual activity could be improved with training (Elkind, Koegler & Go, 1962), it seemed reasonable to suppose that training in perceptual activity might help to improve children's reading skills. To test this hypothesis, we devised a set of nonverbal exercises aimed at getting children to explore, re-organize, schematize, transport, and anticipate perceptual configurations and arrays. The exercises were made nonverbal in the belief that this would force children to really exercise their perceptual activities without the crutch of verbalization. The exercises were also made nonverbal on the basis of our observation that teachers often talk too much or at too abstract a level and are consequently often "tuned out" by just those children most in need of instruction. After considerable pilot work with these exercises, the present investigation was designed to test the effects of this form of training in a more rigorous fashion.

It should perhaps be said that we do not regard the proposed exercises as a total reading program or as a panacea for all reading ills. On the contrary, we regard them as an adjunct to other methods which are necessarily verbal in nature. Ideally, of course, one would wish to provide individual diagnosis and teaching geared to the particular needs of a given child. It is probably fair to say, however, that we are far from that ideal and that, for now and for a considerable time to come, reading will continue to be taught on on a group basis. Under the circumstances, it seems reasonable to provide teachers with material and procedures that they can use now and that require little in the way of special preparation or equipment. The nonverbal exercises described here have the advantage that they require little in the way of special training on the part of the teacher and nothing more than a blackboard and chalk in the way of equipment.

METHOD

Subjects. The original subjects for the study were 60 second-grade Negro children attending school in the inner city of Rochester. These 60 were selected from a larger sample of second graders who had been tested on individual tests of perceptual activity (the

TABLE 1

Pretraining Mean Scores and t Tests for Experimental[a] and Control Groups[b]

GROUP (N)	PIT	PAT	Word Form	Word Recog.	Mean. of Opp.	Picture Assoc.	Read. Comp	Calif. Total[c]
					Test			
Control (29)	10.48	8.74	21.66	15.97	7.56	10.86	8.14	2.08
Exper. (25	9.08	9.02	19.08	14.72	8.84	10.56	7.40	1.92
t	1.53	0.35	2.32*	1.30	1.60	0.39	0.73	0.11

a Mean age (in mos.) = 96.5; means SD (in mos.) = 6.97.

b Mean age (in mos.) = 97.0; means SD (in mos.) = 7.32.

c These are transformed scores which represent the child's grade level in whole numbers and decimal fractions.

* Significant at .05 level (two-tailed test).

Picture Ambiguity Test or PAT [Elkind, 1964; Elkind & Scott, 1962] and the Picture Integration Test or PIT [Elkind et al., 1964]) and on Form W of the California Achievement Tests (1957 ed.; 1963 norms). Subjects were selected so as to form two groups matched for perceptual activity and for reading achievement. For reasons to be described later, only 29 of the control subjects and 25 of the experimental subjects actually completed the experiment. It is because of these lost subjects that the matching data, shown in Table 1, are not as consistent and close as they were initially. As examination of Table 1 reveals, however, the loss of subjects worked in favor of the control rather than the experimental subjects, who as a group scored somewhat lower in most of the subtests and significantly so on word-form subtest of the California Achievement Test. Accordingly, any terminal superiority of experimental over control group would be in spite of an initial inequality that was not in their favor.

Procedure. The experimental and control groups were each broken up into two teaching groups of 15 children per group. Throughout the training sessions one of us (S.E.) served as the teacher while the other (J.D.) served as participant observer. We met with each group three times a week for one-half hour for a period of 15 weeks. The control groups met from 1:00 p.m. to 1:30 p.m., and from 1:30 p.m. to 2:00 p.m. The two experimental groups met from 2:00 p.m. to 2:30 p.m. and from 2:30 p.m. to 3:00 p.m.

For the control groups, The Bank Street Readers (1966) were distributed to the children at the beginning of the class period and the half hour was spent in having each child read several paragraphs of a story. In addition, exercises provided in the teacher's handbook were written on the blackboard and were used to teach vocabulary, grammar, and comprehension. Over the 15-week session, the control classes read through two of the readers (one first- and one second-grade reader).

In order to channel the motivation of the children and to maintain order, several devices were employed. At the beginning of the period, children were appointed to various roles. Two children, a boy and a girl, were selected as "choosers". These children sat beside E and took turns choosing the child who was to read. In addition, one child was selected as "Keeper of the Place", and his job was to point out the sentences currently being read, to youngsters who had lost the place. Still another child was chosen as "The Helper" to aid the child who was reading when he ran into difficulty with a word or phrase. A different child was chosen as "Keeper of the Page", and his job was to write on the blackboard the number of the page currently being read. Finally, one child was chosen as a "Shusher" to keep the other children quiet. Other youngsters were chosen to straighten the chairs, collect the books, and clean the blackboards after the session was over. By providing children with these various functions, it was possible to maintain the group at a workable noise and activity level and to keep the reading and the exercises going at a reasonable pace. Each child had at least one opportunity, and usually two, to read during the course of each session.

The experimental groups were trained with our nonverbal exercises, which are described in detail elsewhere (Elkind, in press) and will be described only in a general way here. During the first session, the children were told, "We are going to play a game in which no one talks. I will write something on the board and when you know the answer, raise your hand. I will point to the child who is to go to the board. Remember, no one is to talk. All right, watch me."

At this point, E went to the blackboard and wrote out a simple exercise (the series ABCDE) and then turned to the children after drawing a line under the next position in the series. Most of the children got the idea and raised their hands. The nonverbal training was thus launched. Each session began with a simple exercise and progressed to more difficult ones. The exercises included series of descending and ascending order and of increasing difficulty:

ACEG ‗‗‗‗‗‗‗‗

           P
Anagrams: SIT

Scrambled words: LUBE =

Symbolic transformations: SUN   = ☀

                                   MOON = ∧

Tenses and plurals: SHOE   SHOES
                          TOP   TOPS
                          PIE   ‗‗‗‗‗

Coding: HTAENS   5432 = ‗‗‗‗‗‗‗‗‗
        1 2 3 4 5 6

and many variations of these and similar problems. About midway through the teaching sessions, E chose children to come to the

blackboard and serve as teachers. The children enjoyed this and
did not limit themselves to parroting exercises first employed by
E; that is to say, most of them grasped the principles upon which
the exercises were constructed and were able to create new ones
of their own.

One other point should be made about the exerimental groups.
They spontaneously became competitive, and this competitive
spirit was channeled by having the boys compete against the girls.
The E drew two columns on the blackboard and labeled one "Boys"
and the other "Girls". Each time a boy completed an exercise
correctly, E placed a "1" in the boys' column, and the same held
true when a girl succeeded. Although E was sometimes accused of
showing favoritism to the boys or girls, the competition seemed to
enhance interest and to be, for the most part, constructive. Each
child was given at least one opportunity to go to the blackboard each
day, and most children had two opportunities during any given class
period.

Treatment of Data. After the completion of the training, the subjects were retested on the individual tests of perceptual activity
(the PIT and PAT) and were group tested on the California Achievement Test (Form X). Difference scores based on the pre- and
post-test scores were than tabulated for the perceptual tests and
for various subtests of reading achievement from the California.
Differences between the mean difference scores for experimental
and control groups were tested by the t test procedure.

RESULTS

Because of moves, illness, and incorrigibility, not all the
children who began as participants in the study remained to the
end. There was one loss from the control group and five losses
from the experimental group. Accordingly, all comparisons are
based on the 29 control and 25 experimental subjects who completed
the experiment. Results of the t tests for the various pre- and
post-test difference scores for experimental and control groups
are shown in Table 2.

As Table 2 indicates, there were three significant t tests for
differences between experimental and control groups. In each
case, the higher mean score was made by the experimental groups.
Tests on which the experimental group made significantly greater
improvement than the control groups were the PIT, word recognition, and word form. In addition, the differences between experimental and control groups on the PAT and the Picture Association

TABLE 2

Post-test Mean Difference Scores and t Tests for Experimental and Control Groups

Test

GROUP (N)	PIT	PAT	Word Form	Word Recog.	Mean of Opp.	Picture Assoc.	Read Comp.	Calif. Total
Control (29)	0.31	3.41	0.24	0.57	1.62	0.93	1.41	0.21
Exper. (25)	3.64	4.78	2.52	2.44	0.28	1.88	1.68	0.36
t	1.96*	1.40	2.40*	2.64*	1.61	1.64	0.38	0.11

* Significant at .05 level (two-tailed test).

Test again favored the experimental groups but did not reach statistical significance. Just the reverse held true for the Meaning of Opposites Test, wherein the difference was in favor of the control groups but again did not reach statistical significance.

DISCUSSION

Results of the present experiment suggest that nonverbal training in perceptual activity had a greater effect upon certain aspects of reading achievement than did the more usual type of reading instruction. Before interpreting this finding, however, it might be well to make several general remarks about the experiment as a whole, both to further clarify the context of the experiment and to answer possible objections.

First of all, it must be said that the investigation labored under several unforeseen handicaps. One of these was the problem of discipline. As it turned out, we had fewer discipline problems in the two control groups than we did in the two experimental groups. This was the result of two factors. For one, by chance we got three boys in the experimental group who had been recognized discipline problems prior to the experiment and whom we eventually had to drop from the class because they were so disruptive. In addition, the experimental groups were made up of children from different classrooms so that there tended to be some initial cliquishness. The control groups, on the other hand, were in each case all from the same classroom.

Other handicaps came as a result of teaching the children in the afternoon (when many who had had no lunch were restless as well as hungry) and from taking the children out of their homerooms to the experimental classroom, which meant that valuable time was lost in getting settled and "warming up". In these regards, experimental children were penalized more than control children, because they came later in the afternoon and from a greater variety of homerooms.

Despite these handicaps, which on the whole seemed more detrimental to the experimental than to the control groups, all the children did make improvement, and particularly the experimental groups. It might be argued, however, that the improvement made was a function of experimenter bias (Rosenthal, 1966) and expectation, rather than as a result of the teaching per se. While this is a possibility, since the same experimenter taught all groups and knew whether they were experimental or control, the findings speak against such an interpretation. While the experimental groups did do better on some aspects of reading achievement, they did not do better on all aspects. Indeed, with regard to "Meaning of Opposites", they did more poorly than the controls. It would be hard to reconcile this particular difference with the charge of experimenter bias since, if that were operative, experimental children would be expected to perform at a higher level on all counts. Accordingly, while the possibility of experimenter bias was certainly present in this experiment, the results are not consistent with such an interpretation.

What do these findings mean, then, with respect to reading achievement and perceptual activity? For one thing, they seem to support our theoretical analysis of what is involved in this relation. Practice in visual exploration schematization, reorganization, transport, and anticipation clearly improved the performance of the experimental group on the recognition of words and word forms to a significantly greater extent than was true for the control subjects. That such training did not differentially affect reading comprehension was to be expected, since the exercises were not designed to alter this aspect of reading achievement. In the case of the Meaning of Opposites Test, wherein the experimental subjects did more poorly than the controls, an artifact may have played its part. Since many of the nonverbal exercises resembled some of the items on this subtest, but had to do with differences and similarities, there may have been some inappropriate generalization to the test items. This possibility needs to be tested in our subsequent research. In general, however, by training children in the processes which we regard as basic to certain aspects of reading achievement, we have improved performance on these aspects, and this, in some degree, argues for the validity of the analysis.

It should be said, in closing, that, while the use of classroom teaching as an experimental training technique has many drawbacks, it also has special virtues. Not the least of these is the opportunity to observe the role of group processes in learning--something which is not often possible when children are seen and trained individually. Although we lack a model or a language for describing these group factors, their potency can hardly be denied. We were repeatedly impressed with the difference in the approach to learning of our several training groups. One was a cohesive group with the children accepting and reinforcing one another. Another group was fragmented with several cliques and isolated sniping at one another. Such group esprit, or lack of it, is clearly important in the learning activity of any individual within the group. This view is supported by the findings of the recent Campbell and Coleman (1966) report, which suggests that the single most important factor in school achievement is neither teacher nor facilities but rather the educational background of the classroom group. Teaching in a class-room setting is one way in which to explore the role of such group factors in learning.

REFERENCES

The Bank Street Readers. New York: Macmillan, 1966.

California Achievement Tests, Monterey, Calif.: McGraw-Hill, 1957 (1963 Norms).

Campbell, E.Q., & Coleman, J.S. Inequalities in educational op-portunities in the United States. Paper read at the American Socio-logical Association, Miami Beach, Florida, August 31, 1966.

Elkind, D. Ambiguous pictures for the study of perceptual develop-ment and learning. Child Development, 1964, 35, 1391-1396.

Elkind, D. Reading, logic and perception: An approach to reading instruction. In J.F. Hellmuth (ed.), Educational therapy, Vol. II. Seattle: Special Child Publications (in press).

Elkind, D., Horn, J., & Schneider, G. Modified word recognition, reading achievement and perceptual decentration. Journal of Genetic Psychology, 1965, 107, 235-251.

Elkind, D., Koegler, R.R., & Go, E. Effects of perceptual train-ing at three age levels. Science, 1962, 137, 3532.

Elkind, D., Koegler, R.R. & Go, E. Studies in perceptual develop-ment, II: Part-whole perception. Child Development, 1964, 35, 81-91.

Elkind, D., Larson, M.E., & Van Doorminck, W. Perceptual learning and performance in slow and average readers. Journal of Educational Psychology, 1965, 56 (1), 50-56.

Elkind, D., & Scott, L. Studies in perceptual development, I: The decentering of perception. Child Development, 1962, 33, 619-630.

Elkind, D., & Weiss, J. Studies in perceptual development, III: Perceptual exploration. Child Development, 1967, 38, 553-561.

Holmes, J.A., & Singer, H. Theoretical models and trends toward more basic research in reading. Review of Educational Research, 1964, 34, 127-155.

Piaget, J. Les mécanismes perceptifs. Paris: Presses Universitaires de France, 1961.

Rosenthal, R. Experimenter effects in behavioral research. New York: Appleton-Century-Crofts, 1966.

III. READING PROBLEMS

LINGUISTIC CONSIDERATIONS IN READING DISABILITY

by David W. Reed and Jesse O. Sawyer

Language is more an intellectual than an "environmental" or "physiological" component of the process of reading, and therefore it must be an intellectual component of the disabilities suffered by some persons in learning to read.

The analysis and treatment of reading disability may be separated into those considerations which are appropriate to psychology, to pedagogy, and to linguistics. After any such division the linguist is likely to see his role as most important in diagnosis and important in treatment perhaps largely to the extent that he views his function as that of writing a better grammar of the language being taught.

If linguistic factors are not viewed as a major causal element in reading disability--conceivably pedagogy or psychology might be-- we take it that we are here because linguistics is somehow involved either as a subsidiary feature of the reading process or more likely a discipline suspected of being a tool in the analysis and treatment of reading disability. The linguist can indeed suggest areas in which not reading disability so much as reading difficulty can be obviated by a better understanding of the patterns of the language being learned, and ultimately he can solve a few problems by writing grammars which are more humanely and humanly oriented. He also has something to say about distinguishing between genuine disability and those troubles which arise when different aspects of language are associated in the teaching-learning situation.

The idiolectal system that a child has fully learned by the time he is five or six, that which enables him to communicate orally about most of his needs, is simpler and more fragmentary than the language system shared by highly literate adults, upon which the system of English writing is based. Therefore, as soon as

---

This paper was originally presented at the annual convention of the International Reading Association, May 2, 1969.

children have begun to acquire the mechanics of reading and writing
sentences that they might utter or orally understand, they need to
expand their knowledge of the system of the English language they
will use as young adults.

This is not to deny that the language of an individual at all stages
has centain features which are unique to that particular stage in the
development of language skills. The very fact that a child lacks
certain vocabulary items must mean that he handles the vocabulary
he does have in a somewhat different way from the habit of adults
or children of other ages. Or one can guess that certain communication features proliferate in their own times. For instance, the
affective vocabulary, the vocabulary of groans, grimaces, laughter,
and tears, is obviously very large in the child who has yet to learn
to read and it possibly becomes progressively smaller as the child
learns words which can take the place of or describe his feelings.
The strongest statement we have ever heard of the unique characteristics of the language and language experience of the child was
made by Kenneth L. Pike, who suggested that language is trans-
mitted from generation to generation by the young school child,
who was in his view also responsible for most important language
change.

As he begins his reading--his formal educational experience--
the child is occupied with a series of problems. In the most general sense he faces the problems of matching his speech to a set
of written symbols and of associating ideas he already has with
written symbols. Closely connected to the development of his
skill in matching speech to writing and writing to speech will be
the matching of new concepts with vocabulary, and where vocabulary is "taught", of matching new concepts to both printed symbols
and spoken sounds.

Complicating this rather straightforward set of matching problems
will be the business of learning a new style of speech that exists
only in writing and in certain formal presentations, such as this
one today. It is not by chance that we are haunted by the idea that
a sentence expresses a complete thought in arrangements that our
teachers would accept as sentences. For the child, normal problems in reading and writing consist of the matching problems, the
problem of redundancy, or style, and the problem of new words
and ideas. His experience up to the time of learning reading and
writing has demanded neither frequent arbitrary visual symbolization nor completeness beyond the assurance of knowing he is understood. The child has demanded only momentary functional utility
from language. At the age of five or six, he is asked to seriously
consider that language may not be momentary but capable of artificial extension in time. And he is asked to consider it as some-

thing else than merely functional. As he learns formal reading and
writing, he begins the business of learning that language may also
have and does indeed in all its occurrences have culturally determined aesthetic values.

In all of this the linguist plays a humble role. First, the matching problems.

The child's idiolect contains many homonyms that he will discover are spelled differently, e.g. pair, pare, pear, and so on.
What he may have thought to be one word with several different
meanings turns out to be two or more words, and he must match
up the semantic differentiae that correlate with the different spellings. Presented such groups as the /pehr/ group, he must adjust
among other things his definition of "word". When a child speaks
of a word he means one sequence of sounds that designates a loosely
associated set of objects and ideas around him; the grouping is not
necessarily rational in any sense that he can conceive. It is arbitrary. Once he has learned a few sound-alikes that are spell-
differents, the least adjustment he can make in his definition of a
word is that it is any isolable sound sequence which sounds the same
and is spelled the same. We have no idea whether or at what stage
in his development a child includes different meanings as establishing
different words. Certainly his definition of a word is largely shaped
by his reading experience, until finally a word may become anything
he sees written or can write between spaces.

Once he has learned that homophones are not homographs he will
also discover the obverse, that one spelled sequence can represent
confusingly different sets of sounds, as in read pronounced /red/
and read pronounced /riyd/. In the physical process of actual reading or reading aloud, pair, pare, and pear offer visual clues to
meanings and are confusing for pronunciation where /riyd/ and /red/
can be absolutely ambiguous both as to meaning and pronunciation.

We think it is worth noting that there are at least two and probably
many kinds of interference involved in problems of homophones and
homographs. The case of pair, pare, and pear must be analyzed at
first blush as helpful to the reader, for here the child is given three
different clues to meaning for which the speech he has learned up
to then has given him only one set of sounds, /pehr/. The written
forms are more redundant and one might hope somehow easier.
But they do extract their pound of effort. The help offered by the
written distinction is only available if the three have been
memorized--learned--and to the linguist it seems likely that the
three must be learned separately and at different times, although
here we would want to wait for the psychologist's advice. /riyd/
and /red/, on the other hand, seem at first glance to create no
problems. Since the context may tell the reader which to expect,

he will not be troubled and will supply the form which his pronunciation of the language tells him is required. But the answer is not all
that easy. If at a guess we way that most ea spellings in English
are pronounced /iy/, then our reader should probably be protected
from /e/ words spelled ea until he has reached a stage of development in which the introduction of read, lead, dead, and so on, will
not be sounded out.

If the /e/ words come early we can expect our reader to be no
leader in the eager attempt to reach success. He will have become
a casualty of the course.

In one case--pare, pear and pair--we have a written distinction
that is a learning problem. The student cannot escape the force of
the association of the three in that he is obliged to cut up the meaning area which has been to him simply the /pehr/ area. If, on the
other hand, he has kept three meaning areas separate in his mind,
each different and each labelled /pehr/, the discovery of convenient
different written tags may be a matter of small joy and comfort.
In /riyd/ and /red/, however, two semantic units which have partial
semantic-phonetic similarities are ruthlessly brought together by
his knowledge of reading.

It is problems of these kinds that characterize the complexities
of the matching process. The varieties are many and deserve to
be rather carefully worked out and classified. They are certainly
among the building blocks that the textbook author ought to bring
to his job of creation.

Some of the child's homonyms that are differently spelled are
also differently pronounced in dialects with which he may not be
familiar. Most speakers of American English today make no distinction in the pronunciation of pairs like hoarse, horse; four, for;
and mourning, morning but many older persons, most Southerners,
and some New Englanders, have "close o" in the first word of each
pair and "open o" in the second--a contrast that can be predicted
from spelling in the vast majority of cases. Even unconscious
knowledge of these dialect features helps to explain what otherwise
must appear to be arbitrary differences in spelling, although such
knowledge may come for some dialect speakers at a much later
time in the language learning process.

An immediate problem exists for the child whose native dialect
varies from the standard dialect of the schools, but the case is a
pseudo-problem, no matter how serious. Ideally, the young child
should learn to read under the guidance of a teacher who speaks the
child's dialect. Failing this, the teacher must know the dialects
of his students and adapt to their exigencies, remembering when he
is teaching reading and when speech. As a rule of thumb, we
should think a good reading teacher might eschew correcting dialect

pronunciation in the reading class. The child ought not to be expected to do two jobs at once. He ought to be allowed to read in his own dialect. He will in any case. Nevertheless, we are sure that some teachers correct as misreadings, errors which arise out of their ignorance of the dialect of the reader. Consider such traps as to, two, and too. The dialect of many American Negroes also pronounces tour and tool as /tuw/. It is too much to expect that /tuw/ and /tuw/ for tour and tool can have gone unnoticed. I can hear it now: "Johnny, you said /tuw/. The word is tour." "That's what I said, teacher. I said /tuw/."

The teaching of spelling has been handled in a variety of ways. By and large the presentations are guided, so far as we can see, mainly by principles for which psychology or educational psychology should provide the reasons. The principles we have observed in a relatively lay contact with a few spelling and reading books are efforts to present groupings of words with common patterns, and the reverse but often transgressed rule that items of symbolization which are certain to be confused with each other are relegated to opposite ends of the book; that is, if ie words are on page 5, then ei words may appropriately appear on page 105. It has been obvious to the teacher that sets of words that are similar can be grouped in the reading or spelling lesson, and in most textbooks there is an effort to make such sets integral parts of the presentation. Although such grouping is little more than a mnemonic device, it is as far as we have gone in many cases. Certainly a student learns from juxtaposing similar things, but this is only a small part of what we ought to be doing. The sets should themselves be arranged in a sequence that moves from easy to difficult, and opposing sets for which interference will be great should be presented in a way that minimizes the inherent oppositions. As a matter of fact, to say that elementary reading materials should be arranged in sequences moving from easy to difficult is the same as to say arranged in a way that minimizes interference. Here, however, we know relatively little. We do not know that items X and Y are best learned if X precedes Y. The linguist can give some help in predicting likely sequences, and the practical teacher can suggest various typical results, but ultimately we have no real choice yet except to measure relative difficulty by adding up the errors children make and the difficulties they have in learning to read. The necessity of avoiding mixing or juxtaposing items which create interference has not been sufficiently stressed in view of the fact that most people can remember at least one pair of words which they have eleminated from their personal spelling control by the simple device of juxtaposition. In my own case I have lost the ability to predict whether medial English -ng- will be /ŋ/ or /ŋg/

by the simple device of bringing large numbers of examples together
in haphazard fashion in preparation for some work I wanted to do
with the set of such words.

Of spelling, it seems useful then to point out that whatever problems are reading problems are also probable spelling problems.
Where dialect enters into reading, it enters into spelling. Homonyms that are reading problems are also spelling problems.
Given this, it seems sensible that spelling is taught as a function
of reading and is based on the reading assignment. I believe that
such is not always true, although the principle seems to exist in
the idea of a language arts program as distinct from special programs in individual language skills.

We have given a somewhat simplified picture of the matching
process; unfortunately, such a simplification comes only part way
to the truth. The speech learned by the child includes a complicated
set of changes and adjustments, a set of rules, if you wish, that
allow speech to exist in rather different ways. Mostly what the
child hears is presented in a rapid-fire barrage which really is
imcomprehensible if taken out of its natural, supportive environment. Most such talking has all the comprehensibility of a recording made of a family Christmas party on a new Christmas tape
recorder--all taken out of context, of course. The written version
the school child learns is so far from the colloquial that it must
appear at times to be almost a different language. The difference
is one of speed and completeness as well as grammar. The
slower, more detailed, version serves to clarify or to make comprehension possible in conditions in which talking would otherwise be difficult. Within the child's experience the more detailed
kind of speech comes closest to and is usually used as a bridge
into the formal written language. The ability to apply a whole
range of complex sound shifts that change slow into fast speech is
part of that unconscious idiolectal system that the five-year-old
brings with him to school.

At a later point in his education a parallel but more arbitrary
kind of morphophonemics becomes available to him. Expansion
of the child's reading vocabulary in the learned disciplines will
introduce large numbers of works from Greek, Latin, and Romance
sources that obey rules of pronunciation that are largely unknown
to him from his early speaking vocabulary. Knowledge of these
rules will explain what would otherwise be exceptions to generalizations about phoneme-grapheme correspondences. For example,
awareness of the existence of legality, rebellion, civilian, Mon-
golian, and cherubic explains the different spellings of the identical
second vowel sounds in legal, rebel, civil, Mongol, and cherub.

As the child's vocabulary enlarges through reading, he may become aware of other anomalies in spelling that are understandable if one knows what the source language of the word is--e.g. ph as a spelling for /f/ is found primarily in words borrowed from Greek; the "silent" gh after i is limited to words of native English origin.

There seems to us to be some evidence for assuming that the period of learning to read is one in which each child develops an extensive internal and private grammar and phonology for his language. The arguments are fairly uncomplicated. Up to the time of learning reading a child is asked only to mimic what he hears. He uses words which he has heard from others. He is not asked to guess or to create. Now suddenly at the age of five or six he is faced with a set of symbols for sounds he has probably never viewed as separable entities or manipulable. The problem he is faced with once the shock of recognition is past is the problem of prediction. He is asked on the basis of his six years of language and six months of instruction to predict what sounds a sequence of symbols can have and he is even asked, although much later, to predict the meaning that can be assigned to the sequence on the basis of the context of the sequence and his previous experience. The whole problem of reading and the really new thing that faces the child is this requirement for prediction.

The first result, we believe to be that at this period the child develops his phonology and grammar for his native language from a much simpler to a much more complex instrument. Moreover, the decisions of his new tools are enormously powerful in their ability to persist through time and later reading experience. Some evidence for at least the effects in phonology are well known to us all. I suppose no one has failed to discover at some time that he is mispronouncing a word which by chance he has neither ever spoken nor heard spoken by anyone. The words belong to his reading vocabulary and he has learned a pronunciation and finds that his pronunciation is perhaps reasonable but certainly not accepted. I remember having such experiences with vagary and paucity, which I pronounced /véygiriy/ and /pókitiy/, although these were certainly not early acquisitions in my reading vocabulary. The point is that such mispronunciations tell us quite clearly that we internalize certain rules and predict sounds and even accept our own versions of new reading materials. Usually, the errors we make in applying our rules or in making our rules are corrected by hearing the words read or used by others, but there is always a residue which survives into high school and college. The kind of experience which discovers these came late to me when I was a freshman in college--presumably a backward child if not absolutely subnormal.

More esoteric than our set of rules of sound-making are the rules
of formal grammar which we suppose are also receiving some extensive development at this time. With much hesitation I would argue
that the survival of substandard speech, that a child may have
learned at home, into adult speech is achieved at this time by being
made to fit the grammar that is evolving in the child's mind. Sub-
standardisms are either eliminated, relegated to a separate dialect
which may be spoken at home or with friends, or survive into the
child's grammar of the language by being incorporated into his idea
of the standard. In my own case I managed to continue using "he,
she, and it don't" until the usage was scared out of me by the critical sarcasm of a college sophomore roommate. I suppose I knew
the rules, and yet I was totally unaware of my own usage.

There is one feature of prediction in learning one's own language
which we suspect is not formed and settled during any early period.
This is the ability of native speakers of a language to create new
words or to refuse to allow new word creations. To use examples
which are familiar, I suppose one would accept such a word as
disambiguate, although I suspect it is an egregious neologism.
You feel, for instance, in such sequences as brute, brutal, brutality;
cause, causal, causality; and coast, coastal, coastality, that causal
and causality are mildly suspect, while coastal is acceptable and
coastality unacceptable. If the unique language activity of the adult
is vocabulary expansion and control, it is not surprising that this
particular kind of prediction is not possible until long after the business of learning to read is completed. Nevertheless this control
is a final expression of the grammar the child begins to construct
as he learns to read. It is even possible to view this skill as the
highest language achievement, the true test of nativeness at which
all abstract language skills are aiming. It is, after all, easy to
write a grammar of what occurs, but the grammar that predicts
that coastality cannot occur is quite a different creation. It is easy
enough to chart the boundaries of words in final -al and -ality, but
to abstract from the patterns of all such examples in the language
the possibility that a word one has never heard may either exist
or not exist is a major accomplishment. Nor can we say that the
skill is achieved by simply learning all of the vocabulary of the language, because even a vast vocabulary would only allow us on the
basis of comparison with what we know exists to say "This word
exists" or "It doesn't exist," not "This is possible, that impossible."

We have not yet touched on the child's problem with redundancy,
style, the complete sentence, beyond a suggestion that some difficulties may exist here and that they are related to the aesthetic
aspects of the formal language. Certainly the child has existed in
an environment in which his language is mostly functional, serving

to supply him with his physical needs and such pleasures as he requires. He may have been exposed to complete sentences during
the period when his own grammar created mostly pivot sentences
of the order "Car break," to which his mother may have replied,
"Your toy car has broken down," in an attempt to figure out for
herself what he was trying to say, perhaps, as much as to correct
him. It is probably not relevant to reading problems whether the
imposition of formal language style on the child is dictated by real
problems of communication or simply the traditional artistic prefer-
ences of the community. I am inclined to favor allowing the latter
its share, and having admitted this clarifies the situation a bit.

From the point of view of the child the requirement is largely
arbitrary. If our demands are essentially aesthetic, only aesthetic
rewards--an appreciation of beauty--could be used as a justification
for our demands. Written language is complex in part because it
is limited to a single modality, the printed word. In actual talking,
of course, tremendous amounts of information are never verbalized.
Gestures, body and head movements, and a variety of references to
the surroundings in which a conversation takes place all contribute
their share. It is not our intention here to suggest ways of getting
out of this quandary which we have labelled the complete sentence
problem. We want only to call your attention to this demand as one
of the real difficulties for the child who must learn to read and write.

We want to return now to the subject of the section meeting which
emphasized disability. So far what we have said has scarcely
touched on such problems. We have outlined some of the thoughts
linguists come up with when faced with problems in reading disability. Our conclusion is that in the case of severe physical or
psychological trauma, the linguist is needed just about as much as
a father at a birthing. In the more subtle occasions of dyslexia or
comparable complaints a linguist might be of some use in describing
the symptoms, but a psychologist would be more useful in almost
every possible respect. We see the function of the linguist as con-
sultative but without much promise of great advantages accruing
from the consultation.

We do find a place for the linguist in any case in which actual language materials are prepared for student use, whether in testing,
teaching, or treatment. With respect to the learning task in a more
general sense we can state our belief that the disabilities experienced
by some children in learning to read and write may be overcome if
these activities are taught, not as purely mechanical skills, but as
part of a unified program of instruction in language, in which the
patterns of the total language are well understood by the teacher
and become at least matters of unconscious knowledge to the
learner.

READING RETARDATION: I. PSYCHIATRIC AND SOCIOLOGIC ASPECTS

by Leon Eisenberg, M. D.

The modern species of the genus <u>Homo</u> has been christened variously: <u>sapiens</u>, the wise; <u>faber</u>, the tool-maker; <u>loquens</u>, the speaker; but man's most extraordinary accomplishment warrants the epithet: <u>Homo scribens et legens</u>, man the writer and reader. Contemporary man, wherever he has been found and whatever his state of culture, has possessed a spoken language; every language thus far encountered has been complex and sophisticated. The origins of the faculty of speech are lost in antiquity. It can be deduced confidently that Cro-Magnon man, who lived from 25,000 to 10,000 years ago, possessed language; his fabrication of tools, his ceremonial burials, and, most of all, his cave paintings, all bespeak the necessary level of conceptualization. It seems not unreasonable to suppose that Neanderthal man, the maker of stone tools and of fire, knowledgeable enough to cook his food, a man with a cranial capacity in no wise inferior to our own and with endocranial markings indicative of frontal and parietal lobe differentiation, may have possessed the gift of tongues as long as 50,000 years ago.[1] The invention of writing, on the other hand, dates no earlier than the fourth millenium before Christ.

Consider the exponential rate of development of society in the 5,000 years since written language as against the limited progress in the 50,000 years of spoken language that preceded it. True, technological advances other than literacy have been catalysts of this revolutionary transformation but few are the advances that have not been mediated by written symbols. The magnificence of this accomplishment transcends the creature comforts it has enabled man to attain. The ability to read makes available to the least of men direct commerce with the great minds of all times. It opens vistas of sensitivity and understanding that liberate

---

Reprinted by permission from <u>Pediatrics</u> 37:2 352-365 (February 1966).

men from the parochialism of individual experience. Reading of
our brothers half a globe away cannot but quicken the pulse of our
common humanity. Writing confers immortality; the fame of
Ozymandias may crumble with the decay of his colossal monument,
but time does not dim the poet's luster. Yet today fully half the
world's adults are wholly illiterate and not one-third are "function-
ally" literate by the criterion of a fourth grade reading level.[2] By
that standard in 1956, 11% of U.S. citizens could not read, the proportions varying by states from 3.9 to 28.7%.[3] This is a measure
of our failure and their failure, for to them are denied the riches
of literature and the necessities of life. Employability is increasingly contingent upon literacy; those who fail to learn to read today
will be the disadvantaged of tomorrow, impoverished in body and
in soul. Clearly, then, just as the pediatrician concerns himself
with the correction of physical defect, the prophylaxis of infection,
and the adequacy of nutrition, all to ensure the healthy physical development of the children under his care, he must be concerned
with physiological characteristics of the individual child, the preschool intellectual environment of the family, and the psychological
nutrients provided by the educational system, all precursors to the
attainment of skill in reading. Few issues bear more directly upon
the future of his patients.

METHODS

What is the magnitude of the problem? How many children are
defective readers and where are they to be found? What personal
and familial characteristics are associated with reading difficulty?
If the answers to these questions are to be interpretable, we must
first consider methods of measurement of reading competence.
Surveys of reading performance are based upon group tests of
reading such as the Iowa, Stanford, California, Gates, and others.
Typically, the test is standardized by scoring the results of its ad-
ministration to a sample of children drawn from selected and presumably representative communities throughout the United States.
Practical considerations determine that the test must be relatively
brief in order to avoid fatiguing the child and in order to recommend
itself to school administrators for periodic system-wide surveys.
Scoring must be simple; hence stems the reliance on multiple
choice answers which permit machine scoring. In general, the
tests that are given to upper classmen assume reading competence
at the elementary level, again in keeping with the necessity for
brevity; consequently, a child may receive a minimum non-zero

score simply by appearing for the test and signing his name to it.
To this basement grade score may then be added additional credit
for sucessful guessing at answers; most standard tests do not pena-
lize for errors (the Gates is an exception). As a result, clinical
reading specialists usually report functional reading levels based
upon individual examination that are one or more grades lower than
those derived from the group tests.

The skills measured by the elementary reading tests are different
from those demanded for successful completion of the intermediate
and advanced batteries. At the lower levels, little more is required
from the child than the ability to decode the visual symbols into
recognizable words. At intermediate and advanced levels, comprehension is called much more directly into play; in consequence, performance will vary with vocabulary, level of reasoning, and general
intellectual facility. One would expect, therefore, that the child
with limited exposure to intellectual stimulation would be progressively more penalized at ascending grade levels. One final caveat
is in order. The great variability in individual response at primary
grade levels, together with the limited discrimination of the test
instrument at the lower end of the scale, restricts the confidence
to be placed in group testing methods in the first grades of school.
I would commend to every pediatrician that he familiarize himself
with the tests used in his community by reading through the test
forms with some care.

EPIDEMIOLOGY

With these general considerations in mind and the further re-
striction that comparisons between systems employing different
tests must be made with caution,[4] let us look at the facts and figures
that we can summon. In Figure 1, I have plotted the 1964 reading
performance on the Stanford Test of the entire sixth-grade population of a large urban center here named "Metropolis". (It should
be noted that children in special classes for mental retardation are
not included). Though the figures in this graph are precise and
based upon actual figures from a single city, I shall not name the
city, as naming would invite invidious comparisons. The findings
serve to condemn not it but urban America. Twenty-eight percent
of the sixth-grade children are reading two or more grades below
expected grade level, the conventional definition of severe reading
retardation! With a median reading level of 5.2, the distribution
is shifted significantly to the left; by definition of test construction,
the median should lie at 6.5, the grade and month at which the test
was administered.

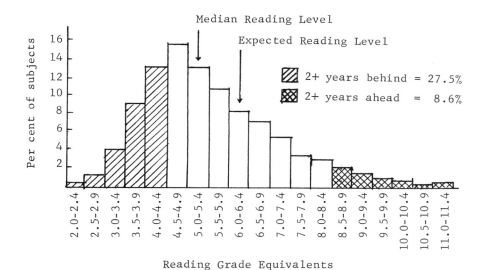

Grade 6.5
Reading Levels in Metropolis
(Stanford Test—1964)

Fig. 1. Reading levels for all sixth-grade children (except those in special classes for the retarded) in a large city in the Eastern United States. The data are based on 12,000 children. On the abscissa are plotted reading scores by half-year intervals, on the ordinate the percentage of the total sample scoring in each range.

Group intelligence tests administered to these children at the same time revealed a median I.Q. between 94 and 95. This may appeal to school personnel as a rationalization for the reading scores on the grounds that, had the children had the expected I.Q. median of 100, the theoretically constructed reading curve would be shifted well toward a more normal distribution. Before we buy this reassurance that all is well with the educational establishment, let us remember that the group I.Q. test requires reading for its comprehension; success with it no less than with the reading test is a function of the educational experience of the child. It would be more accurate to state that both group I.Q. and reading levels are depressed in contemporary American urban school populations, given the circumstances of education and of life for the children who reside in the gray areas of our cities.

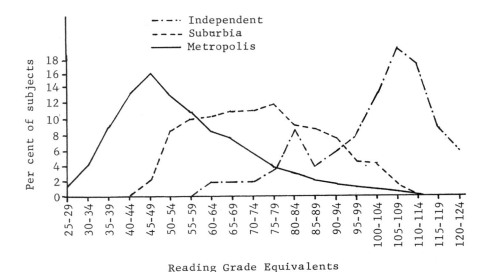

Reading Grade Equivalents

Fig. 2. Reading levels in 1964 for sixth-grade children in Metroplis, Suburbia, and Independent. Plot is as in Figure 1. Number of subjects in each sample: 12,000 for Metropolis, 8,000 for Suburbia, and 200 for independent. Expected mean based on national sample is 6.5 (i.e. 5 months into the sixth grade).

The epidemiologic significance of these data can be heightened by comparing them with those from other population groups. Figure 2 plots the reading scores for "Metropolis", for "Suburbia" (a county immediately outside Metropolis), and for children attending independent (that is, private) schools in Metropolis. So enormous are the differences that one could almost believe three different biological populations are represented here; yet what we know would indicate that the children of Metropolis have a potential not different from that of Suburbia[a] and, I would add, not substantially different from that of the independent schools[b]. If this be so, or even approximately so, then we have here in the difference between what the children of Metropolis do do and what they could do, a scathing indictment of the indifference of our cities to the education of their children.

Table 1 sets forth key reading parameters for the school populations of "Metropolis", "Suburbia", the independent schools, and "Clinicounty", a bedroom county (for exurbanite white-collar workers) that includes pockets of rural, largely Negro, poverty. If we focus our attention on the percentage of children more than

TABLE 1. Sixth-Grade Reading Levels by School System

| System | Test | Percentage Retarded | | Percentage Advanced |
		2 yr	1 yr	2 yr
Metropolis	Stan.	28	57	9
Clinicounty	Cali.	15	35	8
Suburbia	Iowa	3*	19	34
Independent	Stan.	0	1	82

*Because of the Iowa Scoring System, this figure is almost certainly an underestimate, by half or more, of the actual prevalence of children two or more years retarded in reading in Suburbia.

one year retarded in reading, Metropolis has failure rates two-thirds higher than Clinicounty, three times higher than Suburbia, and more than fifty times higher than the independent schools. Similar discrepancies obtain at the other end of the reading spectrum. Success rates, as measured by the percentages of children more than two years advanced in reading, are nine times higher in the independent schools than in Metropolis or Clinicounty and 2.4 times higher than in Suburbia.

Let us now turn to other demographic characteristics as a basis for comparative analysis of population groups. Rates by sex (for Clinicounty) reveal that the number of retarded readers among boys (19.5%) is more than twice as high as that for girls (9.0%), a finding consistent with other surveys of reading performance[5,6] and a point to which we shall return.

We have thus far examined rates by area of residence and by sex. What of rates by race? This question is not readily answerable for many urban school systems; for, although the schools may not be fully integrated, the records are; much, one suspects, to the relief of administrators when irate citizen groups raise questions about the adequacy of education for Negro children. The data from Clinicounty, however, did permit computation of rates by race.

Whereas 12% of the white children were two or more years retarded in reading, a failure rate alarming enough in itself, the corresponding figure for Negro children was 36%, three times as great! (Within each ethnic group, the male rate remains significantly higher than the female rate, 16.8% to 7.1% for whites and 42% to 26% for Negroes.) These figures become somewhat more explicable when we add the information that only 7% of the white families in Clini-county as against 62% of the Negro families fall into social class V, the very bottom of the economic heap.

SOURCES OF RETARDATION IN READING

Epidemiologic surveys employing a crude measure like group reading levels suffer from the inherent limitation that they treat by a common statistic cases that vary widely in the nature of the underlying pathology. We would not expect to learn much useful about the epidemology of infections if we studied the distribution of fever in a population without regard to its source. Yet this has been the common practice in respect to reading. It is not therefore surprising that competent investigators have been led to contrary conclusions about the role of handedness, heredity, perceptual handicap, and the like, when each has examined a heterogeneous sample of cases defined only by its reading performance.

TABLE 2. Provisional Classification: The Sources
of Reading Retardation

A. Sociopsychological factors

  1. Quantitative and qualitative defects in teaching
  2. Deficiencies in cognitive stimulation
  3. Deficiencies in motivation
    (a) Associated with social pathology
    (b) Associated with psychopathology ("emotional")

B. Psychophysiological factors

  1. General debility
  2. Sensory defects
  3. Intellectual defects
  4. Brain injury
  5. Specific (idiopathic) reading disability

PROVISIONAL CLASSIFICATION OF SOURCES
OF READING RETARDATION

To order our further inquiry, it is convenient to divide the sources of retarded reading into two major groups; the sociopsychological and psychophysiological, with full realization that this dichotomy is both arbitrary and inaccurate. Given the differential by social class of the complications of pregnancy and parturition, of the availability of adequate nutrition and medical care, one could equally well classify brain injury under the heading: sociophysiological. However, the axis of classification employed in Table 2 can provide a useful basis for a preliminary examination of the types of retarded readers.

SOCIOPSYCHOLOGICAL FACTORS

Defects in Teaching. We should not expect that a child who had not been taught would learn to read. Yet there are children in the United States who are late in beginning school, who attend irregularly, whose school year is foreshortened to conform to the farming season, and who therefore experience a significant loss of exposure to teaching. These are the children of sharecroppers and of migratory workers. Similar academic ills befall children of disorganized families who move from one tenement, and hence one school district, to another.

But even those urban or rural children of the poor who attend school more or less as required by law suffer a serious deficit in teaching. The schools they attend are likely to be more overcrowded, are more often staffed by less qualified teachers, are more beset by problems of discipline to the detriment to teaching time, and employ traditional methods of teaching that, however adequate they may be for the middle-class child, are highly inappropriate for the special educational needs of the disadvantaged. No less devastating is the pessimistic conviction of many teachers and many administrators that such children lack the necessary wherewithal to learn. This belief may be couched in terms of the restricted intellectual stimulation in the child's home or may be more nakedly racist in adherence to beliefs in biological inferiority. Whatever the source of the conviction, it influences the performance of the teacher, the expectations he sets for the child, and the ultimate attainment in the classroom. Without a direct challenge to these conventional beliefs, educational progress will not be possible.

Under the heading of teaching defects, most physicians will expect to hear some discussion of the "look-say" (whole word) method
versus phonics. Attacks on the look-say method have their fad;
they appeal to traditionalism and suggest a cheap and easy answer
to contemporary problems by returning to the ways of the good old
days. Such evidence as there is indicates that the average first
grader learns equally well by either method but somewhat faster
by look-say, whereas the potential dyslexic child may have his
disability magnified by exclusive reliance on the whole word method.
That the look-say primers have been full of drivel: "Here, Tip!
Run, Jane! Look, look, look!" (Damn, damn, damn!) is not inherent in the whole word method but must be attributed to the
vacuous authors of these non-books. Pending the accumulation of
definitive evidence based upon controlled studies,[c] we can only conclude that the excellence of the teacher and a class size small
enough for individualization of instruction are far more important
than the choice of method. An either-or formulation is in any event
absurd; a competent teacher should know the several ways of teaching
reading in order to capitalize on the ability profile of the particular
child. Nostalgia for the McGuffey reader and a "no nonsense" approach to education will not solve the reading problem.

Deficiencies in Cognitive Stimulation. Although the formal education of the child by definition begins when he enters school, there
has in fact been a quite extraordinary transformation in his mental
function during the first six years of life at home. From a largely
vegetative, only intermittently conscious newborn with a limited
repertoire of reflexes, he has become a self-conscious, speaking,
reasoning, and imaginative being. This developmental explosion
accompanies a tripling of brain weight and an uncountable proliferation of dendrites and synapses, but is in no sense a mere unfolding
of a process predetermined from within. How fast it happens and
how far it goes are, within limits, a direct function of the amount
and variety of patterned stimulation supplied by the environment[7]

We know that if a child does not hear language, he will not speak.
We tend to overlook the corollary proposition that if he is exposed
to a less-differentiated language experience, he will speak and
understand less well. The slum child has, on the average, had
less training in listening to sustained and grammatically complex
speech, had less exposure to the extensive vocabulary of our language, and had less reinforcement for his own verbal efforts. He
exhibits defects in auditory attention and perception, performs
less well on vocabulary tests (especially when challenged by abstract words), and is less responsive to verbal instructions in the
classroom[8,9]

Many inner-city children have never been more than a few blocks
from their home; the museums, symphony halls, even the zoos and
amusement parks of their communities are foreign territory to them.
Books, magazines, even newspapers are infrequent companions;
they are not often read to. Exercises with paper and pencil, puzzles,
and sedentary games with formal rules are uncommon. They have
been short-changed of experiences that, for other children, serve
to build concepts and set the ground for learning to learn.[10] Yet
their lives have, in no sense, been blank. Scrounging in the streets,
dodging cars for a game of stick ball, avoiding cops, defending
themselves from youthful and adult predators alike, they have had
to learn the complex arts of survival in the slums. In so doing,
they acquire behavior traits that <u>interfere actively</u> with the acquisition of the patterns required for success in the classroom. To
note that these children are different is not to convict them of being
defective. The figures from Metropolis make appallingly clear
their failure to learn <u>as they have been taught</u>. This, however, is
a failure of the teaching, not the children.[11]

<u>Deficiencies in Motivation</u>. Intelligence tests have been the best
available single predictors of academic success, but the highest
correlations obtained between I.Q. and grade averages have been
on the order of 0.5 and 0.6. Statistically, then, "intelligence" (or
whatever I.Q. tests measure) accounts at best for one-quarter to
one-third of the variance in academic performance. This is hardly
surprising; we all recognize it when we choose students, house
officers, and colleagues by estimating their motivation in addition
to their talent. Motivation, like intelligence, is shaped by the environment; in this shaping, both social class values and idiosyncratic life experiences play a role.

When parents fail to reinforce a child for good school performance
or to chastise him for academic misbehavior; when they convey a
belief that school success bears little relationship to ultimate occu-
pational attainment; when they share with the child a view of school
authorities as repressive agents employed by a society hostile to
their values, they provide little support for the development of
achievement motivation. The beliefs on which these behaviors are
predicted are not myths; they are constructed from the social
reality of the slum dweller. These beliefs may lead--indeed, they
do lead--to the self-perpetuation of defeat and alienation, but that
does not make them untrue. The Negro high-school graduate is
more often unemployed and, when employed, earns less than the
white graduate. Unemployment rates for young workers, white
and Negro, are disproportionately high; unchecked, the crisis will
grow worse as population trends lead to an increase in this age
group.[12] The examples of success that sustained previous genera-

tions of immigrants from abroad have been replaced by examples of
failure in homes and on street corners that discourage all but the
hardiest of today's domestic immigrants from farm and mine. For
this, the solution will not lie in the schools but in the creation of
job opportunities with equal access to all.

However, teacher attitudes may serve to consolidate a conviction of
the hopelessness of it all. Educators are satisfied with less from the
lower-class child because they expect less; their expectations form
part of the social field that molds the child and determines, in part,
what he does. He arrives at school ill-prepared; his initial poor
performance leads to "streaming" in low-ability sections; the limited
teaching further retards his learning; he completes his "education"
less able than others; ironically, the terminal product is used to
justify the system.[13] But is it not apparent that the operation of the
system has guaranteed fulfilment of the prophecy? ·Schiffman[14] in
a study of 84 elementary school children referred for placement in
classes for "slow learners" because of academic failure, found that
78% had Wechsler performance quotients in the average or better
range; yet only 7% of their teachers identified them as other than
dull and only 14% of their parents recognized their potential. Need
it suprise us that 86% of the children rated themselves as dull or
defective? With such a self-image, affirmed at school and at home,
what shall it profit a child to try?

With or without social disadvantage, though all too commonly associated with it, individual psychopathology is a frequent concomitant of retardation in reading. On the one hand, school difficulties
are among the major presenting complaints at every psychiatric
clinic for children; on the other, physicians who have studied retarded readers have uniformly noted a high association with
emotional disturbance.[15,18] The correlation with antecedent family
pathology[18] indicates that, in a substantial number of cases, the
psychiatric disorder is the source of the reading problem. No
single pattern of psychopathology is characteristic; among the more
common patterns are: anxiety states that preclude attention to academic tasks; preoccupation with fantasy such that the child is
psychologically absent from class; passive-aggressive syndromes
in which resistance to parental coercion is subtly executed by a
hapless failure to learn; low self-esteem based upon identification
with an inadequate parent; schizophrenic thought pathology in which
letters and words become invested with idiosyncratic meanings.
Reading failure is a final common pathway for the expression of a
multiplicity of antecedent disruptions in learning.

At the same time, it must be recognized that the reading difficulty
is in itself a potent source of emotional distress. Embarrassed by
fumbling recitations before his peers, cajoled, implored, or bullied

by his parents and his teachers to do what he cannot, the retarded
reader is at first disturbed and finally despondent about himself.
His ineptness in reading penalizes him in all subjects and leads to
his misidentification as a dullard. With class exercises conducted
in what for him is a foreign language, he turns to other diversions,
only to be chastised for disruptive behavior. However begun, the
psychiatric disturbance and the reading disability are mutually reinforcing in the absence of effective intervention. For such children,
psychiatric treatment may be necessary before response to remedial
techniques can be expected.[19]

PSYCHOPHYSIOLOGICAL SOURCES

   The psychophysiological sources of reading reterdation can be
divided into five major categories: general debility, sensory defects,
intellectual defects, brain injury, and idiopathic or specific reading
disability. Overlap and multiple conjunction of causes are common.
   General Debility. Discussions of reading retardation do not list
general debility among its causes but this is a serious oversight.
The child who is chronically malnourished and the one who is
chronically ill can hardly be expected to perform adequately in
school. I mention them here only to stress the importance of a
thorough pediatric examination as the first step in the evaluation
of any child with a learning failure.
   Sensory Defects. Defects in seeing and hearing impede information transmission over the primary channels whose integration is
required for reading. Visual defect leads to reading handicap only
when acuity is reduced by half or more[20] With respect to hearing,
however, there is increasing evidence that children with normal
pure tone auditory thresholds may nonetheless suffer from perceptual
handicaps in discriminating speech sounds[21] and from defective
intersensory integration, as in the task of converting auditory to
visual signals,[22] both disorders being associated with poor reading.
These deficits may stem from central nervous system pathology or
from faulty auditory experience. In either case, corrective training
to minimize this source of difficulty would appear logical though
the effectiveness of such training remains to be established.
   Intellectual Defects. Intellectual defect can be expected to limit
reading achievement as a function of its severity. The assessment
of this factor requires individual clinical examination by a competent
psychologist and cannot be based upon group testing. The prognosis
will, of course, vary with the nature of the underlying disorder as
well as the degree of mental deficiency. However, even moderately

retarded children can learn to read enough to transact the ordinary business of life, if teaching methods take into account the learning characteristics of the defective child.

Brain Injury. Children with chronic brain syndromes are at high risk for learning disabilities, though there is no simple one-to-one relationship between amount or locus of damage and ultimate academic achievement[23] Whether the category: "brain injury" or its various extensions, "minimal cerebral dysfunction", "diffuse brain damage", etc., are useful concepts has been challenged,[24] but the clinician should be alerted to the search for learning problems and to the importance of special teaching techniques for children with borderline as well as overt neurological findings. Occasional children with brain tissue damage sufficient to result in mental deficiency of moderate degree are nonetheless able, in the elementary grades, to attain above average fluency in oral reading, although their comprehension of what they have read is minimal. Such instances are instructive in several respects. They serve to remind us of the variability of the clinical patterns observed in brain-injured children; they indicate the complex nature of the reading process, in which word recognition and sentence comprehension are separable skills; they emphasize the importance of a thorough reading analysis in complement to a comprehensive pediatric assessment in the work-up of each case of reading retardation.

Specific Reading Disability. We turn now to the important residual category of specific reading disability also known as congenital word blindness,[25] primary reading retardation,[26] and developmental dyslexia.[27] The adjective "specific" calls attention both to the circumscribed nature of the disability and to our ignorance of its cause. Operationally, specific reading disability may be defined as the failure to learn to read with normal proficiency despite conventional instruction, a culturally adequate home, proper motivation, intact senses, normal intelligence, and freedom from gross neurologic defect. Hinshelwood's statement,[28] is not less relevant today than when it was written in 1902: "It is a matter of the highest importance to recognize the cause and the true nature of this difficulty in learning to read which is experienced by these children, otherwise they may be harshly treated as imbeciles or incorrigibles, and either neglected or punished for a defect for which they are in no wise responsible."

There are no reliable data on which to base a secure estimate of the prevalence of specific reading disability; such surveys as exist record only the extent of retardation in reading on group tests without differentiation as to cause. Clinical reports indicate a much higher rate of occurrence among boys, the male/female ratio generally exceeding 4 to 1.[27] This disproportion is similar to, but

higher than, the surplus of boys among retarded readers from all
causes, among children designated as academically backward,[5] and
among children referred to psychiatric clinics.[29] Some have sought
to explain these figures on the grounds of greater cultural pressure
upon boys for academic success; this may account for some differential in rates of identification in so far as standards for boys may
be more exacting. But it is noteworthy that boys are in general
slower to acquire verbal facility and are more prone to exhibit behaviors in the early school grades that teachers label "immature".
It would seem more parsimonious to relate these disproportions to
the greater biological vulnerability of the male to a wide variety of
ills; from the moment of conception onwards, there is a highly
significant differential in morbidity and mortality between the
sexes, such that an original surplus of males is converted to its
opposite by the time adulthood is attained.[30,31]

Many authorities have called to attention, as though they were
diagnostic of specific reading disability, such phenomena as: re-
versals (was for saw, gril for girl), mirror writing, confusion of
certain letters (b, d, p, q, g), omitted or added words, perseverations,
skipped or repeated lines, and the like. These very same errors
occur as the normal child learns to read; what distinguishes the
dyslexic is the frequency and persistence of these errors well beyond the time at which they have become uncommon in the normal.

The failure of many investigators to adhere to defined criteria
for the diagnosis and to recognize the importance of the age variable accounts for some of the contradictory findings reported in the
literature. It does seem that sinistrality and, more especially,
delayed or inconsistent laterality occur more often among dyslexics
(though many are typical dextrals), but it is quite another matter to
suggest that "incomplete cerebral dominance" accounts for the
reading problem. The determination of laterality is not so simple
a matter as once thought[32] nor is "brainedness" so readily to be
inferred from handedness.[33] The apparent association between delayed establishment of laterality and the reading defect seems more
probably related to a common underlying developmental antecedent
than as cause and effect. The confusion about the proportion of
dyslexics with perceptual deficts takes on some order when it is
realized that perceptual handicaps are more often found in younger
than in older dyslexics.[34] This change with age may reflect the
developmental course of perception.[35] The older child may no longer
exhibit the handicap which may have been prominent at a critical
stage in the learning process and have contributed to the failure to
learn to read.

Etiologic studies have also led to apparently contradictory conclusions. Kawi and Pasamanick[36] have presented evidence of a

much greater frequency of pregnancy complications and premature births in the obstetrical histories of retarded readers than those of control cases. The differences are well beyond chance expectancy. However, the index cases were selected from school records because of retarded reading and screened only for an I. Q. above 81. It seems probable that cases with a variety of reading disorders were included, the proportion of specific dyslexia being unknown. On the other hand, many clinicians have been impressed with the regularity with which a history of reading difficulty is obtained from the parents and collateral relatives of children with specific reading disability. In the most comprehensive study of its kind, Hallgren[37] concluded that the data from a genetic survey of 276 cases support a dominant mode of inheritance.

We are left with the unanswered question of the nature of the defect, even if we accept the proposition that it is biological. Critchley supposes it to be due to "specific cerebral immaturity", but adds that he doubts the existence of "a structural lesion recognizable by present day techniques".[38] Geschwind[39] has advanced the notion that there is "delayed maturation of the angular gyrus region, probably bilaterally". From the evolutionary standpoint, this region is not recognizable in the macaque and is only imperfectly developed in the higher apes. The human inferior parietal lobule (including the angular and supramarginal gyri) matures very late cytoarchitectonically, often not until late childhood.[40] Geschwind argues that, since lesions of the angular gyrus in the adult result in word blindness, delay in its development might account for specific reading disability in childhood. Against this thesis is the opinion of other neurologists that pure word blindness is neither so "pure" nor so consistently associated with specific lesions as classical doctrine alleges. Autopsy material being unavailable, the argument rests upon its plausibility and the way the clinical evidence is evaluated.

Problems of diagnosis, treatment, and outcome are the topics of Dr. Klapper's paper and for that reason will not be further considered here.

THE DEVELOPMENT OF READING SKILL: A PEDIATRIC ACTION PROGRAM

The evidence marshaled in this paper has, I trust, persuaded you of the integral relationship between reading and intellectual development, of the appalling extent of retardation in reading among American school children, of the multiple sources of interference to the acquisition of literacy, and of the relevance of the

foregoing to the pediatrician's role in the maintenance of health and
the correction of disability. Permit me, in my concluding remarks,
to outline the areas in which the informed pediatrician, as professional and citizen, has the opportunity and the responsibility to
provide leadership for social action to promote the healthy development of children. Those areas, as I see them, are (a) maternal
and child health programs, (b) health and education programs for
the preschool child, and (c) revised curricula and classroom conditions throughout the years of public schooling.

Maternal and Child Health Programs. At the level of primary
prevention, there is a clear need for comprehensive maternal and
child health programs to diminish the complications of pregnancy,
parturition, and the neonatal period that lead to insult to the central
nervous system of the infant.[41] Malnutrition, poor hygiene, and
inadequate medical care are among the causal factors subject to
control if we but have the determination to apply present knowledge
and resources.[42-44] Current federal legislation provides us with
a splendid opportunity for progress but money and initiative from
Washington alone will not suffice to guarantee quality of services.
Pediatricians in every community will have to participate in the
planning and the execution of new and imaginative programs. More
is needed than the customary 3-minute-per-child schedule of traditional health department well-baby clinics, more than the mere
advertisement to the community of their existence. Medical interest
will have to extend beyond vaccinations and cursory physical examinations to sensitive concern with cognitive as well as physical development; notices of clinic hours must be augmented by an active
recruitment of the families not now making use of these services.
The index patient may be the pregnant woman or the infant but the
physician's curiosity must extend from them to the welfare of all
members of the family unit. Special programs will be necessary
for mothers at highest risk: the unmarried, the very young and the
old, the Negro, the mother with prior history of obstetrical difficulty. It should not be tolerated that the pregnant high school
student is merely dismissed from school; health care and provision
for supplementary education are essential. In these tasks, medical
specialists and generalists, nurses, social workers, health educators, nutritionists, and others will have to function as a team if the
disadvantaged family is to be rehabilitated. The call for pediatric
leadership is not an appeal to establish hegemony but rather a re-
minder of the proudest tradition in pediatrics: its concern with prevention.

Preschool Programs. The emphasis on preschool enrichment via
Project Head Start, directed by an eminent Fellow of this Academy,
Dr. Julius Richmond, opens the vista of large-scale efforts to

foster early cognitive development. Pilot studies indicate that inner-
city children exposed to nursery enrichment programs function
more effectively than their peers when they enter first grade. For
the first time, funds are available to extend this opportunity to
several hundred thousand children. Funds, though necessary, are
not sufficient to ensure quality. Thought and effort will have to be
devoted to curricula to promote intellectual growth rather than
baby-sitting services. The shortage of professional personnel requires that imaginative use be made of talent wherever it exists in
the community without getting hung up on formal criteria created
to preserve the educational power structure and without opening the
doors to politically controlled job handouts. If the children are to
be served with greatest effect, there must be parallel parent-
education programs couched in terms that make sense to urban
slum-dwellers. They love their children no less than we; what
they need to understand is how they can help their children to
achieve the goals they long for but see as unattainable. The preschool program will serve as a catchment area for pediatric identification of medical defects and the mobilization of corrective measures. If these are to be more than the mere compilation of records,
vigorous pediatric procedures for follow-up together with the establishment of medical responsibility will be required.

Improved School Programs. If preschool enrichment is not augmented by substantial revision of traditional school services, there
is little reason to anticipate significant long-run benefit. None of
us would expect a good diet at the age of 3 to protect against malnutrition at 6. The brain requires alimentation both biological and
psychological at each stage of the life cycle; early nourishment is
necessary but not sufficient to guarantee its development. The
precedent-shattering federal aid-to-education bill recognizes for
the first time a national responsibility to improve the quality of
education; the funds made available are but a token of what will be
required ultimately. If we allow them to be used to supplant state
funds or merely to be spread thinly throughout the system, no
palpable changes will result. The best teachers must be attracted
to slum area schools; class size must be reduced to private school
levels: 15 to 20 pupils per class; curricula must be modified.
School programs will have to be extended to include after-school
tutoring and recreational activities. What I am emphasizing is
capital investment in human renewal, the very principle that has
paid off so handsomely in our industrial enterprise. The proposals
will not be welcomed by those school boards and those professional
educators threatened by any change in the status quo. The pediatrician can play a significant role as citizen in mobilizing community
support for the intent of this legislation.

I would urge upon you one final task. Most school systems introduce remedial reading instruction at the third grade or later (if they have it at all). The justification is one of economy. Of those children not reading at the end of first grade, perhaps half manage to pass muster by the end of the second grade, a few more of the remainder learn to read by standard instruction by the end of the third grade. These children are the "late bloomers", youngsters who, for unknown reasons, acquire late, but do acquire, the capacity to profit from conventional teaching. By waiting till the third grade, the school system has spared itself the cost of extra teaching for children who were going to make it on their own. This "economy" however, must be balanced against the cost to those children who, by the third grade, are deeply imprisoned in faulty learning habits, have become convinced of their ineptness, and now respond poorly to any but the most expert individual clinical instruction. Surely, this country can afford to do better by its children. It is essential that we identify the child who is not beginning to read by the second semester of the first grade, institute a careful diagnostic study, and provide the appropriate remedial education. If this means that we will be giving extra help to a child not in need of it for each child who requires it, then I urge that we do so. The surplus child will not be harmed and may be benefited; the dyslexic child will be reached at a time when the chance of success is greatest. We would not hear of delaying therapy for rheumatic fever because not every patient incurs a valvulitis; we would not consider deferring laparotomy for a suspected appendicitis because diagnosis is imprecise and not every case perforates; how then can we tolerate a view that is equivalent to saying: Let us make certain the child cannot read and is really in trouble before we give him extra help? An effective program for early identification and treatment might even produce long-run savings if we take into account the cost of prolonged treatment and ultimate losses in the economic productivity of the handicapped readers. But my argument places no weight on such matters. Where the healthy development of children is concerned, financial considerations are simply irrelevant.

If this call to political action on behalf of children seems out of keeping with your conception of a physician's role, let me recall to you the words of Dr. Benjamin Rush, signer of the Declaration of Independence and the first American psychiatrist. In his final lecture to medical students,[45] he placed prominent among the duties of a physician: "a regard to the interests of your country. The education of a physician gives him a peculiar insight into the principles of many useful arts, and the practice of physic favors his opportunities of doing good, by diffusing knowledge of all kinds. ... In modern times and in free governments, they [physicians] should disdain an ignoble silence upon public subjects. The history of the

American Revolution has rescued physic from its former slavish
rank in society. For the honor of our profession it should be recorded, that some of the most intelligent and useful characters,
both in the cabinet and the field, during the late war, have been
physicians. "

Let it be said of us that we were among the most intelligent and
useful characters, both in the cabinet and the field, in the late war
against poverty by helping to create a healthy and a literate population.

NOTES

a. To the extent that the slum dwellers of Metropolis suffer a
heavier burden of C.N.S. injury stemming from social-class-
related complications of pregnancy, parturition, and early life (see
later sections of this paper), we encounter a true biological difference; but one that is far less in magnitude than that evident in the
reading figures and one that is preventable by the vigorous application of health and welfare measures. It has been argued that assortative migration and assortative mating have engendered substantial hereditary differences between these populations. This remains to the present an hypothesis whose validation would require
that differences in educational performance persist even after
equality of life experience has been afforded the less privileged
group. The repeated demonstration of I.Q. gains after special
programs of educational enrichment for slum children makes
equally tenable the view that the greatest part (if not all) of the
class-related variance in school performance is attributable to
differences in experience. At the least, this viewpoint has the
heuristic advantage that it suggests, at one and the same time, a
possible remedy for the educational deficiency and a test of validity
for both hypotheses.

b. Independent schools routinely employ entrance tests; to the extent that these tests screen out slow-learning and handicapped
children, the admitted group will be superior to the general population of children.

c. There is some early evidence that the Initial Teaching Alphabet,
employing 43 symbols, may be a superior method for teaching reading in the early elementary grades. The augmented alphabet allows
a one-to-one correspondence between sound and symbol.

REFERENCES

1. Critchley, M. The evolution of man's capacity for language. In S. Tax (ed.), The Evolution of Man, Vol. II. Chicago: University of Chicago Press, 1960.
2. Gray, W. S. The Teaching of Reading and Writing Pairs. Unesco, 1956, p. 29.
3. Gray, W. S. The Teaching of Reading (Burton Lecture). Cambridge, Massachusetts: Harvard University Press, 1957, p. 2.
4. Millman, J., and Linlof, J. The comparability of fifth grade norms of the California Iowa and Metropolitan achievement tests. J. Educ. Meas., 1:135, 1964.
5. Bentzen, F. Sex ratios in learning and behavior disorders. Amer. J. Orthopsychiat., 33:92, 1963.
6. Miller, A. D., Margolin, J. B., and Yolles, S. F. Epidemiology of reading disabilities. Amer. J. Pub. Health, 47:1250, 1957.
7. Hunt, J. McV. Intelligence and Experience. New York: Ronald Press, 1961.
8. John, V. The intellectual development of slum children. Amer. J. Orthopsychiat., 33:813, 1963.
9. Deutsch, M. The role of social class in language development and cognition. Amer. J. Orthopsychiat., 35:78, 1965.
10. Harlow, H. F. The formation of learning sets. Psychol. Rev., 56:51, 1949.
11. Gordon, E. A review of programs of compensatory education. Amer. J. Orthopsychiat., 35:640, 1965.
12. Freedman, M. Perspectives in youth employment. Children 12:75, 1965.
13. Wilson, A. B. Social stratification and academic achievement. In A. H. Passow (ed.), Education in Depressed Areas. New York: Columbia University Press, 1963.
14. Schiffman, G. Personal communication.
15. Missildine, W. H. The emotional background of thirty children with reading disability. Nerv. Child., 5:263, 1946.
16. Fabian, A. A. Clinical and experimental studies of school children who are retarded in reading. Quart. J. Child Behavior, 3:15, 1951.
17. Blanchard, P. Psychogenic factors in some cases of reading disability. Amer. J. Orthopsychiat., 5:361, 1935.
18. Ingram, T. T. S., and Reid, J. F. Developmental aphasia observed in a department of child psychiatry. Arch. Dis. Child., 31:161, 156.

19. Eisenberg, L.   Office evaluation of specific reading disability. Pediatrics, 23:997, 1959.
20. Irvine, R.   An ocular policy for public schools.   Amer. J. Ophthal., 24:779, 1941.
21. Goetzinger, C. P., Dirks, D. D., and Baer, C. J. Auditory discrimination and visual perception in good and poor readers. J. Otol. Rhinol. Larying., 69:121, 1960.
22. Birch, H. G., and Belmont, L.   Audiovisual integration in normal and retarded readers. Amer. J. Orthopsychiat., 34:852, 1964.
23. Eisenberg. L.   Behavioral manifestations of cerebral damage in childhood. In Birch H. G. (ed.), Brain Damage in Childhood. Baltimore: Williams & Wilkins, 1964.
24. Herbert, M.   The concept and testing of brain-damage in children: A review. J. Child Psychol. Psychiat., 5:197, 1964.
25. Morgan, W. P. A case of congenital word blindness.   Brit. Med. J., 2:1378, 1896.
26. Rabinovitch, R. D., Drew, A. L. DeJong, R. N., Ingram, W., and Withey, L.   A research approach to reading retardation. Research Publ., A. Nerv. Ment. Dis. Proc., 34:363, 1954.
27. Critchley, M.   Developmental Dyslexia.   London: Heineman, 1964.
28. Hinshelwood., J.   Cited in Critchley; see Reference 1.
29. Bahn, A., Chandler, C., and Eisenberg, L. Diagnostic and demographic characteristics of patients seen in outpatient clinics for an entire state. Amer. J. Psychiat., 117:769, 1961.
30. Childs, B.   Genetic origin of some sex differences among human beings. Pediatrics, 35:798, 1965.
31. Washburn, T. C., Medearis, D. N., and Childs, B.   Sex differences in susceptibility to infections. Pediatrics, 35:57, 1965.
32. Benton, A. L.   Right-Left Discrimination and Finger-Localization: Development and Pathology. New York: Hoeber, 1959.
33. Mountcastle, V. B. (ed.).   Interhemispheric Relations and Cerebral Dominance. Baltimore: Johns Hopkins Press, 1962.
34. Benton, A. L.   Dyslexia in relation to form perception and directional sense. In J. Money (ed.), Reading Disability. Baltimore: Johns Hopkins Press, 1962.
35. Birch, H. G. and Belmont, L.   Audio-visual integration, intelligence and reading ability in school children. Percept. Motor Skills, 20:295, 1965.
36. Kawi, A. A., and Pasamanick, B.   Prenatal and paranatal factors in the development of childhood reading disorders. Monogr. Soc. Res. Child Develop., 24: No. 4, 1-80, 1959.

37. Hallgren, B. Specific dyslexia: A clinical and genetic study.
    Acta Psychiat. Neurol. , Suppl. 65, 1950.
38. Critchley, M. See Reference 1.
39. Geschwind, N. Disconnection syndromes in animals and man.
    Brain, 88:237, 1965.
40. Yakolev, P. Cited in Geschwind, Reference 39.
41. Eisenberg. , L. Preventive pediatrics. Pediatrics, 30:815,
    1962.
42. Pasamanick, B. Socioeconomic status: Some precursors of
    neuropsychiatric disorder. Amer. J. Orthopsychiat. , 26:594,
    1956.
43. Scrimshaw, N.S. , and Behar, M. Malnutrition in underde-
    veloped countries. New England J. Med. , 272:137, 193, 1965.
44. Cravioto, J. , and Robles, B. Selected Writings. D. D. Runes
    (ed.), New York: Philosophical Library, 1947, p. 311.
45. Rush, B., Selected Writings. D. D. Runes (ed.). New York:
    Philosophical Library, 1947, p. 311.

A NOTE ON THE RELATION OF READING FAILURE TO PEER-GROUP STATUS IN URBAN GHETTOS

by William Labov and Clarence Robins

For the past several years, we have been studying certain conflicts between the vernacular of the urban ghettos and schoolroom English, especially in relation to reading failure.[1] We work primarily with peer groups of Negro boys within the culture of the street, since we believe that the major controls upon language are exerted by these groups rather than the school or the home. Our research has recently revealed a sharp and striking relationship between participation in this street culture and reading failure. The pattern is so clear and plainly so important in understanding the educational problems of ghetto areas, that we are sending this brief note to all those who have shown interest in our progress reports.

The Populations Concerned. In the summer of 1965, we interviewed a sample of 75 Negro boys, age 10 to 12 years, in a geographically random sample of "Vacation Day Camps" in Harlem. Boys had to be enrolled by their parents in these recreational programs, held in schoolyards and playgrounds, so that there was a bias of selection for children from intact families with support for educational goals. Nevertheless, we found that the majority of these 10-to-12-year-olds had serious difficulty in reading aloud such second and third grade sentences as

Now I read and write better than Alfred does.

When I passed by, I read the sign.

In August of 1965, we turned to the study of groups of boys in their natural associations on the streets of South Central Harlem. Our normal method of work was to interview a few individuals, locate their peer group and become acquainted with it; we then studied the language of the peer group in spontaneous interaction, and recorded the remaining individuals in face-to-face interviews.

Reprinted by permission from The Record—Teachers College 70:5.395-405 (February 1969).

We used this approach first in studying two pre-adolescent groups
in a low-income project, the "Thunderbirds" and the "Aces",
against the general population of the project. We then began the
study of the major adolescent groups that dominated the tenement
areas from 110th Street to 118th Street between Sixth and Eighth
Avenues. One of our staff members, Mr. John Lewis, acted as a
participant-observer in the area. With his help, we followed two
major adolescent groups, each composed of many subgroups, for
two years. These groups were known as the "Cobras" and the
"Jets".[2]

Our knowledge of the social structure, history, activities, and
value systems of these groups is an essential aspect of the finding
to be presented in this note. We traced the history of group relations and explored the value systems through individual face-to-face
interviews, meetings with small groups of two or three close friends,
and group sessions with six to twelve boys. In all these sessions,
involving the most excited physical and verbal interaction, each
person's statements and ideas were recorded on a separate track
from a microphone several inches away from his mouth. We also
studied group behavior in various field trips with the boys, and recorded their interaction en route. Most importantly, our participant-
observer saw the boys every day on the streets, and met with them
in their hang-outs and our "club-house". He was present at several
moments of crisis when fighting was about to break out between the
two major groups.

We also interviewed a number of isolated individuals in the same
tenement areas, who were definitely not members of these groups,
but who often knew about them. We are able then to assert that we
reached all the major "named" groups in the area, although we did
not have a representative sample of all adolescent boys. In the
same areas we completed a stratified random sample of 100 adults,
but only in the low-income projects did we relate our groups quanti-
tively to the total population.[3]

The Street Groups. The larger associations which bear the names
"Jets" or "Cobras" are known to the boys as "clubs". They are not
to be confused with the groups which are organized within recreation
centers by adults, which are also called "clubs" and sometimes overlap in membership. The groups we studied are initiated by the boys
themselves, and are disapproved of by the adults in the neighborhood.[4]

The structure and value systems of these groups are partly in-
herited from the period of gang violence of the 1940's and 1950's.
The frequency of group fighting, however, is comparatively low.
These are not "gangs" in the sense of groups with frequently fight
as a unit. Nevertheless, a major source of prestige for the leaders

is skill in fighting, and individual fights are very common. The
inter-group conflicts which do occur are the most important sources
of group cohesion; they become a fixed part of the mythology and
ideology of the group, and the obligation to support one's fellow
members in a group fight is strongly felt by many members.

The general value systems of these groups conform to the lower-
class value pattern which has been described by Walter B. Miller.[5]
The focal concerns of the groups are toughness, smartness, trouble, excitement, autonomy, and fate. Intelligence or smartness is
used and valued as a means of manipulating others, rather than a
means of obtaining information or solving abstract problems. The
specific values of the Negro nationalist movement are reflected in
some groups more than others. The members of the "Cobras",
within the period that we worked with them, moved from a moderately nationalist position to deep involvement with the militant
Muslim religion and its complex ideology.[6] This ideology involved
the members in a strong interest in learning and abstract knowledge;
but the general value systems of all the groups were such that
school learning was seen as hostile, distant, and essentially irrelevant.

The groups have a formal structure which may include four officers: president, vice president, prime minister and war lord.
Junior organizations are often formed by the appointment of a
younger brother of an officer to a leading position among the 10-to-
13-year-olds. However, this formal structure can be misleading.
The day-to-day activities of the boys[7] are in smaller, informal
hang-out groups, determined by geography and age; an individual's
association with the larger group is often a matter of formal definition of his identity more than anything else.[8] Yet the ultimate sanc-
tion of the larger group and its fighting role is often referred to.

Sources of prestige within the group are physical size, toughness,
courage and skill in fighting; skill with language in ritual insults,
verbal routines with girls, singing, jokes and storytelling; knowledge of nationalist lore; skill and boldness in stealing; experience
in reform schools; and connections with family members or others
which provide reputation, money, hang-outs, marijuana, or other
material goods. Success in school is irrelevant to prestige within
the group, and reading is rarely if ever used outside of school.[9]

Group Membership. Full participation in the group consists of
endorsement of this set of values, and acceptance of a set of personal obligations to others within the same environment and value
system. The criterion of formal membership ("you are a Jet" or
"you are not a Jet") is often disputed. A few individuals want to be
members and are rejected; others could easily be members but do
not care to. Full membership, as we define it, means that the indi-

vidual is thoroughly involved with the values and activities of the group, and is defined as a member both by himself and by others. If some but not all of these criteria are fulfilled, we term the individual a "marginal member". The clearest evidence for full membership as against marginal status is provided by the symmetrical relations in a sociometric diagram.[10] If an individual on the outskirts of the group wants to be a member, yet is prevented by the influence of other environments (family, school) and other value systems, he is classed with other non-members. In each area there are "social groups" which are strongly influenced by adult organizations: we do not include membership in such groups in the category of membership which we are studying.

It has been shown in many similar situations that group membership is a function of age.[11] Boys 8-to-9 years old are definitely outsiders for the groups we are studying, and they have only a vague knowledge of group activities. Membership is strongest in the 13-to-15-year-old range, and falls off rapidly in the later teens. A few 18-or-19-year-old boys act as seniors, especially if younger brothers are serving as officers, but as a rule boys drift off into different activities.

It is difficult to estimate the percentage of boys who are full participants in the street culture. However, in the one 13-story low-income project which we studied intensively,[12] there were 22 boys 10-to-12 years old. Their relationships to the major peer group, the "Thunderbirds", were as follows:

members	marginal members	non-members
12	3	7

Our general experience would indicate that 50 to 60 per cent of the boys in the age range 10-to-16 are full participants in the street culture we are studying here.

Reading Records. In all of our individual interviews, we used a number of special reading tests developed to yield specific information on the vernacular phonology and grammar.[13] However, the most direct evidence for reading performance in schools is obtained from the Metropolitan Achievement Test given every year in the New York City Schools. With the help of the New York City Board of Education, we were able to study recently the academic records of 75 pre-adolescent and adolescent boys with whom we had worked in the years 1965 to 1967. The substance of this report is the correlation between the Metropolitan Achievement Reading Test and group membership.

Figure 1 shows the correlation between grade level and reading achievement for 32 boys we interviewed in the 110th-120th Street

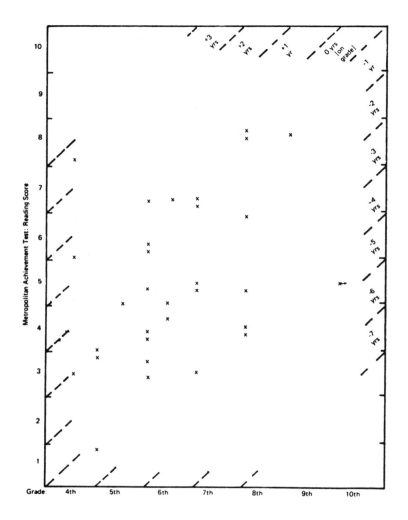

Fig. 1. Grade and reading achievement for 32 non-members of
street groups in South Central Harlem.

area who are not members of the street culture, or whose group status is unknown (from the Vacation Day Camp series). The horizontal
axis is grade level at the time of the test; the vertical axis the Metropolitan Achievement Test score. Each individual's score and grade
are indicated by the location of an x. The diagonal lines group together
those who are reading on grade level [0]; one to three years above
grade level [+3] - [+1]; or one to six years behind grade level
[-1] - [-6]. As one would expect, there are a good many boys who

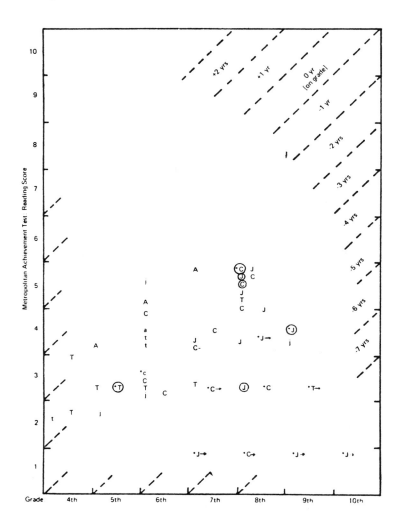

Fig. 2. Grade and reading achievement for 43 members of street groups in South Central Harlem.

T, t = Thunderbirds
A, a = Aces
C, c = Cobras
J, j = Jets
other symbols: see text

are two years behind grade, which is average in New York City, but there are also quite a few on grade and some ahead of grade level. Eleven of the 32 boys are on grade or above. The general

direction of the pattern is upward, indicating that learning is taking
place.

Figure 2 shows the same relationships for 43 boys who are members or marginal members of street groups in South Central Harlem. Each individual is represented by a letter symbolizing the
group of which he is a member or to which he is most closely related. Upper case letters are full members, and lower case marginal members. The overall pattern in entirely different from
Figure 1: no one is reading above grade, only one boy reading on
grade, and the great majority are three or more years behind.
Moreover, there are no boys who are reading above the fifth grade
level, no matter what grade they are in. At each grade, the reading achievement for these boys forms a lower, more compact group
than for the same grade in Figure 1. The close concentration of
boys in the eighth grade below the fifth grade level shows a limitation on achievement which is quite striking. On the whole, Figure
2 shows very little learning as compared to Figure 1.[14]

The lower achievement of group members does not indicate overall deficiency in verbal skills. Many of these boys are proficient
at a wide range of verbal skills appropriate for group activity: the
verbal leaders are indicated by circles in Figure 2. While several
are clustered near the highest point of achievement, there are other
verbal leaders near the bottom of the diagram.

These findings are merely preliminary to our main body of correlations; we will shortly be able to provide more detailed data on
a larger sample. There are a total of 170 boys whose reading
abilities and language scores have been studied, and we will be able
to correlate reading skill with many other factors besides membership in the street culture. However, the patterns revealed by
Figures 1 and 2 are so striking that we thought all those interested
in the problem should be aware of them as soon as possible.

What Is To Be Done? The overall view given by Figure 3
strongly reinforces our view that the major problem responsible
for reading failure is a cultural conflict. The school environment
and school values are plainly not influencing the boys firmly
grounded in street culture. The group which does show learning
contains a large percentage of boys who do not fit in with street
culture--who reject it or are rejected by it. For the majority,
Figure 3 confirms indirect evidence that teachers in the city schools
have little ability to reward or punish members of the street culture, or to motivate learning by any means.

The usual statistics on reading achievement in urban ghettos are
alarming, but they do not reveal the full extent of reading failure.
Research inside the schools cannot discriminate membership in
the street culture from non-membership, and educators are there-

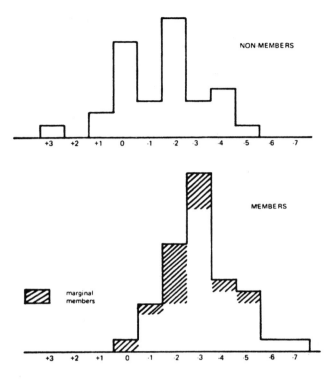

Fig. 3. Distribution of non-members, marginal members and members of street culture by years behind grade.

fore not aware of the full extent of the cultural barrier between them and their students.

It should be understood that the educational goals of the adult Negro community are the same as that of our society as a whole. Our subjective evaluation tests, for example, show that adults in Harlem are almost unanimous in their norms of correct speech and the goals for language teaching in school. Many of the members of the street culture gradually break away and acquire these adult norms in their twenties. However, these norms are of little value for those who do not have the skills to put them into effect.

The reading failure that we have documented here is typical of other performance on the academic records. The pattern of failure is so widespread, in many urban areas, that one cannot hold respon- sible any one system, school or teacher. The majority of these boys have not learned to read well enough to use reading as a tool for further learning. For many of them, there is no realistic possibility

of graduating from high school and acquiring the skills needed for
the job market. In this particular note we are dealing only with the
formal aspect of educational failure. In later publications, we will
attempt to document the pessimism and despair with which these
adolescents view their immediate future.

The absolute ceiling of Figure 2 is of course an artifact of the
limited sample. We know from our own tests that there are group
members who read very well, whose school records are not pres-
ently available. But even these rare individuals view the educational
system with a profound cynicism. The majority of those who learn
from the system are located in Figure 1.

We do not believe that the present college-educated teaching staff,
Negro or white, has the specific knowledge of the street culture to
to solve this problem alone. Negro teachers raised in ghetto areas
are not members of the current street culture. With a few rare
exceptions, we find that success in education removes the individual
from his culture so effectively that his knowledge of it becomes
quite marginal. The specific knowledge of the street culture which
is needed is only available to those who are in constant interaction
with the peer groups on the streets. Part of the reason is that the
value system, though quite general, is intensely local in focus. The
factors that control language behavior are often local and immediate:
what happened last year, last month, or yesterday to that particular
sub-group is the best stimulus for evoking spontaneous speech.
And the general configurations of the culture change rapidly even
though the value system remains intact: a teacher raised in Harlem
in the 1950's, returning to the streets today, would find it difficult
to understand how and why gang fighting is no longer in style.

We hope to elaborate on these problems of communication in
later publications. Here we would like to indicate briefly the form
of one proposal we believe will be effective in solving the problem
of Figure 2.

We propose that a cultural intermediary be introduced into the
classroom in the person of a young Negro man,[15] 16 to 25 years
old, with high-school level reading skills, but not a college graduate. We propose the creation of a special license to allow this
young man to carry out the following functions:

1. To acquaint the teacher with the specific interests of members of the class and help design reading material centering
   on these interests;
2. To provide effective rewards and punishments that will motivate members of street culture for whom normal school
   sanctions are irrelevant;
3. To lead group discussion on topics of immediate concern
   to members of the class;

4. To lead boys in sports and other recreational activities in school time;

5. To maintain contact with boys outside of school, on the streets, and help organize extra-curricular activities.

We are well aware of the difficulties that any school system will have in absorbing such outside elements. The situation in most ghetto schools is plainly desperate enough so that many educators will be willing to endorse a proposal that may create such difficult-ies. We suggest that summer training schools be held for such special-license teachers, in which regular teachers will participate to develop jointly techniques for cross-cultural cooperation. At such training schools, it will also be possible to provide regular teachers and special-license teachers with specific linguistic data of the type generated by our principal direction of research.

NOTES

1. Data in this research note is the product of cooperative Research Project 3288, "A Study of the Non-standard English of Negro and Puerto Rican Speakers in New York City", under OE-6-10-059. Preliminary linguistic findings of this research are published in "Some Sources of Reading Problems for Negro Speakers of Non-Standard English", in A. Frazier (ed.), New Directions in Elemen-tary English (Champaign, Ill.: N.C.T.E., 1967), pp. 140-167, and available in "Some Suggestions for Teaching Standard English to Speakers of Non-Standard Urban Dialects", submitted to the Bureau of Curriculum Research of the Board of Education of the City of New York.

2. The names "Cobras" and "Jets" are here used as cover symbols for a complex of formal groups which changes over time. The "Co-bras", in particular, was originally a group formed by mergers of several groups which in turn underwent mergers with other groups under successive changes in nationalist orientation.

3. See below for relative sizes of street groups and isolated popu-lation in one project.

4. The "Thunderbirds" are a partial exception here, since the club was formed in a recreation center (and was successively re-formed with different names); however, the identity of the group was not confined to the center, and it contained members who had been ban-ned from the center.

5. "Lower Class Culture as a Generating Milieu of Juvenile De-linquency", Journal of Social Issues, 14, 1958, pp. 5-19.

6. As noted above, the "Cobras" underwent a number of organizational transformations, with new officers, and merged with other groups as nationalist orientation increased.

7. Major activities are flying pigeons, playing basketball, playing cards, petty theft, playing pool, smoking marijuana, hanging out ... although not all members participate in all of these activities. The groups as formal wholes have relatively few activities.

8. The problem of group identity, and the obligations which accompany membership, is not fully solved.

9. As one indication of the importance of reading in the group, we may consider one pair of boys who were best friends and saw each other every day. One read extremely well, the other not at all: the other's performance was a total surprise to each.

10. The most important data is derived from the question, "Who are the guys [cats] you hang out with?", supplemented with other questions on group leaders, best friends, and all other mentions of individuals in relevant roles.

11. Cf. Peter Wilmott, Adolescent Boys in East London, London: 1966, p. 35. In answer to a question on main companions in spare time, 57 per cent of those 14-51 years old indicated a group of other males; 44 per cent of those 16-18 years old; and only 32 percent of those 19-20 years old.

12. The building studied here is 1390 Fifth Avenue.

13. Gray's Oral Reading Test was also given to a section of the population for further calibration on school approaches to reading

14. There is a close correlation between reading achievement and the Pinter Cunningham IQ test (given in the early grades in New York City in former years) in Figure 1, and less markedly in Figure 2.

15. We specifically designate a male for this role, in contrast to a number of proposals for "para-professionals" in the schools which utilize women from the community or from college training courses. We cannot elaborate on the importance of sex differentiation here, except to indicate that we believe it is a matter of prime importance.

DYSLEXIA: A PROBLEM OF COMMUNICATION

by Jessie F. Reid

In her paper to the Education Section of the British Psychological Society in 1964 (Vernon 1964) Professor Vernon referred to the continuing controversy between those who maintained that all reading delay was environmentally caused, and those who believed that in some cases a 'more fundamental constitutional condition' was involved.

In the following year, in the autumn issue of the AEP News Letter, there appeared a group of articles on dyslexia, contributed respectively by a neurologist (Reinhold 1965), an educational psychologist (Bannatyne 1965), and a college lecturer (Walbridge 1965), all of whom accepted that the term 'dyslexia' has some meaning. The issue for March 1966 contained, in answer to these, an article by Burt (Burt 1965) headed 'Counterblast to Dyslexia', in which arguments about intelligence, motivation, emotional disturbance, and suitable instruction were advanced.

In the latter part of the same year, two substantial works on reading were published in the United States and Britain. The Disabled Reader: Education of the Dyslexic Child, edited by Money and Schiffman in America, can be regarded as a sequel to the research symposium edited by Money which appeared some five years ago (Money 1962a). It contains sections on phenomenology and theory, teaching methods and programme organization, case-studies illustrating different types of difficulty, and a final summing up, with a glossary, a bibliography of some 300 references, and a bibliography of tests.

There are seventeen contributors, some of them British. Money's preface makes it clear that the terms 'dyslexic' child, or 'disabled' reader cover many types of disability, but indicates that the word 'disability' implies failure to learn in circumstances where learning

Reprinted by permission from Educational Research 10:2, 126-133 (February 1968).

might have been expected, and that it particularly excludes failure attributable to 'educational neglect or inadequate instruction'.

Standards and Progress in Reading (Morris 1966) contains the results of a detailed longitudinal survey of children in Kent. It is mainly concerned with the school conditions in which two selected groups, a group of 'good' readers and a group of 'poor' readers were taught, but pays attention also to domestic, social and personal characteristics. In the concluding chapter of The Disabled Reader, Edwards says: 'Unquestionably, there are special types of genuine learning disability'. In the concluding chapter of Standards and Progress in Reading Morris says: 'It was concluded ... that the study as a whole lends little support to the idea that "specific developmental dyslexia" is an identifiable syndrome distinct from "reading backwardness".'

This article has been written in an attempt to clarify some of the issues involved in these conflicts of judgement. It is not a comprehensive review, even of recent literature, but is selective in an effort to make certain points clear and is perhaps less about dyslexia than about attitudes to it. For comprehensive bibliographies and reviews the reader is referred to Benton (1962), Vernon (1964), Critchley (1964), Kinsbourne and Warrington (1966) and to the symposia in which the first and last of these references appear.

The conflict exemplified above is, of course, not new, nor are the origins of it easy to trace or explain in purely rational terms. But some explanation has to be found for the fact that side by side with the increasing recognition of backwardness and retardation, the development of more 'child-centred' methods of teaching, the growing body of knowledge about the effect on learning of emotional stresses and cultural deprivation, the development of the Child Guidance Services, and the enormous expansion of special provision for the handicapped, there has persisted among administrators, psychologists and teachers a resistance to the notion that a condition describable as 'specific reading disability' exists. Most have wanted to regard all retardation (i.e. a state in which a child's reading ability was demonstrably below some level regarded as his 'potential') in terms of other causative factors. But some have tried to explain retardation away, as largely a statistical artefact (Vernon 1956), and to deny that any 'expectation' of achievement other than a statistical one, based on observed correlations, is justifiable.

The assertion that the condition does exist (that is, that 'dyslexia' is a name for something more than the behavioural state of 'retardation in reading', in the same way that 'measles' means more than 'the state of being covered with a blotchy red rash') has come mainly from people in the medical profession; the history of medical

interest in the topic is outlined by Critchley (1964). The resistance
amounts, therefore, to an unwillingness among certain educators to
accept medical opinion on an educational matter. To try to trace in
detail the origins of the conflict of opinion would be a historical exercise outside the scope of this article. It is important, however,
to look further at some of the things that have been said on both
sides, not only as illustrations of the amount of feeling the topic
has generated, but as clues to the possible resolution of what is,
after all, a rather unproductive state of controversy.

On page 9 of his book on Developmental Dyslexia, Critchley (1964)
accuses sociologists and educational psychologists of having 'invaded
... what had hitherto been a medical province or responsibility'.
'Invaded' is an emotive term, and a derogatory one, and the passage
from which this quotation is taken seems to imply clearly that
sociologists and psychologists, by trying to relate a child's educational history to a whole network of genetic, economic, social,
cultural, emotional, and pedagogic influences, were arrogating to
themselves the right to pronounce on what was, in fact, a medical
condition; that they had succeeded in casting doubt on reputable
evidence, and that they had obscured a distinction of great educational importance.

It is not hard, however, to find equally harsh words uttered from
the other side. For instance, Wall, speaking at the Nottingham
refresher course held by the English Division of Professional
Psychologists, had this to say: 'The word "dyslexia" seem to be a
jargon at its worst.... It means bad reading, and nothing is added
but its Greek form ...' (Wall 1961).

Going on to point out that reading is a culturally-determined
activity, he asserted that 'pseudo-medical terms seem to be not
merely out of place but dangerously so.... Let us call our examinations and tests examinations and tests and not diagnoses'.
Words such as these coming from the Director of the National
Foundation for Educational Research make it hard not to conclude
that the source of the 'resistance' has been the feeling that from
the educationist's standpoint it was the medical specialists who had
'invaded' an educational domain and that the disagreement constitutes a battle for professional possession. But the skilled collaboration of doctors in the ascertainment and treatment of mental sub-
normality, severe emotional disturbance, and infantile autism, all
of which are, in part, cultural problems, has become accepted
practice. What is different in the situation under review here? For
one thing, the fact that neurologists and ophthalmologists have taken
a keen interest in the particular difficulties and errors exhibited by
children referred to them for reading and writing failure, and that
they have often conducted psychological and educational examinations

without calling on the help of a psychologist, may have put them in
a special position. It is also, unfortunately, true that the descriptions given, and the labels and explanations proposed, have produced a multiplicity of obscure terms, and great deal of conceptual
confusion.

That medical men should have shown interest in the particular
manifestations of reading/writing difficulty is completely understandable if we remember that the earliest thinking on the subject (Morgan
1896, Hinshelwood 1917) was in terms of analogy with acquired
aphasia (i.e. that resulting from 'damage' by injury, vascular
disease, or tumours) and that the study of aphasic disorders in relation to brain function was in the early part of this century an im-
mensely exciting new discipline in which it was believed that the
key to understanding lay in trying to list, classify and systematize
the varieties of receptive and expressive disorders displayed by
patients with known cortical lesions. It is now fairly generally
acknowledged, however, that the analogy is unsound and misleading,
and that a diagnosis of 'developmental dyslexia' does not imply
cortical 'damage' (i.e. the disruption of a previous state of normality)
and may indeed exclude it.

The nature of the terminology evolved (such as Orton's 'strephosymbolia', or Critchley's 'dyssymbolia', or Claparède's 'bradylexia')
is a result of standard medical practice in naming 'conditions'. The
variety arises from the fact that attempts to identify what the children are suffering from have not led to uniform conclusions. All
children have not exhibited identical abnormalities, samples of
clinic cases have varied, and--more seriously--the same behaviour
can be attributed theoretically to a variety of 'causes' or categorized
in a variety of ways. This is, of course, a very general problem
in the study of behaviour. But the profusion of terms, such as those
exemplified above, has produced considerable bewilderment. There
has also been serious confusion of a different kind over the exact
meaning of the qualifying words 'specific', 'developmental' and
'congenital', and over the terms 'word-blind' and 'syndrome'. I
should like, however, to leave consideration of these till later.

The discussions reported in the Invalid Children's Aid Association
symposium (Franklin 1962) testify further to the fact that many non-
medical participants (though not the parents of non-reading children)
found the concept of 'specific dyslexia' difficult--or else provocative
of hostile feelings. Several speakers appeared to dismiss the
clinical procedures used in identification of cases as 'unsound',
while others who would admit to the existence, in retarded readers,
of particular difficulties with orientation or space perception simply
saw (to quote one speaker) 'no theoretical or practical use for the
concept'. The claim was made that the description 'reading retarda-

tion' was quite adequate as a basis for remedial tuition. This is substantially what Wall (1961), Malmquist (1958) and Morris (1966) also claimed. The objection is to the notion that 'a condition' or 'a clinical entity' is involved--something to which the terms 'specific' of 'syndrome' are applicable.

At one point in the ICAA discussion Meredith remarked that he would very much like to know what underlay this 'resistance to the idea of something specific', and asked a very pertinent question: namely, whether a remedial worker would attempt to differentiate between different causes of retardation, and what action he would take if told that, of two retarded readers, one had many associated spatial and motor difficulties while the other had not. No clear answer appears to have been given to this very important question. Daniels, however, gave his own personal objections to the notion of specific dyslexia. These rested largely, it seemed, on his own experimental evidence about the effect, on a 'hard core' of non-readers, of intensive phonic training, which left only one child out of ten still unable to read. To have labelled these children 'dyslexic' (or, even worse, 'word-blind') would, he claimed, have been to discourage at the outset all attempts to teach them. That is to say, he admitted that they had some special difficulty which caused them to need tuition which their classmates did not, and even said at one point that their 'disability' was 'akin to tone-deafness', but he rejected the labels because they carried the connotation of an incurable condition. Daniels, in other words, views the concept of 'dyslexia' not as useless, or bewildering, but as dangerous.

In his review of the literature, and of the history of attitudes towards the belief in specific dyslexia, Critchley (1964) obviously with this sort of pronouncement in mind, says that neurologists have been to blame for allowing psychologists to assert that neurologists believed the condition irremediable. He cites Burt as one originator of this erroneous idea. Burt, writing in The Backward Child (1950), did indeed talk of 'so-called "word-blind" children... who have made rapid and remarkable progress after a few weeks' intensive training at the hands of a psychological specialist', and Critchley points out that the adjective 'so-called' is objectionable, and that the claim about 'a few weeks' training' is doubtfully true. Burt's remarks do exemplify a view which not only calls the concept in question but almost holds it up to ridicule. But it must be asked whether the underlying attitude here is simply one of rational disbelief, or whether it is one of justifable fear of what the term 'word-blind' may become in the minds of the inexperienced or unreflecting teacher or parent.

In their contribution to The Disabled Reader, Kinsbourne and Warrington (1966) make a similar point. They refer to the 'naive

notion' that 'impairment due to disease states is necessarily total
and irremediable' and to the equally mistaken idea that thinking of
reading disability as representing one extreme of a normal continuum
of competence will dispose of these unfortunate connotations. They
imply that such connotations do not need to be disposed of because
they are not carried by the terms in question, namely 'cogenital'
and 'specific'.

The force of the term 'congenital' is to make a distinction between
a condition acquired through disease or injury and one existing from
birth. But again, doctors should remember that to the layman the
term is known principally through its attachment to states that may
be distressing and in many cases in fact irremediable, such as
mental deficiency, or spina bifida, or syphilis, and that it functions
in their minds almost as a 'pathic sign'. It is therefore understandable that there should have been resistance to the apparent finality
of the term, and of the companion term 'word-blind'. But it would
appear that a failure of communication has existed in this area for
many years, and it can only be a matter for regret if educators
have spent time and energy strenuously opposing neurologists over
something they did not say.

Critchley, besides describing psychologists as having been on oc-
casion 'muddled and opinionated', criticizes them for having been
'more concerned with aetiology than with cure'. This is a puzzling
charge, but one which touches on a crucial issue. Concern with
aetiology has been the principal feature of medical intervention in
the problem of the retarded reader--indeed it might be said to be
in some cases the sole reason for that intervention. And, as we
have seen, certain features of the way in which medical opinions
have been expressed have probably helped to arouse resistance. It
cannot be that aetiology is here being set aside as of lesser importance than cure. What must be meant is that matters of aetiology
and diagnosis are a medical concern, while cure is the business of
the psychologist and the remedial teacher. A view which might be
thought to be similar is put forward by Reinhold (1965) who states
that 'the final diagnosis of this condition should, of course, be left
to the neurologist, as there are many conditions of organic brain
damage whose symptoms mimic those of congenital dyslexia.' But
there is a vast difference, if not a complete contrast, between feeling the need to call in the opinion of a medical specialist to assist
in a differential diagnosis, and abandoning all interest in the origins
of an educational difficulty. A remedial worker who did not retain
a lively speculative interest in aetiology would be reduced to the
level of a technician, carrying out remedial exercises to someone
else's specification. Moreover, the remedial worker has to deal
with the emotional reactions of the child and of his parents, and an

understanding of causes is a necessary part of the process of re-
lieving anxiety. It might even be more true to say that educators
have not concerned themselves sufficiently with aetiology, in that
they have sometimes put together for remedial purposes children
who were retarded for a variety of reasons and who perhaps required very different sorts of help. It is possible that important
distinctions have thereby been obscured. Edwards (1966) suggests
also that educators have been slow to develop adventurous thera-
peutic techniques based in any scientific way on their findings. But
such an undertaking is inseparable from an interest in causation
and indeed presupposes it, so that Critchley's criticism seems here
not only unjust, but misguided.

In his own contribution to the 1962 Symposium on Dyslexia, Money
(1962b) remarks on the slowness which medicine and pedagogy have
shown in coming together in joint study of problems of mutual interest, and on the desirability of greater collaboration. It is true,
as any survey of the literature will show, that interdisciplinary
studies have been very few in number. This fact has, no doubt,
been part cause and part effect of the lack of understanding and trust
between the disciplines concerned. The last twenty years have seen
some improvement in this state of affairs, together with a move
away from the more anecdotal method of recording case-studies to
the collation and systematic analysis of test results, and from boldly
speculative theorizing to more cautious and tentative explanatory
attempts. But a study of these discussions (Money 1962a, Shankweiler 1964, Ingram 1965, Williams 1965, Money and Schiffman
1966) reveals how much methodological and theoretical difficulty
still exists, and the extent to which attempts at rigorous study are
beset by problems of identification and classification, and by the
danger of circularity in reasoning.

Those who publish clinical studies of dyslexic children, who attempt theoretical systematizations, and who argue for the early recognition and special treatment of these cases, assume (a) that the
category exists and (b) that members of it can be identified. To assert (a) without (b) would, of course, be not a scientific statement
but an expression of faith. But how, in fact, do they claim to identify these children?

In the ICAA Symposium those in clinical practice frequently asserted that they could recognize a case of specific dyslexia almost
unerringly, by a number of signs and symptoms. They also, however, admitted that no one of these signs was, by itself, definitive:
any one might appear either in a retarded reader not suffering from
dyslexia or, in passing, in a normal reader. The signs formed, that
is, a 'variable syndrome', the uniquely distinguishing mark being the
clustering--the coincidence of several signs together. Money (1962b)

defends this as a respectable concept. 'It is', he says, 'not at all
rare in psychological medicine, nor in other branches of medicine,
that a disease should have no unique identifying sign, that uniqueness
being, in the pattern of signs that appear in contiguity'. But it is
difficult to see how, unless certain of the signs are regarded as
necessary, and perhaps even if they are so regarded the identification can ever, on this basis alone, be more than a probabilistic one,
with the probability increasing as the number of signs--or the
severity of those present--increases.

A study of the writing of different neurologists will further show
that they do not agree on the criteria by which they diagnose.

Critchley bases his belief in the existence of the condition on four
crucial criteria: persistence into adulthood; the peculiar and specific nature of the errors in reading and writing; the familial incidence of the defect; and the frequent association with other symbol
defects. But the first of these is diagnostic only in retrospect and
the fourth leaves room for considerable variation. Other workers
(e.g. Reinhold 1965; and see Vernon 1964) select other criteria, too
numerous to list here, with the distinction between 'necessary' and
'sufficient' not always clear. It is probably these uncertainties, together with the need to show that alternative hypothese about causation will not suffice, that has led to the practice of identification by
elimination, resulting in some such statement as this: 'This child
is a very retarded reader of good intelligence. He has had an enlightened home and normal schooling. His vision and hearing are
intact, and he has no overt neurological damage. He has no history
of emotional upset prior to going to school and starting to learn to
read. He wants to learn, but has failed. He must be dyslexic'.

The important point to note about this mode of identification is that
it is negative not positive, and that it does no more than place the
residual cases in a category which medically is termed 'idiopathic'
--that is, of unknown origin (Money 1962b). This is also, of course,
a perfectly respectable notion, representing a state of knowledge in
which one can recognize a condition operationally, or behaviourally,
but give no explanation of its aetiology. Eisenberg (1962) states
exactly this position with regard to 'dyslexic' cases when he writes:
'The adjective "specific" calls attention both to the circumscribed
nature of the disability and to our ignorance of its cause. Operationally specific reading disability may be defined as the failure
to learn to read with normal proficiency despite conventional instruction, a culturally adequate home, proper motivation, intact
senses, normal intelligence, and freedom from gross neurological
defect'.

There is, however, one totally unsatisfactory feature about this
mode of definition, namely, that it appears to imply that 'specific

dyslexia' --as a condition--will exist only if all these other conditions obtain, i.e. that it will not occur in a child with defective eyesight or hearing, or in a child whose life is culturally deprived or
whose school attendance has been disrupted, or who does not want
to learn! One has only to write this to see that it makes nonsense
of the notion of a 'congenital' or 'developmental' condition. What
is being said is that the condition can be identified with certainty
only if it exists in isolation; otherwise it will be impossible to dis-
entangle it completely from other possible 'causes' of retardation.
In the earlier Johns Hopkins Symposium (Money 1962a), Rabinovitch
shows awareness of this difficulty, noting that very often he and his
co-workers find themselves making a 'double-barrelled diagnosis--
secondary reading difficulty with a touch of primary disability. (It
should be remarked in passing that the difference between the general population of clinical referrals in Child Guidance and the highly
selected population of severe cases seen by neurologists may account for the contrast between views such as those of Rabinovitch,
that admit of degrees of dyslexia and of mixed aetiology, and views
such as Critchley's, which emphasize 'purity and gravity'.) But it
will be immediately obvious that this 'double-barrelled' diagnosis
must be made by the use of positive clinical signs on the probabilistic
basis indicated above, and that the point at which 'significance' is
reached may well be somewhat arbitrary. Moreover, it is here
that supporters of the doctrine of the parsimony of hypotheses find
grounds for criticism. Why, they ask, invoke a cause which you
cannot demonstrate when other perfectly feasible explanations are
present?

The somewhat perplexing status of the individual 'clinical signs'
which collectively add support to the diagnosis of dyslexia has also
not been clarified by their heterogeniety. A rough four-fold classification of them might, however, be made on the following basis:

(1)   Signs of perceptual difficulties of a more general kind
      ('spatial' difficulties, 'visuo-motor' difficulties, and so on).
      Statements about these are normally inferences from results
      on performance tests, although they may also be based on
      observation of other behaviour (for instance, drawing) or on
      reports.

(2)   Signs of anomalies in development (of laterality, of speech,
      of motor control). Again, test results, observations and
      history-taking are the sources.

(3)   Circumstantial evidence (such as familial incidence of simi-
      lar educational difficulties to those of the patient, handed-
      ness in the families, etc.).

(4)   The precise nature and severity of the difficulties themselves
      (e.g. the kind of errors made in spelling, the movements of
      the hand in writing, the speech rhythm in reading).

It is not always clear from discussions of the first three kinds of sign whether they are being regarded as clues to a cause, or whether they are merely being regarded as 'associated' difficulties, the cause remaining unknown. Especially has this been true of the discussions of the importance of laterality characteristics, which, once noticed, invited much speculation about corresponding anomalies of cerebral dominance. But Zangwill (1962) makes it very clear that inferences about cerebral dominance from observations of laterality in hand, eye and foot are unjustified in the present state of knowledge.

Doubt has also been cast on the validity of the 'signs' in the great numbers of group studies which have investigated the correlation between ability in reading and other 'abilities' inferred from test results. Most of these studies have been done on heterogeneous groups of backward or retarded readers, and the effect has been to produce results that are inconclusive, or which contradict one another, and frequently appear to cast doubt on the notion that groups of associated difficulties exist. This point is made by Eisenberg (1966) and also by Vernon (1960, 1961, 1962), whose remarks are especially interesting, following as they do so soon after her comprehensive review of such studies (Vernon 1957). In a recent investigation, Belmont and Birch (1965) found no difference in laterality characteristics between backward readers and controls. But evidence of this kind does nothing to refute the claims of those who believe that 'dyslexia' exists. No one claims that all backward readers will show anomalies of laterality, and the same argument holds for any other characteristic investigated in this way. Likewise, Morris's correlational studies were bound to obscure rather than to highlight the few cases that might have an aetiology which differed from the majority. This is not a criticism of her studies, but it is a criticism of the implication in her conclusion (quoted at the beginning of this article) that her studies cast doubt on the existence of dyslexia as a variety of reading disability.

What seems to emerge from the foregoing review is an overwhelming need for rigorous study in this area, study which would be undertaken at an interdisciplinary level and which would courageously submit the contentions of those who believe in dyslexia and those who do not to the most searching reappraisal and testing that can be devised. Since one of the standard scientific methods of demonstrating that a difference exists between two events or states of being is to make predications the outcome of which will be different for the two events or states in question, it seems reasonable to suggest the setting up of a controlled experiment involving remedial methods. (This was in fact adumbrated by Vernon in 1962.) Two matched groups of 'dyslexic' children and two matched groups of retarded readers who are thought not to be 'dyslexic' could be selected. Within each pair one would receive tuition, from teachers who 'believed in' dyslexia, based, in the case of the dyslexic children, on a close diagnosis of the variety of disorder they were suffering from, while the other group would receive tuition of equal duration from teachers who did not believe in dyslexia but worked presumably at a phenomenological level. An analysis of variance design would be appropriate and would show whether (a) the dyslexics' as a whole made slower progress than the others, (b) whether 'dyslexics' taught on the basis of a diagnosis of dyslexia got on better than those who were not, and (c) whether there was any overall difference between the results of the two groups of teachers.

An experiment of a different sort might pair children diagnosed as dyslexic by one specialist, with children whose retardation, equally severe, was of a different origin, and then set another specialist the task of picking the 'dyslexic' child from each pair. This may sound a slightly frivolous suggestion, but it is prompted by a consciousness of the confusing variety of criteria used, by the conviction that the notion of dyslexia would become more respectable if a greater degree of unanimity could be reached, and by the thought that such an exercise might help those taking part to analyse their dependence on scientific analysis and on intuition and clinical awareness of subtle kinds.

A third type of experiment might investigate, with suitable controls, the effect of training in the more general perceptual skills thought to be deficient, in an effort to see whether (a) improvement occurred in the skill in question (e.g. retention of shapes), and (b) whether any transfer took place to reading and writing. All investigations carry the limitation, of course, that it is not possible to discover whether 'dyslexics' are or are not characterized by 'X', unless 'X' is not one of the criteria by which they have been initially identified.

The mention once more of variety in criteria leads to a further final point with which this discussion has not concerned itself so far. Current opinion seems to be moving in the direction of recognizing 'sub-types' of dyslexic disorder, thereby further complicating the notion of 'variable syndrome'. Some writers have suggested that the postulating of an entity--a 'condition'--is thereby rendered meaningless. But if all these sub-types should prove to have in common a basis in some developmental anomaly or delay, then it would seem that the use of one term to classify them would still, both theoretically and practically, make sense.

REFERENCES

Bannatyne, A.D. (1965). 'The Word Blind Centre for Dyslexic Children', AEP News Letter, No. 4, Autumn 1965, pp. 17-9.

Belmont, L. and Birch, H.G. (1965). 'Lateral dominance, lateral awareness and reading disability', Child Develop., 34, pp. 257-70.

Benton, A. (1962). 'Dyslexia in relation to form perception and directional sense'. In: Money, J. ed. Reading Disability. Baltimore: Johns Hopkins Press.

Burt, C. (1950). The Backward Child. Edinburgh: Oliver & Boyd.

Burt, C. (1966). 'Counterblast to dyslexia', AEP News Letter, No. 5, March 1966, pp. 2-6.

Critchley, M. (1964) Developmental Dyslexia. London: Heinemann Medical.

Edwards, T.J. (1966). 'Teaching reading: a critique'. In: Money, J. and Schiffman, G. eds. The Disabled Reader. Baltimore: Johns Hopkins Press.

Eisenberg, L. (1962). Introduction to: Money, J. ed. Reading Disability. Baltimore: Johns Hopkins Press.

Franklin, W. ed. (1962). Word Blindness or Specific Developmental Dyslexia. London: Pitman Medical.

Hinshelwood, J. (1917). Congenital Word Blindness. London: H.K. Lewis.

Ingram, T.T.S. (1965). 'Specific learning difficulties in childhood'. Public Health, Vol. LXXIX, No. 2, January 1965, pp. 70-80.

Kinsbourne, M. and Warrington, E.K. (1966). 'Developmental factors in reading and writing backwardness'. In: Money, J. and Schiffman, G. eds. The Disabled Reader. Baltimore: Johns Hopkins Press.

Malmquist, E. (1958). Factors related to Reading Disabilities in the First Grade of the Elementary School. Stockholm: Almqvist & Wiksell.

Money, J. ed. (1962a). Reading Disability. Baltimore: Johns Hopkins Press.

Money, J. (1962b). 'Dyslexia: a post-conference review'. In: Money, J. ed. Reading Disability. Baltimore: Johns Hopkins Press.

Money, J. and Schiffman, G. eds. (1966). The Disabled Reader. Baltimore: John Hopkins Press.

Morgan, W. P. (1896). 'A case of congenital word blindness', Brit. Med. J., 2, 1378.

Morris, J. M. (1966). Standards and Progress in Reading. Slough: NFER.

Rabinovitch, R. (1962). 'Dyslexia: psychiatric considerations'. In: Money, J. ed. Reading Disability. Baltimore: Johns Hopkins Press.

Reinhold, M. (1965). 'Congenital dyslexia', AEP News Letter, No. 4, Autumn 1965, pp. 13-7.

Shankweiler, D. (1964). 'A study of developmental dyslexia', Neuropsychologia, Vol. I, pp. 267-86.

Vernon, M. D. (1957). Backwardness in Reading. Cambridge: Cambridge University Press.

Vernon, M. D. (1960). 'The investigation of reading problems today', Brit. J. Educ. Psychol., Vol. 30, pp. 146-54.

Vernon, M. D. (1961). 'Dyslexia and remedial education'. In: Proceedings of a Refresher Course on Dyslexia and Remedial Education. British Psychological Society: English Division of Professional Psychologists. (In cyclostyle.)

Vernon, M. D. (1962). 'Specific dyslexia', Brit. J. Educ. Psychol., Vol. 32, pp. 143-50.

Vernon, P. E. (1956). 'Dullness and its causes', Times Educ. Suppl., 26 October.

Walbridge, A. (1965). 'A view of dyslexia by an educational psychologist', AEP News Letter, No. 4, Autumn 1965.

Wall, W. D. (1961). 'Recent research into dyslexia and remedial education'. In: Proceedings of a Refresher Course on Dyslexia and Remedial Education. British Psychological Society: English Division of Professional Psychologists. (In cyclostyle.)

Williams, D. J. (1965). 'A five-year follow-up study of fifteen children assessed as possibly dyslexic in 1960'. Unpublished dissertation presented for Diploma in Education of Backward Children, University College, Swansea.

Zangwill, O. L. (1962). 'Dyslexia in relation to cerebral dominance'. In: Money, J. ed. Reading Disability. Baltimore: Johns Hopkins Press.

THE RARITY OF READING DISABILITY
IN JAPANESE CHILDREN

by Kiyoshi Makita, M.D.

While the problem of dyslexia causes a formidable number of
psychiatric casualties in Western countries, this difficulty is seldom
encountered in Japan. Not a single such case has been brought into
our children's psychiatric service since its opening in 1965. Reports
on this topic thus far have been almost nonexistent in our child
psychiatric meeting.

On congenital word-blindness, a few but noteworthy contributions
are to be found in our psychiatric leterature. In 1957, Obi[26] reported a case of a 9-year-old girl with congenital word-blindness
and provided a stimulating discussion of its pathology pertinent to
the specific features of the Japanese language. The work of Kuromaru and Okada on a similar topic, referred to in a monograph by
Weinschenk,[37] also stresses specific characteristics of the Japanese
language. A recent addition to our psychiatric literature is a work
by Anzai, Iwata, and Ikeda,[1] but it is primarily concerned with congenital word-blindness, considered to be the most severe and nuclear type of dyslexic difficulty. Strange as it may appear to
Western researchers, in Japan there has not been a single report
on dyslexic difficulties in the broader sense usually applied to the
major portion of Western "poor readers," the sense for which
Rabinovitch[29] preferred the term "reading retardation" and to which
Bach[2] referred as "normal Leseschwierigkeit."

Setting the criteria for reading disability has been a difficult
task. The classical German school tended to view these difficulties
with emphasis on the organic background. Hence some researchers
limit the implication of dyslexia only to congenital word-blindness.
On the other hand, many Anglo-American researchers emphasize

Reprinted by permission from the American Journal of Orthopsy-
chiatry 38:4. 599-614 (July 1968).

QUESTIONNAIRE

1. In what grade is your class? _____

2. How many children do you have in your class?

    Boys: _____ Girls: _____ Total: _____

3. Do you have mentally retarded children in your class for whom you think special education is necessary?

    Yes _____ No _____

    If "yes," how many do you have? _____

4. Do you have children in your class who show specific difficulty in learning "reading" with ordinary teaching methods regardless of their normal intelligence?
   [An elaborated explanation for the criteria was added.]

    Yes _____ No _____

5. If "yes," how many children do you have? _____

6. If "yes," are they more backward than the expected level of the last grade? For instance, supposing you have a third grade class, how many children do you have whose backwardness in reading correspond to the level of:
    (a) the end of the second grade? _____
    (b) the end of the first grade?   _____
    (c) in between (a) and (b)?   _____
    (This answer is not necessary if you have a first grade class.)

7. If "yes," on what kind of script did the children show their foremost difficulty?

    (a) HIRAGANA script _____   How many? _____
    (b) KATAKANA script _____
    (c) KANJI script   _____
    (d) NUMERALS   _____

8. Do you have children in your class who caught up to the standard level in reading regardless of their obvious backwardness in their first or second grade levels?

    Yes _____ No _____

9. If "yes," how many? _____

10. If "yes," on what kind of script did the children show their foremost difficulty?

    (a) HIRAGANA script _____   How many? _____
    (b) KATAKANA script _____
    (c) KANJI script   _____
    (d) NUMERALS   _____

11. Are there any children to your knowledge (not necessarily in your own experience) who had difficulty in scholastic achievement in higher grades owing specifically to reading disability?

    Yes _____ No _____

12. If "yes," how many of such children have you heard about? _____

13. Would you write briefly on such children if you have any:

Table I

CHILDREN WITH READING DISABILITY

GRADE	Surveyed Population	Number of Dyslexic Children	Percentage of Dyslexic Children
1st grade	2,234	28	1.2
2nd grade	2,830	33	1.1
3rd grade	2,307	20	0.8
4th grade and over	1,824	8	0.4
TOTAL	9,195	89	0.98

Table 2

NUMBER OF DYSLEXIC CHILDREN IN RELATION TO VARIOUS SCRIPTS

GRADE	KANA Scripts		KANJI Script	NUMERALS
	HIRAGANA	KATAKANA		
1st grade	15	8	10	1
2nd grade	11	6	26	1
3rd grade	1	1	17	0
4th grade and over	0	0	8	0
Total	27	15	61	2

the functional and developmental aspects, which results in the inclusion of milder cases. In this paper, the definition of reading disability is directed to children with normal eyesight (or corrected visual capacity) and with normal intelligence who show difficulty in learning how to read with ordinary teaching methods. In consequence, not only the rare severe cases of congenital word-blindness but also the majority of poor readers are included.

Method and Results

Based upon the above criteria, the questionnaire opposite was sent to school teachers of primary schools (public and private), randomly sampling metropolitan Tokyo so as to include both urban and rural areas.

In answer to 323 questionnaires, 247 school teachers (73%) gave replies which covered 9,195 children. The result of the survey is shown in Table 1. As the table indicates, the total number of children reported to have some degree of reading difficulty was only 89—0.98% of the population. A small number of these children were judged to be generally retarded, on the basis of additional explanations by teachers. As a consequence, the real prevalence of reading disability was somewhat less than the figure of 0.98%. In any event, the responses suggest that the rate of reading disability is less than 1% among Japanese school children.

If we consider the three varieties of script used in Japanese, the reading disability on each variety is indicated by Table 2. It is interesting to note a marked drop of reported difficulty with both Kana scripts among the third grade children and none beyond fourth grade, whereas the prevalence of difficulty on Kanji script increases relatively from the third grade.

A second questionnaire asking about experience with reading disability was sent to more than 30 institutions such as child guidance clinics, educational guidance bureaus, and other child study institutions. Cooperation was poor and the results negative. Only a few institutions responded, and those that did reported that they did not see any children with reading disability other than cases of general mental retardation. As the only exception, one institution reported a case of congenital word-blindness. Poor response from institutions might be interpreted as implying little or no experience with this problem. If we add impressions of leading child psychiatrists in Japan to this poor response from institutions, we may assume that the incidence of reading disability in the broader sense is extremely rare in Japan.

Discussion

The criteria for reading disability differ so much between various investigators in many countries that the comparison of its prevalence is a difficult task to carry out properly. Bach[2] reported that 10% to 20% of the school population falls within his normale Leseschwierigkeiten (with a figure of 0.2% to 7% for congenital word-blindness). Reviewing the literature, Weinschenk[37] wrote that the prevalence of normalbegabten Legastheniker fluctuates between 2% and 15%. While Lotte Schenk-Danzinger[31] in Austria found 22% of the school children to be having Legasthenie of varying degrees, Monroe[23] declared that 12% of school children were "poor readers." In comparison with such figures, our finding that the prevalence of

poor readers in Japan does not reach even 1% of school population
must be considered striking. How can this remarkable difference
be explained when there are no such discrepancies in the prevalence
of other psychiatric disorders ?

On the etiology of reading disability, there have been various
theories. Hinshelwood[13],[14] was the first to look for an analogy
between acquired word-blindness and specific reading disability.
He felt that the latter is caused by unknown injury or faulty development of the left angular gyrus in the righthanded person. Critchley[6],[7]
supposed its origin to be due to "specific cerebral immaturity, " but
questioned the existence of a structural lesion recognizable by
present-day techniques. Geschwind[11] related reading difficulty to
delayed maturation of the angular gyrus region (probably bilaterally),
basing his theory on the fact that the human inferior lobule (including the angular and supramarginal gyri) matures very late cytoarchitectonically. Kawi and Pasamanick[17] presented evidence of a
greater frequency of pregnancy complications and premature births
in the obstetrical histories of poor readers than in those of control
cases. In his textbook, Kanner[16] concluded that "we may have to
assume a very mild degree of some mal-formation or mal-develop-
ment of certain parts of brain more or less analogous to pathology
of congenital word-blindness, although we know nothing about the
etiology of reading disability at present. "

An approach to the genesis of reading disability from the physiological point of view was initiated by Orton.[23] He ascribed the
etiology of reading disability to conflict of hemispheral dominance.
There are many children among the poor readers in English-speaking
countries, he pointed out, who will do mirror reading (b for d,
p for q) and backward reading (was for saw, no for on). Orton
coined the term "strephosymbolia" for such phenomena and attributed the phenomenon of reversal to a failure to establish unilateral
cerebral dominance. But there is another type of confusion which
cannot be directly linked with strephosymbolia in strict terms.
There are children who read felt for left, could for called, under
for uniform, steady for straight, etc. Such a confusion cannot
easily be ascribed to dominance conflict and could more easily be
explained by a difference in modes of perception: total and partial.
Moreover, it has become clearer that the determination of laterality
is not as simple a matter as once thought, nor is "brainedness" so
readily to be inferred from handedness.

On the other hand, Blanchard,[3-5] Missildine,[22] Gann,[10] and others
have reported that children with poor reading display emotional
conflict, and they have emphasized emotional factors in the pre-
cipitation of reading disability. However, they have given no adequate explanation of the mechanism by which emotional tension

manifests itself through reading disability rather than in other possible manifestations. Furthermore, as was pointed out by Eisenberg[8] reading difficulty is in itself a potent source of emotional distress; even when an emotional maladjustment is inferred from clinical interviews or psychological tests, it can as well be an outcome of the reading difficulty as its cause.

Another school of investigators, such as Hallgren,[12] emphasize genetic inheritance.

At any rate, none of these theories is sufficient to explain the etiology of reading disability. This is understandable since the reading disability, the object of the investigation itself, occurs in such wide variation from nuclear congenital word-blindness to peripheral "poor reader." Rabinovitch[20] preferred to use the term "reading retardation" for the entire group and proposed to subdivide it into three major groups:

1. Those in whom the reading difficulty is based on demonstrable brain damage and is associated with varying degrees of aphasia.
2. Cases of <u>primary reading retardation,</u> presenting a basic defect in the capacity to integrate written material and to associate concepts with symbols. "A neurological deficit is suspected in these cases ... a developmental discrepancy rather than a brain injury."
3. Cases of <u>secondary reading retardation</u> as a result of personality or educational neglect factors.

Theoretically speaking, this approach seems to be convenient for finding a more direct relationship between clinical types and etiological factors. Eisenberg[8] proposed a provisional classification for the sources of reading retardation which is as follows:

A. Sociopsychological factors
  1. Quantitative and qualitative defects in teaching
  2. Deficiencies in cognitive stimulation
  3. Deficiencies in motivation
    (a) associated with social pathology
    (b) associated with psychopathology ("emotional")
B. Psychophysiological factors
  1. General debility
  2. Sensory defects
  3. Intellectual defects
  4. Brain injury
  5. Specific (idiopathic) reading disability

It is remarkable, however, that none of those investigators refers to specific features of language and script, the direct object of reading behavior. Transcultural epidemiology of reading disability is hardly found in psychiatric literature. Perhaps it is because the

problems of reading disability have so far been studied in Western
countries, where the use of the Roman alphabetical script was accepted as a given. It may now be fruitful to look at reading disability from a transcultural aspect.

Why, then, is the reported prevalence of dyslexia in Japan some
ten times lower than the figure which may be taken as median (10%)
for Western countries? It is unthinkable to assume that the Americans and the Europeans have ten times the population with malde-
velopment or malformation of cerebral gyri than do the Japanese.
It is hardly believable that the prevalence of hemispheral dominance
conflict or split laterality is ten times less in the Japanese than in
Westerners. It is equally absurd to suggest that children with
emotional distress are ten times less frequent in Japan, for the
prevalence of behavioral problems and psychosomatic manifestations in Japan is as high as it is in Western countries. Why, then,
is "emotional tension" not leading to the manifestation of reading
difficulty? Do we have to speculate about a different "pathway" between emotional difficulty (or cerebral dysmaturity or genetic factors) and reading behavior in the Japanese than in Western children?
The distinct difference of the actual scripts, the very objects of
perception, has to be taken into consideration at this point.

The Specificity of the Japanese Scripts

The Japanese scripts (Figure 1) include first of all two series of
Kana scripts, namely, Hiragana and Katakana, each series consisting of 48 phonetic letters. Japanese script secondly has numerous
ideographs called Kanji script, which originally were borrowed
from Chinese classics but read differently and which are, at present,
limited to 1,850 ideographs for daily use. The mechanism of reading, accordingly, is entirely different from that in Western cultures
where reading is based on combinations of 26 Roman letters.

A unique difference between the Japanese and Occidentals in cases
of alexia has been described by Sakamoto[30] Imura,[15] Kuromaru
and Okada,[30] and others: in the process of destruction of reading
capacity in acquired diseases or injuries, Kanji, the ideograph,
remains more resistant than Kana, the phonetic letter. The difference of vulnerability is ascribed to the difference of the mode
of perception between the ideograph and the phonetic letter. And
the difference of the mode is derived from the difference of total
and partial grasp in visual perception. Hence, in transcultural
comparative study, it is more appropriate to compare reading difficulties based on alphabetical letters and Kana script, both being

Figure 1

3 VARIETIES OF THE
JAPANESE SCRIPTS

a) KATAKANA

ア	イ	ウ	エ	オ
[a]	[i]	[u]	[e]	[o]

カ	キ	ク	ケ	コ
[ka]	[ki]	[ku]	[ke]	[ko]

サ	シ	ス	セ	ソ
[sa]	[si]	[su]	[se]	[so]

b) HIRAGANA

あ	い	う	え	お
[a]	[i]	[u]	[e]	[o]

か	き	く	け	こ
[ka]	[ki]	[ku]	[ke]	[ko]

さ	し	す	せ	そ
[sa]	[si]	[su]	[se]	[so]

c) KANJI

山	川	花	鳥	魚	人
[yama]	[kawa]	[hana]	[tori]	[uwo]	[hito]
(mountain)	(river)	(flower)	(bird)	(fish)	(human)

児	童	精	神	医	学
[ji -	do	sei -	sin	i -	gaku]

(child psychiatry)

Figure 2

A FEW EXAMPLES OF THE
MIRROR WRITING OF
JAPANESE KANA SCRIPTS

ま [ma]   　a
ま 　b
ヨ [yo]　c
E 　d

phonetical symbols. In Japan, primary instruction of reading begins with Kana script. It has to be noted that reading disability based on alphabetical letters is ten times more frequent than the same disability based on Kana script in spite of the fact that both are phonetic symbols. Let us take the question of strephosymbolia for an example. Such letters as p and q or b and d are mutual mirror figures. If confusion in reading is so derived, it is true that there are no Kana symbols which stand in mirror relationship to each other. But we must discriminate between strephosymbolia in reading and in writing. In the process of learning to write, a formidable number of children in Japan pass through a transient stage of writing the erroneous Figure 2(b) for the legitimate letter in Figure 2(a) or the incorrect Figure 2(d) for Figure 2(c). As learning progresses, however, such mistakes in writing disappear. Since we do not have any readable letter in a mirror-figure situation like p and q or b and d in Kana, mirror reading cannot come into existence.

When the letter g becomes involved in the confusion of p and q it has to be understood as a different matter. The letter g certainly looks like p or q, but it is not their mirror image. The relationship between those letters is nothing but "alike but ambiguous." Similar ambiguous letters are found in the Kana scripts, examples of which are shown in Figure 3. In fact, however, such confusions do not develop into reading difficulty at a clinical level.

Figure 3	Figure 4
"ALIKE BUT AMBIGUOUS" LETTERS IN THE JAPANESE KANA SCRIPTS	EXAMPLES OF CONFUSION DUE TO THE ORDER OF LETTERS IN KANA SCRIPTS

Figure 3

"ALIKE BUT AMBIGUOUS" LETTERS IN THE JAPANESE KANA SCRIPTS

は [ha] and ほ [ho]　　シ [shi] and ツ [tsu]

き [ki] and ま [ma]　　ソ [so] and ン [n]

た [ta] and な [na]　　タ [ta] and ク [ku]

め [me] and ぬ [nu]

Figure 4

EXAMPLES OF CONFUSION DUE TO THE ORDER OF LETTERS IN KANA SCRIPTS

a. さ か な [sa ka na] (fish)　and　さ な か [sa na ka] (in the midst)

b. ニ キ ビ [ni ki bi] (pimple)　and　ビ キ ニ [bi ki ni] (Bikini)

Phonation is indicated in the brackets, while meaning is indicated in the parentheses.

Another similarity is found in both languages. Confusion between whole words—was and saw, left and felt— are said to be a source of reading difficulty in English. Similar ambiguous words exist in Japanese and particularly in Kana scripts, as the examples in Figure 4 indicate.

There are also some counterparts in Kana scripts for such confusions as steady and straight, under and uniform in English (a few examples are illustrated in Figure 5). The difficulty can be attributed to the resemblance of total visual appearance of such words. Confusion of this sort might be expected also in Japanese, but, nevertheless, does not occur in reality. Transient errors in discriminating such words can be found in the learning process in lower grades; however, they are corrigible and do not persist so long as to become the object of clinical practice. The difficulty is likely to be derived from the dominance of intuitive perception of the total figure of a word as a whole over its comprehension by analysis and synthesis. The nature of the difficulty is somewhat akin to a sort of paralexia in Kanji script. In English, such a reading difficulty has to be attributed to the disturbance of correct grasp of each individual letter, the disability of partial perception in one single word. In spite of the similarities of such confusing situations, why should the incidence of poor readers be more frequent in English-speaking communities and so scarce in Japan? One answer, at least, has to be in the difference of specificities of both languages and scripts.

Figure 5

EXAMPLES OF CONFUSION
DUE TO TOTAL FIGURES OF
WORDS IN KANA SCRIPTS

a. だ　い　た　い
[da　i　ta　i]
(approximately)

b. だ　い　た　ん
[da　i　ta　n]
(bold)

c. な　ん　だ　い
[na　n　da　i]
(difficult task)

d. だ　ん　た　い
[da　n　ta　i]
(group)

When the Roman alphabet and <u>Kana</u> scripts are compared, a few distinct differences can be characterized:

1. While letters like <u>a</u>, <u>b</u>, <u>c</u>, <u>d</u> represent either a consonant <u>or</u> a vowel, a letter in the <u>Kana</u> scripts is always a representation of a combination of a consonant <u>and</u> a vowel with which a phoneme ends. Five notations of vowels are exceptions, but the only exception to this general rule in consonants is the notation of the sound of <u>n</u> with which a phoneme ends. A letter in <u>Kana</u> is otherwise always a representation of a syllable ending with the sound of a vowel (Figure 6).

2. In the alphabet, particularly in English, a letter is pronounced in various ways in accordance with how it is spelled with other letters. A letter in <u>Kana</u> scripts, on the contrary, is always read in one consistent way. From a phonetical aspect a sound of /f/ is represented in English by <u>f</u>, <u>ph</u>, and <u>gh</u>. The letter <u>f</u> must sometimes be sounded as /v/. The combination of <u>gh</u> can be silent (requiring no sound) or sounded as /f/. In representations requiring a sound of /n/ there are <u>n</u>, <u>kn</u>, <u>gn</u>, etc. When a sound of /ai/ is required, you find such a variation of spellings as: <u>i</u>, <u>y</u>, <u>igh</u>, <u>eye</u>, <u>ay</u>, <u>ei</u>, <u>aye</u>, <u>ye</u>, <u>ie</u>, <u>ais</u>. In Japanese, in contrast, phonetic units of the /n/ family are always represented by five letters, each of which is a

Figure 6

DIFFERENCE OF CHARACTERISTICS BETWEEN ALPHABET AND KANA SCRIPT

ALPHABET		KANA SCRIPT	
LETTER	SOUND	LETTER	SOUND
a	[a][e][ei]	い *	[i]
b	[b] or silent	ろ	[ro]
c	[k][s]	は	[ha]
d	[d][t]	に	[ni]
⋮		⋮	
a consonant or a vowel		a syllable a combination of a consonant and a vowel with which the uttering ends.	
SOUND	REPRESENTATION	SOUND	REPRESENTATION
[f] ———f, ph, gh, [f][v] [f] or silent [n]——— n kn, gn [ai]———ais ay, aye, ei, eigh, eye, i, ie, igh, y, ye,		na ** ——— な ni ——— に nu ——— ぬ ne ——— ね no ——— の	
direct link of 2 or more consonants.		no direct link of consonants. consonants are always linked through a vowel or vowels	
Unstable script-phonetic relationship: every sound IS NOT represented by corresponding specific letter.		Stable script-phonetic relationship: every sound IS represented by corresponding specific letter. (like in I. T. A.)	

notation of combined sounds of /n/ plus five vowels, as illustrated in Figure 6. And those five letters are consistently read in no other way than /na/, /ni/, /nu/, /ne/, and /no/, respectively.

3. While two or more letters representing consonants may be put together in a word in English, not infrequently resulting in inconsistent pronunciations, there is no way of representing the sound of a consonant alone in Japanese and each consonant is always phonetically tied to another by an intermediate link of a vowel or vowels.

Thus, the script-phonetic relationship, i.e. the relationship between visually perceived letters and corresponding phonetic expressions, is more stable in Japanese Kana script than in the Roman alphabet. While every sound is not represented by a corresponding

Table 3

READING REQUIREMENT IN PRIMARY
EDUCATION

| GRADE | KANA Scripts | | KANJI Script |
	HIRAGANA	KATAKANA	
1st grade	48		46
2nd grade	"	48	105
3rd grade	"	"	187
4th grade	"	"	205
5th grade	"	"	194
6th grade	"	"	144
TOTAL	48	48	881

specific letter in alphabetical language, every sound is represented
by a corresponding specific letter in Kana script. It might be of
interest at this point to call attention to Pittman's "Initial Teaching
Alphabet" ITA). It is comprised of the ordinary 26 Roman letters
plus 22 extra augmented "letters." Forty-eight notations have
been devised to correspond one to each sound. With this ITA, reading capacities of dyslexic children have been said to show formidable improvement. Moreover, the emergence of poor readers has
been reported to be much decreased in primary reading education
when ITA is applied before the ordinary alphabet. The successful
results of Pittman seems, in a way, to explain the rarity of poor
readers among Japanese children in that both use systems of notation in which each individual sound is always represented by a cor-
respondingly exclusive letter.

Kana and Kanji Scripts

A few remarks should be made here on the difference between
Kana and Kanji scripts as reflected in the reading difficulties of
Japanese school children. When these children are divided into
poor Kana readers and poor Kanji readers (Table 2), the poor
Kana readers in the first and the second grades show a marked
drop in the third grade and almost fade away from the fourth grade
on. Although the figures in Table 2 are not the result of follow-up
studies, we know there is scarcely a child who has a formidable
degree of difficulty in reading Kana script in the third grade. But

numbers of poor Kanji readers remain relatively large. In our
primary educational program, the standard reading requirement is
to comprehend the number of letters shown in Table 3. At the end
of the first grade a child is expected to be capable of reading 48
Hiraganas plus 46 easier Kanjis. At the end of the second grade,
48 Katakanas have to be read in addition to the 48 Hiraganas. The
requirement for Kanji is raised to 105 letters. In the higher grades,
more Kanjis of increasing complexity are added. At the end of the
sixth grade, a child has to have mastered 977 symbols in total.
The situation differs entirely from that of reading in alphabetical
language in that the number of characters being read becomes increasingly expanded up to almost innumerable symbols (although
the number in daily use is tentatively restricted to 1,850). The difference between 26 and 1,850 means much. As the requirements
grow harder in advanced grades, the reading of some complicated
characters becomes difficult even for children with normal endowment. The reading difficulty in Kanji script may be related more
to the individual difference of relative learning capacities within the
range of normal intellectual endowment.

Kanji script is composed primarily of classical Chinese characters, as its literal translation indicates (Kanji stands for the character of ancient China). Most are derived from hieroglyphs as
shown in the few examples cited in Figure 7. One character may
may indicate a monosyllabic reading while another could be the
representation of polysyllabic word. For instance, the character
in Figure 8(a) is read as me in a monosyllabic sound (meaning "eye"),
while the character in Figure 8(b) is read in a quadrisyllabic sound
as kuchibiru (meaning "lip"). The process of reading such Kanji
script differs from the reading of a word in alphabetical language or
in Kana script because a symbol is grasped with the total perception
of its figure at a sight, the perception being directly linked to the
meaning represented by that symbol and the pronunciation being deduced from the comprehension of its meaning. In other words, a
total visual perception of a symbol is primarily connected with its
meaning in reading Kanji, and how it is pronounced becomes secondary. A Kanji character usually has two or more pronunciations,
and the way it is correctly read differs depending on how that particular Kanji is combined with other Kanjis or Kanas. For instance,
the character in Figure 8(a) is read as me when it is used in combination with another character representing the meaning of "medicine," the whole word being me-gusuri (literally, "eye drop") as
shown in Figure 9(a). The same letter is also read as gan Figure
9(b). When the character in Figure 8(b) is used with an adjective
meaning "red", as shown in Figure 9(c), it is read as akai kuchibiru,
while the same character is expected to be pronounced as /shin/

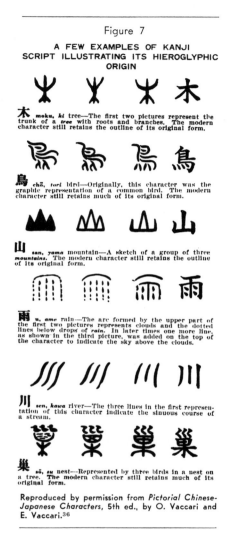

Figure 7

A FEW EXAMPLES OF KANJI SCRIPT ILLUSTRATING ITS HIEROGLYPHIC ORIGIN

木 moku, ki tree—The first two pictures represent the trunk of a *tree* with roots and branches. The modern character still retains the outline of its original form.

鳥 chō, tori bird—Originally, this character was the graphic representation of a common bird. The modern character still retains much of its original form.

山 san, yama mountain—A sketch of a group of three *mountains*. The modern character still retains the outline of its original form.

雨 u, ame rain—The arc formed by the upper part of the first two pictures represents clouds and the dotted lines below drops of *rain*. In later times one more line, as shown in the third picture, was added on the top of the character to indicate the sky above the clouds.

川 sen, kawa river—The three lines in the first representation of this character indicate the sinuous course of a stream.

巣 sō, su nest—Represented by three birds in a nest on a tree. The modern character still retains much of its original form.

Reproduced by permission from *Pictorial Chinese-Japanese Characters*, 5th ed., by O. Vaccari and E. Vaccari.[36]

when in use with another <u>Kanji</u>. Thus the word in the Figure 9 (d) is read as <u>shinon</u> (meaning "labial"). The character in Figure 9 (e) meaning "big" or "large" has at least four ways of being pronounced according to how it is used. The unstable script-phonetic relationship in <u>Kanji</u> is somewhat similar to the unstable script-phonetic relationship in English.

Although the total perception of a visual figure is directly connected with the meaning represented by that figure in the reading of

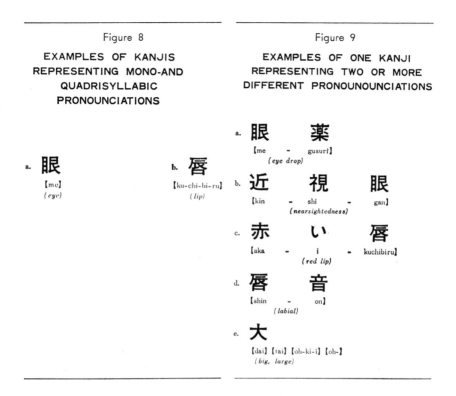

Figure 8

EXAMPLES OF KANJIS
REPRESENTING MONO-AND
QUADRISYLLABIC
PRONOUNCIATIONS

a. 眼
[me]
(eye)

b. 唇
[ku-chi-bi-ru]
(lip)

Figure 9

EXAMPLES OF ONE KANJI
REPRESENTING TWO OR MORE
DIFFERENT PRONOUNOUNCIATIONS

a. 眼　薬
[me　-　gusuri]
(eye drop)

b. 近　視　眼
[kin　-　shi　-　gan]
(nearsightedness)

c. 赤　い　唇
[aka　-　i　-　kuchibiru]
(red lip)

d. 唇　音
[shin　-　on]
(labial)

e. 大
[dai] [tai] [oh-ki-i] [oh-]
(big, large)

Kanji, the process has to be understood as including a function of
discriminating partial details. The discrimination of similar or
ambiguous symbols is accomplished by the differentiation of partial
details in the composition of such ambiguous symbols. For instance,
the characters in Figure 10 may be regarded as somewhat confusing
for foreign readers. Each two characters resemble each other in
their visual figures. However, it can be recognized that in (a) and
(b) the right halves of the characters are different. The characters
in (c) and (d) represent "left" and "right" respectively; the difference lies in their right lower parts. Similarly the characters in
(e) and (f) meaning "flower" and "grass" have their dissimilarity
in the lower parts of their whole compositions. The process of
total grasp of a visual figure runs parallel with a simultaneous function of analyzing and synthesizing partial details. A misconception
due to an erroneous total perception induced by failure to attend to
detail is somewhat like the paralexia between straight and steady
or between left and felt in English. However, there is a significant
difference in the nature of the paralexia. Confusion in partial perception causes paralexic reading faults even in normal subjects in

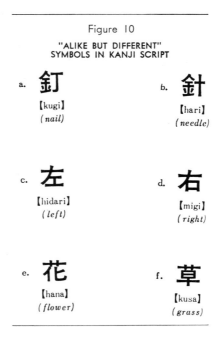

Figure 10

"ALIKE BUT DIFFERENT"
SYMBOLS IN KANJI SCRIPT

a. 釘
【kugi】
(nail)

b. 針
【hari】
(needle)

c. 左
【hidari】
(left)

d. 右
【migi】
(right)

e. 花
【hana】
(flower)

f. 草
【kusa】
(grass)

Kanji, but the mode of such paralexia is usually reading a distortion into a word conceptually related to the written word and is not a misreading into a word with similar spelling or pronunciation. When the localization theory of cerebral functions is introduced, paralexic disorder in English is understood more as a matter of dysfunction in the domain of the visuo-sensory area whereas paralexia in Kanji has to be considered of a transcortical nature, since an additional element of conceptual centrum has to be taken into consideration.

In alexic disturbance due to acquired cerebral lesion in the Japanese patient, it is known that his reading capacity of Kanji remains relatively intact while that of Kana becomes rapidly and massively impaired. The above-mentioned transcortical nature, i.e. the primary connection of a visual perception of a character to its meaning, is assumed as a factor for the higher resistance of Kanji to general reading impoverishment.

It is uncertain, however, whether the specificity of Kanji in acquired alexic disorder could be directly applicable to the process of learning reading. Morphological complexity of Kanji script grows almost endlessly with advanced requirements. It is not an easy task to differentiate the readings of Kanji in two or more ways according to how they are used in combination with other Kanjis or Kanas. Historically, in Japan, uneducated people or those with relatively

poor intellectual endowment managed to read <u>Kana</u> for its simplicity.
To cope with the complexity of <u>Kanji</u> was beyond their reach.

Superficially, there appear to be more communal aspects in reading difficulties between English and <u>Kanji</u> than between English and
<u>Kana</u>, i.e. the difficulty of a total grasp of a word due to perceptual
difficulty of its parts, and the difficulty of discriminating several
ways of reading according to the way a character is used in combination with other characters. However, a distinct difference has to
be accounted as of primary importance—the difference of the mode of
perception <u>per se</u>.

We have to be very careful, therefore, in interpreting the relative
increase of poor <u>Kanji</u> readers in advanced grades. It cannot be interpreted in the same way as is the increase or decrease of poor
<u>Kana</u> readers. Unless we elaborate each individual case, it is dan-
gerous to draw any conclusion, even tentative, on the variability of
such figures. We may speculate (please note that this is a speculation) that the efficiency of learning reading differs with relative general endowment, like efficiencies of any other learning process. It
has to be again emphasized, also, that even with such considerations
the poor <u>Kanji</u> readers are only a part of 0.98%, the total frequency
of children with poor reading capacity in Japan.

CONCLUSION

The fact that poor readers are extremely rare among Japanese
children has to be reexamined from a transcultural philological
point of view. The reason I chose English in making the comparison
with the Japanese language is not only because of the abundance of
reports in English. Some authority has suggested that 60% of reading disability in the world is in English-speaking countries. The
impression I myself gathered in Europe was that the largest numbers
of reading disability were from English-speaking countries, next
from German-speaking countries, and least from Latin-speaking
countries such as Italy or Spain. Impressions of leading child
psychiatrists in Europe almost coincided in this respect. Perhaps
English by far exceeds German or any other Western language in
the number of words in which irregular or unstable relationships
exist between spelling and pronunciation. In this respect Japanese
<u>Kana</u> stands in extreme contrast to English, for in <u>Kana</u> the script-
phonetic relationship is almost a key-to-keyhole situation.

Although the prevalence of reading retardation we obtained through
questionnaires addressed to school teachers was not even one tenth of
that found in Western countries, a reservation must be expressed as

to whether children with poor reading capacity exist "incognito" under the guise of other clinical manifestations. Could there be any possibility that such poor readers are intermingled with mentally retarded children as many autistic children were found in institutions for mentally retarded children in those days when early infantile autism had not been identified? If the child's awareness of reading difficulty itself is a source of emotional distress, as was pointed out by Eisenberg, could there be any instance in which the secondary emotional response reached clinical attention and the primary reading difficulty was overlooked? It will not be justifiable to conclude that the prevalence of reading disability in Japan is really very rare unless such possibilities are finally ruled out. Nevertheless, we have not met with such a report so far and the poor response from child study organizations may be taken to imply the scarceness of such cases.

SUMMARY

Based upon the result of a survey, upon a review of the international literature and upon the specificity of the Japanese language and script, the following tentative conclusions seem warranted:

Theories which ascribe the etiology of reading disability to local cerebral abnormalities, to laterality conflict, or to emotional pressure may be valid for some instances but the specificity of the used language, the very object of reading behavior, is the most potent contributing factor in the formation of reading disability. Reading disability, then, is more of a philological than a neuropsychiatric problem.

REFERENCES

1. Anzai, E., et al. 1966. Lese- und schreibstörungen bei einem 6 jährigen knaben. Psychiat. Neurol. Jap. 68:629-640.

2. Bach, W. 1945. Über die angeborene bzw. frühkindlicherworbene verbale schriebleseschwäche (sogenannte kongenitale wortblindheit) Allg. Z. Psychiat. 124:25-69.

3. Blanchard, P. 1928. Reading disabilities in relation to maladjustment. Ment. Hyg. 12:772-788.

4. Blanchard, P. 1929. Attitudes and education in disabilities. Ment. Hyg. 13:550-563.

5. Blanchard, P. 1935. Psychogenic factors in some cases of reading disability. Amer. J. Orthopsychiat. 5:361-374.

6. Critchley, M. 1960. The evolution of man's capacity for language. In The Evolution of Man, Vol. II, S. Tax, (ed.). Univ. Chicago Press.

7. Critchley, M. 1964. Developmental Dyslexia. Heineman, London.

8. Eisenberg, L. 1966. Reading retardation: I. Psychiatric and sociologic aspects. Pediatrics, 37: 352-365. [Reprinted in the present volume, pages 186-207.]

9. Fabian, A. 1955. Reading disability: An index of pathology, Amer. J. Orthopsychiat. 25:319-329.

10. Gann, E. 1945. Reading Difficulty and Personality Organization. King's Crown Press, New York.

11. Geschwind, N. 1956. Disconnection syndromes in animal and man. Brain, 88:594.

12. Hallgren, B. 1950. Specific dyslexia: A clinical and genetic study. Acta Psychiat. Neurol., Suppl. :65.

13. Hinshelwood, J. 1917. Congenital Word Blindness. Lewis, London.

14. Hinshelwood, J. 1929. Four cases of congenital word blindness occurring in the same family. Brit. Med. J. 2:1229-1299.

15. Imura, T. 1943. Aphasia, its specificity in Japanese language. Psychiatr. Neurol. Jap. 49:196.

16. Kanner, L. 1957. Child Psychiatry, 3rd ed. Charles C Thomas, Springfield, Ill.

17. Kawi, A., and B. Pasamanick. 1959. Prenatal and paranatal factors in the development of childhood reading disorders. Monogr. Soc. Res. Child Develop. 24(4): 1-80.

18. Kirchhoff, H. 1960. Lese- und rechtschreibeschwäche im kindesalter. Basel.

19. Korte, W. 1923. Über die gestaltauffassung im indirekten sehen. Ztschr. f. Psychol. u. Physiol. 93:17-82.

20. Kuromaru, S., Y. Okada, et al. 1962. On developmental alexia and agraphia. J. Ped. Practice, 25:853.

21. Kussmaul, A. 1877. Disturbance of speech. In Cyclopedia of Practical Medicine. 14:581-875.

22. Missildine, W. The emotional background of thirty children with reading disability. Nerv. Child, 5: 263-272.

23. Monroe, M. 1932. Children Who Cannot Read. Univ. Chicago Press.

24. Morgan, W. 1896. A case of congenital word blindness. Brit. Med. J. 2:1378-1379.

25. Mountcastle, V. 1962. Interhemispheric Relation and Cerebral Dominance. Johns Hopkins Press, Baltimore.

26. Obi, I. 1957. Über die angeborne lese- und schreibschwäche. Psychiat. Neurol. Jap. 59:852-867.

27. Ohashi, H. 1960. Aphasia, Apraxia and Agnosia. Igakushoin, Osaka.

28. Orton, S. 1925. Word blindness in school children. Arch. Neurol. & Psychiat. 14:581-615.

29. Rabinovitch, R., et al. 1954. A research approach to reading retardation. Res. Nerv. & Ment. Dis. 34: 363-396.

30. Sakamoto, S. 1940. A contribution to Kanji-Kana problem in dyslexia. Bull. Osaka Red Cross Med. 4: 185-212.

31. Schenk-Danzinger, L. Der zusammenhang der legasthenie mit anderen psychischen faktoren. Bericht d. 3. Int. Kongresses f. Heilpäd.

32. Schenk-Danzinger, L. 1959. Handbuch der Psychologie, 10. Bd.

33. Schenk-Danzinger, L. 1961. Probleme der legasthenie. Schweiz. Ztschr. f. Psychologie, 20.

34. Taguchi, T. 1962. Speech disorders in children. Psychiat. Neurol. Jap. 2:3-14.

35. Tulchin, S. 1935. Emotional factors in reading disabilities in school children. J. Educ. Psychol. 26:443-454.

36. Vaccari, O. and E. Vaccari. 1964. Pictorial Chinese-Japanese Characters, 5th ed. Vaccari's Language Institute Press, Tokyo.

37. Weinschenk, C. 1965. Die erbliche lese-rechtschreibeschwäche und ihre sozialpsychiatrischen auswirkungen. H. Huber, Bern u. Stuttgart.

IV. THE TEACHING OF READING: THE STATE OF THE ART

READING INSTRUCTION 1967

by William D. Sheldon

There are a number of issues raised by teachers, parents, and the press concerning reading instruction in America. Such diverse authorities on learning as psychologists, psychiatrists, optometrists, curriculum generalists, and reading specialists all have something to say about the manner in which reading should be taught and when it should be taught. After careful consideration of the issues, I have selected the six which I consider most pertinent to the development of sound reading instruction. There are many other issues worth discussion, but these seem to merit prior consideration: teaching the preschool or nursery child to read, the role of the kindergarten in the reading program, methods and materials for first grade instruction, teaching disadvantaged children to read, teaching students to read in the secondary schools, and the role of the school in teaching illiterate adolescents and adults to read. Among other issues of less importance but still worthy of comment if space permitted are the value of i.t.a., the use of machines as instructional aids, the place of programed materials, the contributions of linguists to beginning reading, speed reading, and the improvement of perception through special materials created originally for the brain-injured.

Teaching the Preschool or Nursery
School Child to Read

Should we teach preschool and nursery school children to read, or should we spend the years from birth until the time children

---

From The Shape of English (Champaign, Illinois, National Council of Teachers of English, 1967), pp. 49-73. Reprinted by permission of the National Council of Teachers of English and William D. Sheldon.

enter kindergarten or first grade preparing them in a general, informal, and unstructured way to cope with the listening and speaking aspects of their language?

For almost a century it has been customary to begin the teaching
of reading when children entered the first grade. Children were
ordinarily six years of age, and fifty percent of them had attended
a kindergarten designed for the education of the four- and five-year-
old child. A few of these children had attended nursery schools.
These were either the children of the elite or the children of the
poor who, because parents worked, were housed in welfare-
sponsored daycare centers. While some reading instruction did
go on at the pre-six-year-old level, it was random in nature, not
publicized, and usually provided for the very bright three-, four-,
or five-year-old child.

In the last dozen years, however, the laissez-faire attitude toward the formal education of the very young has given way to a
much more academic approach. Now a large number of documented
experiments and demonstrations suggest that the very young can be
taught to read, that some learn to read on their own, and possibly
that young children should be taught to read long before they reach
the age of six.

The principal and most publicized advocates of early reading are
Omar K. Moore,[1] Nancy M. Rambusch,[2] Dolores Durkin,[3] a number
of researchers in Denver Public Schools, a number of psychologists
and sociologists working with disadvantaged children, and Doman.[4]

Moore's work received a great deal of attention in the 1950's
largely because of the dramatic presentation of his experiments
through films entitled Early Reading and Writing. The films pic-
tured Dr. Moore and several associates using an electric typewriter, a tachistoscope, and a chalkboard to instruct two- and
three-year-old children in reading and writing.

Following his first relatively primitive experiment, Dr. Moore,
in cooperation with Mr. Richard Kobler of the Thomas A. Edison
Research Laboratories, developed the Edison Responsive Environment System (ERE), a learning system which has been called the
"Talking Typewriter." The ERE has been established in several
schools and in at least one hospital. In the Freeport, New York,
Public Schools, an experiment, reported by Dr. John H. Martin,
determined the validity of the ERE as a medium for teaching reading to kindergarten and mentally retarded children.[5]

In June 1966, Moore announced that his Responsive Environment's
equipment would be used in Chicago to provide disadvantaged pre-
schoolers with basic intellectual skills.[6] Sargent Shriver, then Director of the Office of Economic Opportunity, stated that his office
would provide twenty ERE machines to help New York's culturally

deprived children and nonliterate adults[7] From the latest announce-
ments of the installation of ERE machines one might conclude that
they are being used largely with primary grade children, brain-
injured and mentally defective children, and nonliterate adults.
Interest in using the ERE with very young children seems to have
waned although unpublicized research and experimentation might
be going on.

Nancy M. Rambusch presented an American approach to the
Montessori method in Learning How to Learn[8] Mrs. Rambusch's
book describes the adaptations of methods originally developed by
Madame Montessori as they are used with three-year-olds and
other children in private schools such as that in Whitby, Connecticut.
Mrs. Rambusch not only discussed what was taking place at Whitby
but depicted her ideal school of the next decade, a school "in which
the arbitrary distinctions of pre-school versus 'real' school have
disappeared, one in which children from age three until age eight
are thought of as being in the first phase of learning." Special
teachers would be available at specific times to help in the first
group acquire the skills of reading, writing, and mathematics as
the academic portion of their learning. One receives the impression from the Rambusch book that the pursuit of reading and writing
is encouraged by the environment and facilitated by direct instruction
after children have tried to learn to read and write by themselves.

During the past several years more than 150 nursery level Montessori schools have developed. The Montessori movement is finding a
reception on the fringes of American public and private education.
Critics of current Montessori schools range from Edward Wakin of
Fordham University, who points out that what was revolutionary in
Montessori's proposals in the early 1900's has become commonplace
today[9] to Evelyn Beyer, Director of Nursery School and teacher at
Sarah Lawrence College, who suggests, among other things: "By over-
stressing achievement and one proper means of achieving, the Montessori method overlooks something of prime importance in any education
of the very young—the children's feelings."[10] Regardless to critical
comment, the impact of formal instruction of three-, four- and five-
year-olds in Montessori and other types of private nursery schools
will have an influence on education in both private and public kindergartens which could lead to a formal structuring of kindergarten programs. It will be virtually impossible for kindergarten teachers to
argue against teaching formal reading in their classes if parents have
already sent their children to Montessori schools where reading and
writing are often taught to three- and four-year-olds.

Although Moore's work and the presence of Montessori schools
will have some effect on the curriculum for young children, the

effect will cause scarcely a ripple compared to the efforts in the
Denver Public Schools. The Denver reading research program consists of two chief studies, one dealing with preschool children and
the other concerned with kindergarten children. Our comments at
this point will relate to the efforts with preschool children. According to a letter received at Syracuse University from the office
of Joseph E. Brzeinski (director, Department of Research Services,
Denver Public Schools), the pioneer parent-education program conducted by the Denver Public Schools during the school year 1960-
1961 and continuing in 1961-1962 provided a program for parents
of preschool children, designed to instruct parents in ways to teach
their children some beginning reading skills. Parents learned from
sixteen taped television programs and were also guided by a manual
entitled Preparing Your Child for Reading.[11] The lessons in the
booklet focus on those prereading steps which help children to discriminate among sounds, relate sounds to letters, and utilize a
combination of initial letter sounds and context to supply words in
sentences. The material is learned through a series of well-planned
lessons which involve a friendly cooperation between parent and
child. Some lessons, such as the one learned through the game
"Giant Steps," require the addition of a neighbor child.

The introduction to Preparing Your Child for Reading provides
the rationale of the program. It states: "Many parents are eager
to help the child become an independent reader as soon as possible.
That is why it is important to teach him an economical and effective
procedure to use in finding out all by himself what are given strange
printed words. Would you like to help your child get ready to learn
this procedure? It is the purpose of this guide to provide you with
definite suggestions for doing just that." I have no quarrel with
the simple steps presented in Preparing Your Child for Reading.
We might well shudder, however, at what could happen when
thousands of eager parents, guided by television lessons and using
this booklet, launch an attack on their young children. Obviously,
we cannot quarrel with the idea that parents should cooperate with
their own children in such a venture. We can only express our
deep concern about what may happen when relatively untutored
parents begin to press very young children into the formal routine
presented in this program.

Bernard Spodek reacted to the parent participation in the Denver
program and the use of the workbook in a review found in Elementary
English. In concluding his article Mr. Spodek writes:

> We do know that there are some activities in which all parents
> can participate that will help their children read sooner and
> better. The support of language activities in the family setting

is such an activity. Parents can read to children and this will
improve their reading achievement. Parents can provide opportunities for speaking to children and listening to them in a
host of informal situations and this will improve their reading
achievement. Similarly, giving children verbal labels for their
experiences as well as providing a rich variety of experiences
will help children read better and, possibly, sooner. These
activities would also provide some concomitant learnings that
early introduction to workbooks would not; a setting would develop that would facilitate positive mental health in the family.[2]
The televised series Preparing Your Child for Reading has been
tested on various educational television stations and has been used
widely by educational television stations throughout the United
States. One of the early stages in the experiment has been described by Anastasia McManus.[13] The Denver Schools coordinated
their preschool instruction with that in the schools and can not report experimental evidence which shows the advantages of early
instruction. Other schools have adopted the Denver approach and
articles describing their programs, which I shall mention later,
have appeared in educational journals.

The long term effect of the Denver and similar experiments and
demonstrations will be hard to measure. The magnitude and apparent success of the program will affect many parents and will
not only encourage them to teach their preschool children to read
but also undoubtedly cause them to put pressure on the schools
to teach reading in kindergarten to the very young.

It is apparent that for the next decade at least we will observe
many programs of preschool reading instruction conducted by
parents or in nursery schools. The overall effect of the program
on children in terms of their interest in reading at a later date or
their general maturation in learning will probably never be evaluated.
However, it is clear that if schools want to maintain an unstructured
kindergarten with a minimum of formal instruction, educators will
have to be persuasive indeed. Parents and educators intrigued by
the published results of the Denver Project might read the reviews
of the study written by Kenneth D. Wann.[14] Wann's specific comments are reported later in this paper.

Dolores Durkin has written a number of articles and a book related to a limited group of children who learned to read before
entering school. From findings elicted from a group of forty-nine
children and a replication of the study, Miss Durkin has encouraged
the idea that because a number of children have learned to read on
their own, revisions need to be made in the curriculum provided
young children in the first days in school. At the conclusion of a
careful summary of her findings, Miss Durkin asks: "What is the

function of the total kindergarten program in the 1960's? It is both
safe and sensible to assume that different communities will find different answers to this most fundamental of questions. It is probably
safe to assume, too, that some of the answers will include help
with reading for some five-year-olds. If this is the case, it is the
sincere hope of this writer that findings from these two studies of
early readers will provide at least a small amount of guidance in
making decisions about what is appropriate help for five-year-old
children who are ready to read."[15]

The reports of those working with extremely disadvantaged preschool pupils are too recent for definitive evaluation. However,
Walter Hodges has reviewed the recent book of Bereiter and
Engleman.[16]   He suggests that the authors propose a departure
from the traditions of early childhood education. Hodges praises
the book as being wonderfully complete and specific but states that
the authors "provide little evidence that the program accomplishes
the goal of helping experimental groups catch up to more advantaged
groups except by presenting larger than typical IQ and ITPA gains."[17]
Hodges' report raises questions about the advantages of the program
which can only be answered by the passage of time and continued
study by the experimenters. The articles of Deutsch[18] and others
raise questions which also demand time and continued study before
definitive answers can be given. However, it is apparent that
educators of very young advantaged and disadvantaged children are
going to pursue experimentation using formal means to open up the
minds of young children and accelerate their acquisition of academic
skills.

The most startling publication related to teaching the very young
was that of Glenn Doman.[19] Among other things, Doman suggests
that two years of age is the best time to teach children to read.
He also says that if one would go to a little trouble he could begin
instruction at eight months or even as early as ten months of age.

The efforts which are being made by teachers, parents, and
psychologists to teach the very young continue. Those who are
particularly interested in the disadvantaged see the preschool period
as one in which there is an urgent need for intervention in the form
of specific education. Whether or not the various preschool programs
will yield valuable results, only time will tell. Opinions at least of
the efficacy of structured, formal reading instruction are sharply
divided, and will probably continue to be until one group yields to
the other or parents and experimenters become tired of the efforts
to teach the very young and move on to other projects.

The Role of the Kindergarten
in the Reading Program

Evidence that there is an issue related to the role of the kindergarten in the reading program can be found in recent issues of such
educational journals as The Reading Teacher, Elementary English,
The Elementary School Journal, and Childhood Education.   The
question seems to boil down to this: Should we or should we not teach
children to read in the kindergarten?

For more than a hundred years the kindergarten in American
schools has served as a nonacademic, unstructured, informal year
aiding the child to make the transition from a home where he often
ruled as the center of attention with few responsibilities to a first
grade program relatively heavy in broad social and academic demands.

During the 1950's surveys of schools in New York State conducted
by the staff of the Syracuse University Reading and Language Arts
Center revealed a definite shift in the kindergarten program from
informality to formality, from unstructured to structured programs,
and from a generally fluid approach to the development of concepts,
listening-speaking skills, and emphasis on the growth of social and
emotional status of individuals to a rather rigid academic approach
to the teaching of readiness for reading and actual reading instruction, plus a gradual overall change from the child's garden to a
rather rigid academic environment.[20]

Educators across the United States, aware that changes were
taking place in the kindergarten, began to search for evidence to
support their heretofore unassailable position on the kindergarten
as an informal learning center. It was noted, for example, that
the Soviets do not begin formal reading instruction until children
are seven. During the kindergarten year the Soviets teach children
to classify, discriminate, compare, and designate what they see
through discussion in appropriate language. The curriculum includes drawing, construction, and general language development.
The teaching of reading and writing is not suggested as starting in
the kindergarten but as growing out of the language development
program of the kindergarten which features oral and prebook learning. The Soviets look upon the kindergarten year as a time of informal learning. Indeed the reported kindergarten resembles the
relatively unstructured program for five-year-olds which has been
traditional in American schools for many years.[21]

In Sweden, according to Malmquist, children start school about
one year later than children in the United States and England.[22]
Swedish educators feel that from both psychological research and

pedagogical experience it is a great advantage for children to start school as late as seven. Many Swedish psychologists and teachers feel that the late beginning age is one of the important reasons why comparatively so few children have reading disabilities in the elementary schools of Sweden.

Other educators noted that children who learn to read and write at a very early age, either on their own or with some slight guidance from others, are present in almost every school in the United States. A survey made by Durkin in Oakland, California, could probably be replicated with similar results in almost any community.[23] Durkin found a number of boys and girls who had begun to read before entering school. During the past year the writer has observed children in a number of schools on Long Island who entered the kindergarten able to identify words and, in several cases, able to read simple material in more or less competent fashion. There is little or no proof, however, that these children maintain their initial advantage when compared with children of similar ability at a later age.

The reports of Brzeinski, Harrison, and McKee,[24] related to the Denver Experiment, and that of Hillerick[25] suggest that children can be taught to read successfully in the kindergarten. No evidence was found that early instruction in beginning reading affected visual acuity, created problems of school adjustment, or caused dislike for reading.

Wann, in a comment on the Denver Experiment, stated that the Denver program merited careful consideration by those interested in developing modern kindergarten programs. After pointing out the balanced approach of the Denver experimenters and noting the following advice given to teachers:

> Go at a rational pace and limit instruction to 20 minutes a day
> Be prepared to stop temporarily or to retrench if necessary
> Excuse from the experiment any child unable to handle the material
> Avoid pushing the children to get through the program by a given date,

Wann stated that these suggestions imply that some pupils can:

> learn all that the activities aim to teach, that others can absorb some but not all of this learning, that still others can absorb little if anything, and that each pupil, without being pushed, should be given the chance to learn all that he can. These are pertinent observations and should be heeded by anyone planning to develop such a program beginning at the kindergarten level.[26]

Wann also suggested that reading must be only one part of a sound
kindergarten program and that "to focus too narrowly on a reading
program is to fail to recognize the great range of experiences five-
year-olds need in order to meet their developmental tasks."[27]

A number of other educators have commented on this issue.
Dolores Durkin presented a bibliography entitled Reading and the
Kindergarten[28] in 1964. In twenty-three articles nineteen educators
presented the pros and cons of the subject. An interesting report
by Elizabeth A. Zaruba presented the attitudes of teachers toward
beginning reading instruction in the kindergarten. Miss Zaruba
concluded that most kindergarten and primary teachers had positive
attitudes toward reading instruction in the kindergarten.[29]

I will restate the crucial question we are asking: Should the kindergarten abandon its traditional unstructured program and become
a first grade in terms of learning activities? Psychologists, pediatricians, and educators in general have contradictory things to say
about the effect of introducing reading and writing to four- and five-
year-olds. One can read research reports and not be entirely convinced one way or the other. The best single procedure might be
to visit a number of kindergartens and observe the reaction of boys
and girls in structured and unstructured classes. A subtle factor
which escapes immediate detection in terms of any comparative
study is the children's interest in reading at a later date. This observer has seen tension and strain in the kindergarten where reading
instruction his been carried on. There is no conclusive evidence
concerning the value or harm done by teaching children to read in
the kindergarten instead of in the first grade. We know that children
can be taught to read at five. Our concerns are, first, whether or
not the advantage of early learning persists and therefore makes the
strain and struggle worthwhile, and second, whether interest in
later reading is increased or diminished by the earlier introduction
of a disciplined approach to learning. My own private plea is for
informality in the kindergarten and a subtle, carefully developed
program which leads children to a step-by-step maturity in conceptual development and listening and speaking skills, a knowledge
of stories and poems, and a sound social and emotional development.[30]

Methods and Materials in
First Grade Reading Instruction

The most hotly debated issue of those considered in this paper
relates to which methods and what materials are the best to use in

teaching in first grade. The debate over the best approach to the teaching of reading to beginners began more than a hundred years ago. Educators such as Horace Mann wrote their views on the problem as early as the 1830's. The argument has not been two-sided but rather has advocates representing many points of view. The most publicized attack on initial reading instruction was that of Rudolph Flesch, and the views expressed in his best seller, Why Johnny Can't Read.[31] Flesch advocated the use of a synthetic system of phonics for first grade reading instruction. Because of the manner of his attack on the then current methods and his denigration of the position of leading United States reading authorities, Flesch drew the fire of virtually the entire reading establishment. The Carnegie Corporation entered the debate, and as a result of a widely publicized meeting of twenty-two nationally known reading experts, published a paper in which the eclectic position attacked by Flesch was defended.

In 1959, between the time of the publication of Flesch's book and the issuance of the Carnegie report,[32] reading specialists from all parts of the United States gathered at Syracuse University to discuss needed research in reading. As a result of three days of discussion, it was decided that the area of reading instruction in greatest need of research was the first grade. From 1959 to 1963 a committee sought funds to carry on a coordinated national research study of first grade reading. In 1964 the USOE awarded approximately $30,000 to each of twenty-seven research centers to carry on the proposed study. Eleven widely different methods, represented by a variety of materials, were tested in some five hundred classrooms of first grade children during 1964-1965. Summary reports of the studies appearing in the May and October 1966 and the March 1967 issues of The Reading Teacher revealed that by and large methods and materials were not the crucial elements in teaching first grade children to read. Such variables as teachers, the intelligence of children, and the socio-economic status of pupils all seemed more crucial than methodology or materials. In fact, I concluded that the most important single factor in developing a successful first grade reading program is the teacher—not a novel idea by any means. The full impact of the first grade experiment has not yet been measured, and it is likely that much of it will be dissipated by a lack of follow-up. While thirteen of the research centers did follow their populations through the second grade, only a few are currently studying the continuing effects on third grade pupils.

Among the procedures and materials used, we find the language-experience approach, a variety of standard basal reading series, an italicized basal version developed by Edward Fry at Rutgers University, the i.t.a., several linguistic approaches, and a variety of phonics programs.

While the initial findings of the studies and the lack of complete follow-up of the children involved is quite disappointing, the studies did encourage the participants to evaluate new methods and materials quite carefully before launching into their use. In the schools in which the Reading and Language Arts Center of Syracuse University studies of linguistics, i.t.a., phonics, and basal readers were made, teachers and administrators learned to appreciate the often overlooked variables mentioned above as ones to be reckoned with in any program of instruction. For example, the effect of continued inservice evaluation of ongoing programs caused teachers to raise questions about what they were doing. The continued presence of supervisors aided teachers in seeking solutions to specific questions and eliminated the feeling of frustration that comes when teachers feel left alone and ignored by the rest of the school.

The several research teams who have continued to evaluate boys and girls in the initial first grade study should be able to present interesting findings in the next few years which might suggest advantages of this method or that material not discovered after one year of study. Positive and negative results on continued learning might be observed as the longitudinal studies are made. We at Syracuse University are interested, for example, in following the boys who, contrary to usual results, were not less able in reading than comparable girls after one year. Will these boys maintain or lose their equal status as the years pass? This and other questions will add to our insights about the learning of reading.

Other studies of first grade or initial reading instruction are contributing to our understanding of best procedures without causing the emotional reactions which accompanied the Flesch book. The study of David E. Bear is typical of those which compare two phonic methods of teaching beginning reading, synthetic and analytic. Bear defined the synthetic method as that of synthesizing of sounds into words as contrasted with the analytic method, which involved the analysis of whole words. Bear found, in a study of two groups of pupils each taught by one of the two phonic approaches, that pupils in the middle range of intelligence received greater benefit from synthetic phonics than pupils in the highest and lowest twenty-five percent. The longitudinal aspect of Bear's study made it particularly valuable as he followed his pupils through the sixth grade and found that initial advantages were maintained. Bear concluded from his study that the proponents of basal readers using an analytic phonics approach and proponents of those using synthetic phonics should abandon their extreme positions and combine the best elements from both approaches.[33] An inspection of several revised basal reading programs suggests that editors of basal readers have modified their positions and use synthetic phonics much earlier in their programs than heretofore in combination with the usual analytic procedures.

The study of Bliesmer and Yarborough, one of the most comprehensive studies on the topic of first grade reading, has elicited a wide response, both postive and negative.[34] It deserves attention because, unlike many studies, the data are drawn from comparisons of five analytic methods and five synthetic methods rather than comparisons of one analytic method and one synthetic method. The researchers found that the synthetic methods in general produced significantly superior results in virtually all measures of reading achievement. While the limitations of this study, indicated by the researchers, suggest broad replication and the need for longitudinal follow-up, it is a valuable contribution to the debate.

The contributions of i.t.a. to first grade reading instruction were explored in several of the USOE first grade studies. In addition, two articles pro- and con- i.t.a. experimentation have appeared recently in the Phi Delta Kappan.[35] I was tempted to consider i.t.a. as a major issue in reading instruction, but the article of Downing, in particular, seems to suggest broad misinterpretation in the use of i.t.a. by Americans and evidence of a family argument between advocates of i.t.a. He suggests more or less that an appraisal of i.t.a. in terms of its contribution to reading instruction should wait for further research and evaluation.

The textbooks used in first grade reading instruction have come in for heavy criticism, particularly from the press. It has been noted that the content of preprimers, in particular, "has been the target of public criticism, scorn or ridicule" in the form of cartoons, jokes, and comments.[36]   Unlike the superficial criticisms of the public and press, based largely on impressions, four University of Colorado researchers studied first grade reading textbooks because of their "concern with the value of preprimers and primer stories in developing children's interest in reading."[37] The researchers centered their studies on finding how appropriate the materials were for boys and girls, how appropriate they are for six-year-old children, and how successfully the activities are carried out.[38]

"The examination led to several impressions. First, the description of primers as pollyannish, as representative of the upper-middle class, and as unrelated to real life situations have some truth. Second, the stories depicted activities that in real life are most frequently engaged in by children younger than most first graders. Rarely did the stories tell of activities appropriate for children older than first graders. Third, the activities were those in which girls rather than boys usually take part. Fourth, frequently stories in which children did not attain the constructive goals of the activities were common. Finally, the activities that boys most frequently engage in were the activities in which the goals were most frequently not achieved. "[39]

The researchers indicate a need for further study, particularly in terms of the effect of the stories on later interest in reading. They cite that the original Hollins study[40] of commonly used first grade readers is now being replicated and the results will establish a more current analysis of first grade texts. There is little debate over the lack of pertinency of much first grade material to today's pupils. Textbook publishers are aware of the issues and are creating multi-ethnic texts with a more mature content emphasizing stories which will appeal to boys as well as girls.

It is apparent in 1967 that much of the former complacency concerning first grade reading instruction has disappeared. No single textbook company or no proponent of the way of teaching beginning reading can hope to engage the serious attention of all or nearly all first grade teachers as was true in the early 1950's. The questions raised by Flesch, the answers given them, and further questions raised by researchers since 1955 suggest that future methods and materials of first grade instruction will be based on sounder research which should do much to obviate the possibility that an inadequate initial reading program is responsible for later failure in reading

Teaching Disadvantaged Children to Read

There is no debate about the necessity of taking special measures to insure success in teaching disadvantaged children to read. Argument does exist, however, concerning these issues: the need for early intervention and whether it should involve direct or indirect language instruction; whether it is better to transport pupils to schools where they learn with predominantly advantaged pupils or make the attempt to improve facilities in the neighborhood school; the approach used in text materials for the disadvantaged; and whether or not the materials should reflect the race, dialects, and environment of the disadvantaged.

There is no easy answer to any of the debated issues concerning the disadvantaged. At the present time educators and others usually refer to the Negro living in the center city ghettos when they talk of the disadvantaged. A recent visitor to a remedial center operated by the writer observed that only three Negro children were present and said, "I see you are not particularly concerned in this center with the disadvantaged." Actually, almost all white children in the group could be labelled as disadvantaged

not only when judged for their inability to read, but also when
measured on any socioeconomic yardstick.

   The literature and the research on the disadvantaged is extremely
limited. The conference reported in the volume Compensatory
Education for Cultural Deprivation gives the reader some general
guidelines in working with the disadvantaged.[41] The previously mentioned book by Bereiter and Engleman is one of the few reports of
actual research which leads to programs for the disadvantaged
young. More than one hundred reports have been written in various
magazines, newspapers, and educational journals related to Opera
tion Headstart, a program designed specifically for the very young,
preschool culturally disadvantaged children. The reactions are
mixed, and one is left with the feeling that an evaluation of the pertinency of the projects under Operation Headstart is very much
needed.

   Ausubel has suggested a teaching strategy for culturally deprived
pupils involving cognitive and motivational considerations. He states
that "an effective and appropriate teaching strategy for the culturally
deprived child must therefore emphasize these three considerations:
(a) the selection of initial learning material geared to the learner's
existing state of readiness; (b) mastery and consolidation of all ongoing learning tasks before new tasks are introduced...; and (c) the
use of structured learning materials optimally organized to facilitate
efficient sequential learning."[42] He believes that "we may discover
that the most effective method of developing intrinsic motivation to
learn is to focus on the cognitive rather than on the motivational
aspects of learning, and to rely on the motivation that is developed
retroactively from successful educational achievement."[43]

   Riessman has helped us understand the educationally or culturally disadvantaged by discussing their characteristics.[44] He describes the deprived individual as being slow at cognitive tasks but
not stupid, appearing to learn most readily through a concrete approach, often appearing to be anti-intellectual, being pragmatic
rather than theoretical, being inflexible and not open to reason about
his beliefs, and being deficient in auditory attention and interpretation skills. Riessman also mentions a number of strengths of the
disadvantaged, many of which unfortunately work to his disadvantage
in a competitive, middle-class school situation.

   A careful perusal of the literature of language arts research reveals little that is related directly to the problems or issues which
we debate. There is some evidence that early intervention does
help the young child participate more fully when he enters formal
education, but this is usually based on observation rather than
research. The problem of whether it is better to transport or "bus"
pupils to schools out of their environment is clouded by the emotion-

ality both of those who see this as the solution and of those who feel
that this is not a good answer to the problem. While the Detroit
Public Schools have participated in the development of a new type
of text specifically designed for the disadvantaged child, we have
yet to see evidence that the material has resulted in advantages for
the children when compared with standard text material.

To date the linguist has suggested that teachers accept the dialect
of their pupils as their standard speech and teach him standard English more or less as a second language. No practical answer has
been presented concerning the reading and writing of standard and
non-standard English.

At the present time we need research into every aspect of the
education of the disadvantaged. There is no doubt that it will be
undertaken, but we are impatient to receive the guidance research
will yield the teacher, parent, school official, and textbook pub-
lisher.

Teaching Students to Read
in the Secondary Schools

It hardly seems possible that an argument exists over whether
or not students in the secondary schools need to be or should be
taught reading. The debate, in which I have participated within the
past school year, revolves around these questions: Who should teach
reading in the secondary school—the English teacher, the content-
area teachers or a special reading teacher? Who should be taught—
the average or above average students who read on grade level, the
student who reads below grade level or the student designated as
remedial and who enters the secondary school reading five or more
years below grade level? At what point should reading instruction
terminate for each of the above groups of students, and what is done
with those who remain semiliterate in spite of the schools' best
efforts?

In a few research centers in the United States, work is being
carried on to determine what the secondary pupil needs in the way
of reading instruction and how he can be best taught. Margaret J.
Early, Harold Herber, and I, working in a Project English center,
have produced a series of ten films in junior and senior high school
settings which demonstrates the full scope of the reading problem
in the secondary school. The films and related manuals suggest
that developmental reading instruction needs to be carried on by
reading specialists during the junior high school years, that corrective and remedial reading instruction is called for throughout

the secondary school for some students, and that teachers of the
content areas must teach the effective reading of their subject to
guarantee its mastery. The goals of secondary reading instruction
have been well stated by Robert B. Heilman:

> The graduating senior high school student should be one who
> has been trained in planning his own reading activities and one
> who has acquired effective study habits so that he can continue
> to use reading to learn. He should have become able to use
> reading as a guide and aid to creative endeavor so that he can
> lead a full, active life. He should be able to read thoughtfully
> and make critical judgments about what is read so that he may
> appraise the validity of the author's point of view and the ac-
> curacy of his statements. The high school reading program
> should develop readers who can and will read for pleasure,
> information, and continued growth in their chosen occupations
> and in their social understandings.[45]

Whether or not a viable program of reading instruction will be
developed in the secondary school is debatable. Most observers,
however, believe that unless the curriculum includes such instruction, the number of semiliterate and illiterate adolescents leaving
high school will continue to increase and in a highly technical
society will need to be maintained by their more literate peers.

The Role of the School in Teaching Illiterate
Adolescents and Adults to Read

The debate concerning the illiterate mainly concerns responsibility. Which institution is responsible for teaching the illiterate
adolescent and adult to read? Several minor issues relate to the
kind of materials, the training of teachers of illiterates, and the
support of the illiterate while he studies.

My position is that it is the duty of the public and private schools
of America to provide for the education of the illiterates in every
community. The problem of illiteracy in the United States is enormous. It is estimated that there are more than eleven million
male adolescent and adult illiterates, and five hundred thousand
semi-literate individuals leave the schools each year.

Despite the scope of the problem of illiteracy, no real action to
reduce illiteracy has been taken by the schools of America. At the
present time educators are trying to determine which agency or
agencies have the major responsibility for teaching the illiterate;

at present all sorts of public-spirited groups—service organizations and churches—are attempting to deal with illiterates in specific communities. The United States government's efforts are sponsored through the Department of Labor, the Office of Economic Opportunity, and the United States Office of Education.

Adult educators have been concerned mainly with the instruction of those in need of continuing education—not basic literacy. It seems apparent that American educators have not been prepared to assume a role in educating the illiterates living in each school district. However, it is expected that through governmental pressure and the interest of industry and individuals, the school will soon have an opportunity to choose whether it or some other agency is to eradicate the blight of illiteracy on the American scene.

Most of the reports on illiteracy and the treatment of illiterates come from agencies other than the school. It is probable that most college reading centers deal with random adult and adolescent illiterates. The report by Rosner and Schatz from the Reading Clinic at Temple University is probably typical of the experiences in most college reading clinics. Rosner and Schatz describe such aspects of their program as evaluation and instruction. They studied ten adults—nine male and one female—ranging in age from 18 to 42. Their description of techniques of instruction and material used could provide others with limited guidance. The results of the program were mixed and no growth patterns were provided.[46]

For many years the Laubachs, Frank and Robert, have worked to provide teachers with the techniques and materials of literacy instruction. The famous slogan of the elder Laubach, "Each One Teach One," is known around the world. At the present time, under the leadership of Robert Laubach, many volunteers teaching in churches and schools are bringing initial literacy to adults in rural areas and city centers. Research, other than the doctoral dissertation of Robert Laubach,[47] is lacking. The efficacy of the program is assumed as an act of faith by men who have seen thousands of men and women take their first steps toward literacy. The book Toward World Literacy provides the neophyte teacher with the basic steps of the Laubach approach.[48] News For You, a weekly newspaper written by the staff of the Laubach Literacy Center, provides up-to-date reading material for new literates. If a program similar to that of the Laubachs were available to adolescents and adults within the framework of our American elementary and secondary schools, it is possible that the first steps towards the eradication of illiteracy would be taken.

TV, as a means of instructing the illiterate, has had some success. The case for the use of TV in coping with the masses of illiterates has been stated by Pauline Hord. Hord reviews the television programs in Memphis and the five years she spent creating lessons which resulted in ninety-eight films now used in TV stations in Alabama, Georgia, Texas, and Arkansas.[49]

The Diebold Literacy Project was a valiant attempt sponsored by the National Council of Churches and the Diebold Group Inc. to provide a well-designed program for the illiterate adult. The fascinating efforts of John Blythe and his staff have been reported in an article by Burrill L. Crohn.[50] It must be noted that in the case of this program, two organizations, both outside the school, provided the money and talent for the project. It is my hope that through the sponsorship of the USOE, with an assist from OEO, the job of developing literacy programs for the millions of illiterates will be assumed by the schools, not as a part of adult education or continuing education, but as a specific program held within the school, during the school day and with a full program provided so that the illiterate not only learns to read and write, but also acquires the job skills needed in an automated society. A staff is needed that is educated for the task of teaching the adolescent and adult illiterates. Heretofore, staff for the most part has been haphazardly recruited from teachers in the elementary and secondary schools who add the teaching of the illiterates to their load as means of supplementing their income. There is no evidence that such a staff has provided adequately for the needs of their illiterate students.

This paper has addressed itself to six issues in reading instruction in 1967. Despite the intensity of some of the conflicts documented here, it is heartening to observe, particularly among teachers and administrators in schools, growing interest in disciplined experimentation and in careful study of research findings and their implications for teaching. The problems which these and similar issues present are clearly ones which American schools are eager to solve.

NOTES

1. Omar K. Moore, Early Reading and Writing, 16mm. film in color (Guilford, Conn.: Basic Education Council).

2. Nancy M. Rambusch, Learning How to Learn (Baltimore: Helicon Press, 1962).

3. Dolores Durkin, Children Who Read Early (New York: Teachers College Press, 1966).

4. Glen Doman, How to Teach Your Baby to Read (New York: Random House, 1966).

5. John Henry Martin, "We've Been Wrong About Early Reading," Grade Teacher Year Book, 1965, 38-40, and Freeport Public Schools Experimenting on Early Reading Using the Edison Responsive Environment Instrument (Englewood Cliffs, N.J.: Responsive Environments Corporation, 1966).

6. Newsletter (No. 13, June 1966), Learning Research and Development Center, University of Pittsburgh.

7. Audiovisual Instruction (September 1966).

8. Rambusch, Children Who Read Early.

9. Edward Wakin, "The Return of Montessori," Saturday Review, 47 (Nov. 21, 1964).

10. Evelyn Beyer, "Montessori in the Space Age," NEA Journal, 52 (December 1963), 36.

11. Preparing Your Child for Reading (Boston: Houghton Mifflin Co., 1963).

12. Bernard Spodek, "The Educational Scene," Elementary English 41 (January 1964), 84-87.

13. Anastasia McManus, "The Denver Prereading Project Conducted by WENH-TV," The Reading Teacher, 30 (October 1966).

14. Kenneth D. Wann, "Beginning Reading Instruction in the Kindergarten," NEA pamphlet, and "A comment on the Denver Experiment," NEA Journal, 56 (March 1967), 25-26.

15. Dolores Durkin, Children Who Read Early (New York: Teachers College Press, 1966), p. 139.

16. Carl Bereiter and S. Englemann, Teaching Disadvantaged Children (Englewood Cliffs, N.J.: Prentice-Hall, 1966).

17. Walter Hodges, Review, American Educational Research Journal, 3 (November 1966), 313-4.

18. Martin Deutsch, "What We Have Learned About Disadvantaged Children in the Preschool," Nation's Schools, 75 (April 1965).

19. Doman, How to Teach Your Baby to Read.

20. Bernard Belden, "A Study of Selected Practices Reported in the Teaching of Reading in the Kindergarten and Primary Grades in New York State," (Doctoral dissertation, Syracuse University, 1955).

21. Eunice Matthews, "What Is Expected of the Soviet Kindergarten?" Harvard Educational Review, 29 (March 1959), 43-53.

22. Eve Malmquist, "Teaching of Reading in the First Grade in Swedish Schools," The Reading Teacher, 15 (September 1962), 22-29.

23. Durkin, Children Who Read Early.

24. Joseph E. Brzeinski, "Early Introduction to Reading," Reading and Inquiry, Proceedings of the Annual Convention, IRA, 10 (November 10, 1965), 443-446; Brzeinski, "Beginning Reading in Denver," The Reading Teacher, 18 (October 1964), 18-19; and Brzeinski, L. M. Harrison, and P. McKee, "Should Johnny Read in Kindergarten?" NEA Journal, 56 (March 1967), 23-25.

25'. Robert L. Hillerick, "Pre-Reading Skills in Kindergarten: A Second Report," Elementary School Journal, 65 (March 1965), 312-17.

26. Kenneth D. Wann, "A Comment on the Denver Experiment," NEA Journal, 16 (March 1967), 25.

27. Ibid., 26

28. Dolores Durkin, Reading and the Kindergarten (Newark, Del.: IRA, 1964).

29. Elizabeth A. Zaruba, "A Survey of Teachers' Attitudes Toward Reading Experiences in Kindergarten," The Journal of Educational Research, 60 (February 1967), 252-255.

30. William D. Sheldon, "Teaching the Very Young to Read," The Reading Teacher 15 (December 1962), 163-169.

31. Rudolph Flesch, Why Johnny Can't Read (New York: Harper and Bros., Inc., 1955).

32. Learning to Read: A Report of a Conference of Reading Experts (Princeton, N. J.: Educational Testing Service, 1962).

33. David E. Bear, "Two Methods of Teaching Phonics: A Longitudinal Study," The Elementary School Journal, 64 (February 1964), 273-279.

34. Emery P. Bliesmer and B. Yarborough, "A Comparison of Ten Different Beginning Reading Programs in First Grade," Phi Delta Kappan, 46 (June 1965), 500-504.

35. John Downing, "What's Wrong with i.t.a.?" Phi Delta Kappan, 48 (February 1967), 262-266; William B. Gillooly, "The Promise of i.t.a. is a Delusion," Phi Delta Kappan, 47 (June 1966), 545-550.

36. Richard R. Waite, G.E. Blom, S.F. Linnet, and S. Edge, "First-Grade Reading Textbooks," The Elementary School Journal, 67 (April 1967), 366.

37. Ibid., 366.

38. Ibid., 366-367.

39. Ibid., 367.

40. W.H. Hollins, "A National Survey of Commonly Used First-Grade Readers," (Unpublished data, 1955).

41. Benjamin Bloom et al., Compensatory Education for Cultural Deprivation (New York: Holt, Rinehart and Winston, Inc., 1965).

42. David P. Ausubel, "A Teaching Strategy for Culturally Deprived Pupils: Cognitive and Motivational Considerations," The School Review, 71 (Winter 1963), 455.

43. Ibid., 461.

44. Frank Riessman, "The Culturally Deprived Child: A New View," Education Digest, 29 (November 1963), 12-15.

45. Robert B. Heilman, "Literature and Growing Up," English Journal, 45 (September 1956), 309.

46. Stanley L. Rosner and G. Schatz, "A Program for Adult Non-readers," Journal of Reading, 14 (March 1966), 223-31.

47. Robert S. Laubach, "A Study of Communications to Adults of Limited Reading Ability by Specially Written Materials" (Unpublished doctoral dissertation, Syracuse University, 1963).

48. Frank C. and Robert S. Laubach, Toward World Literacy (Syracuse, N.Y.: Syracuse University Press, 1960).

49. Pauline J. Hord, "Shall We Use Television in Developing Literacy?" Changing Concepts of Reading Instruction, IRA Conference Reports, 6 (1961), 233-36.

50. Burrill Crohn, "The Diebold Literacy Project: Programing for the Illiterate Adult," Programed Instruction, 3 (June 1964).